D0908638

LEO MELAMED ON
# THE MARKETS

# LEO MELAMED ON
# THE MARKETS

Twenty Years of Financial History
as Seen by the Man Who
Revolutionized the Markets

**Leo Melamed**

John Wiley & Sons, Inc.
New York • Chichester • Brisbane • Toronto • Singapore

In recognition of the importance of preserving what has been
written, it is a policy of John Wiley & Sons, Inc., to have
books of enduring value published in the United States
printed on acid-free paper, and we exert our best efforts
to that end.

This publication is designed to provide accurate and
authoritative information in regard to the subject
matter covered. It is sold with the understanding that
the publisher is not engaged in rendering legal, accounting,
or other professional services. If legal advice or other
expert assistance is required, the services of a competent
professional person should be sought. *From a Declaration
of Principles jointly adopted by a Committee of the
American Bar Association and a Committee of Publishers.*

*Library of Congress Cataloging-in-Publication Data*

Melamed, Leo.
    Leo Melamed on the markets : twenty years of financial history as
  seen by the man who revolutionized the markets / by Leo Melamed.
       p.      cm.
    Includes index.
    ISBN 0-471-57524-0
    1. Finance—United States—History.  2. Futures market—United
  States—History.  I. Title.
  HG181.M45   1992
  332.64'0973—dc20                                            92-22150

Printed in the United States of America

10 9 8 7 6 5 4 3 2 1

*This book is dedicated to my wife,*
*Betty,*
*and my children*
*Idelle, Jordan, and David*
*who were forced to share my attention*
*with a word processor.*

# Foreword

*Milton Friedman*
Hoover Institution
Stanford, California

This book is a selection of talks given and papers published over more than two decades by a remarkable man. Leo Melamed is a successful speculator and a recognized scholar, a far-out visionary and a down-to-earth realist, a skilled performer in Yiddish, dedicated to preserving that dying language, and an author of science fiction, a mover and a shaker, who has had a major influence on both private institutions and public policy. Despite its broad coverage, this book reflects only one side of this many-faceted human being.

He had the independence of mind and foresight to envisage the need for a public market in foreign currency futures, the imagination to invent a mechanism to make such a market feasible, and the courage and leadership ability to persuade his colleagues at the Chicago Mercantile Exchange to establish the International Monetary Market.

In retrospect, that may seem to have been an easy task. But at the time, a widely held view was expressed by one New York bank's foreign exchange dealer quoted in *The Wall Street Journal* on the day the IMM opened for business (May 16, 1972): "I'm amazed that a bunch of crapshooters in pork bellies (a reference to the Mercantile Exchange's major market) have the temerity to think that they can beat some of the world's most sophisticated traders at their own game." The same article quoted as "another skeptic of the IMM's prospects . . . economist Paul Samuelson, who questions whether the IMM can really offer users significant advantages over the current network of banks and money dealers. Also, Mr. Samuelson theorizes that if the IMM proves successful, it may incur the wrath of both the U.S. and foreign governments by fanning currency speculation and thereby disrupting exchange rates." So Leo and his colleagues were certainly not simply enacting received wisdom.

Futures markets in commodities are ancient. However, until the establishment of the IMM there had been, to the best of my knowledge, no successful public futures markets in financial instruments. Under Leo Melamed's leadership, "the crapshooters in pork bellies" pioneered what was to prove a revolutionary change in futures markets. Later, in 1981, by substituting cash settlement for physical delivery, the IMM made it feasible to trade futures in Eurodollars—one of the most successful contracts every devised. Once the ice was broken, trading in other financial futures followed: in interest rates, stock price indexes, and on and on, limited only by the ingenuity of market operators and the interest of market participants. *The Wall Street Journal* carries quotations daily on more than 30 different financial instruments, each for a number of future dates. Financial futures have become a major if not dominant element in futures markets and the "bunch of crapshooters" who initiated trading in such contracts remain the major players—thanks in no small measure to Leo Melamed's guidance of the evolution since.

Part I of this book reflects the wisdom that Leo has accumulated as a speculator. It will interest and be of value to both the individual investor and the professional trader. And the final item in the chapter should be must reading for every citizen. It is an eloquent statement of the case for free and unfettered markets.

Part II tells the fascinating story of the establishment and subsequent growth of the International Monetary Market.

Part III is a spirited and informed defense of the contribution that futures markets make to the operation of a free private enterprise system. An incidental but not unimportant byproduct is an effective attack on legally imposed price controls, whether of individual products or of exchange rates.

Paul Samuelson's early prediction that the IMM "may incur the wrath of both the U.S. and foreign governments" never became a reality with respect to exchange rates, but it did with respect to stock market futures and options. In 1987, when the stock market collapsed, both government officials and private individuals assigned much of the blame to "program trading," which was made possible by the emergence of an active and broadly based market in stock market futures and options. A government commission—the Brady Commission—was established to investigate the collapse.

Leo Melamed played a major role—as a voice of sense and moderation—in the subsequent discussion and helped shape the modest reforms that ultimately were adopted. Part IV tells the story of the initial panicky reaction to the stock market crash and of how Leo and his associates reacted in order to forestall ill-considered measures that could have done serious damage to the whole structure of U.S. financial institutions. When the dust had settled, the government investigation largely exonerated the futures markets. As Leo points out, a paradoxical result was an enhanced appreciation of the constructive role played by futures markets in financial instruments.

The first few papers in Part V explain how GLOBEX developed and the role it is expected to play in integrating world markets in financial futures. The remaining papers offer an eloquent statement of the case for free markets in general, with special reference to international trade.

The collapse of communism plus the technological changes of recent decades—the so-called information revolution—have vastly expanded the possibilities of cooperation between the developed and the underdeveloped countries of the world. The political troubles of communism have made available for participation in multinational production of commodities and services a billion people in China and three or four hundred million in Russia and Eastern Europe. In addition, improvements in communications and transportation, especially the introduction of fax, have made it possible for a company located anywhere to coordinate resources located anywhere to produce a product to be sold anywhere. One result is that Latin America provides a supply of labor available in a way that has not been available before.

These developments offer the opportunity for an enormous expansion in world trade. If that is allowed to develop freely, it can produce a new worldwide economic miracle that will raise living standards around the world, in both capital-rich and labor-rich countries. Unfortunately, the rising tide of protectionist sentiment in the capital-rich countries is a major obstacle to such a development. Instead of welcoming the new opportunities, many people in the developing countries are fearful of the changes that the new world order would require and are trying to withdraw within a sheltered bastion—whether Fortress America or Fortress Europe.

Leo Melamed deserves much credit for speaking out so effectively against the protectionist trend that he labels, in the final item in this book, "the scourge of markets."

I first became acquainted with Leo in late 1971, when he telephoned me in Ely, Vermont, our second home where we were spending the fall quarter, on leave from the University of Chicago. He called to explore the possibility of our meeting to discuss his tentative plans for a public market in currency futures. My name had come to his attention thanks to a news story in *The Wall Street Journal,* which noted my longtime advocacy of floating exchange rates, my expectation that the Bretton Woods system of fixed exchange rates was bound to break down, and my belief in the desirability of a public futures market in foreign exchange. That belief was based partly on a personal experience. In November 1967, it became clear to me and other observers that Britain was going to be forced to devalue the pound. I called all the major banks in Chicago attempting to sell the pound short. No bank would take my order, insisting that they dealt in futures only with their regular customers and only in connection with commercial activities—though when I pressed them, I received the answer that "The Federal Reserve [or perhaps the Bank of England] would not like it." In subsequent *Newsweek* columns, I laid out the case for eliminating government restrictions on trading in foreign currencies and argued for the adoption of a system of floating exchange rates.

So long as the Bretton Woods system of fixed exchange rates guided by the International Monetary Fund was in effective operation, a broad, resilient public futures market was not feasible. Many changes in exchange rates did occur during the Bretton Woods system. However, they were large changes—like the British devaluation in 1967—occurring at widely separated points of time. Between such changes, exchange rates were held within narrow limits by central bank manipulation. Under such circumstances, there is little for a public futures market to do most of the time, and hence it cannot attract traders.

The Bretton Woods system came to an end on August 15, 1971, when President Nixon announced that the United States would no longer live up to its commitment to sell gold to central banks on demand at $35 an ounce. That announcement induced Leo and his associates to move to implement the tentative plans they had developed to initiate trading in currency futures. His phone call to me was one result.

I met Leo and Everette B. Harris in New York on Saturday morning, November 13, 1971.* Leo and Everette arrived, as best I recall it more than two decades later, with a fully fleshed out plan for establishing what was to become the International Monetary Market. They had done their homework. I had little to contribute on that level. However, establishing such a market was clearly a costly and risky enterprise. My role turned out to be to assure them that Bretton Woods was dead for good and that any arrangements that replaced the Bretton Woods system of fixed rates subject to occasional change would involve much wider and more continuous fluctuations in exchange rates of the kind that were necessary to make a public market in currency futures viable.

This done, they contracted with me to write a memorandum under their auspices explaining the need for such a market that they could use in presenting their proposals to the authorities in Washington. The memorandum was completed in late December and issued in printed form under the title "The Need for Futures Markets in Currencies" in early 1972.

With his usual generosity, Leo has publicly given me much more credit for the establishment of the IMM than I deserve (see the third item in Part II). However, over a long life, I have learned repeatedly how large a gap separates the giving of advice from the taking of advice, and how seldom that gap is bridged. I am more than willing to take credit for foreseeing, along with other economists, the weakness of the Bretton Woods system and for recommending the adoption of floating exchange rates as a substitute—I did that first in a paper writ-

---

*At the time, Leo was Chairman of the Board of the Chicago Mercantile Exchange; Everette, its fulltime President.

ten in 1950 and published in 1953; and again in a memorandum
to President-elect Richard Nixon in December 1968.*

However, Leo Melamed deserves the lion's share of credit
for seizing the opportunity offered by Nixon's closing the gold
window, recognizing the importance of taking advantage of
that opportunity promptly, and having the courage to do so,
despite the risks. It took real persistence and diplomacy to get
a prompt go-ahead from government officials much more
prone to delay than to act. In retrospect, it is remarkable that
the IMM opened for business less than ten months after President Nixon closed the gold window. That was possible only
because of advance planning that long preceded the President's action.

The rest is history: Chicago is today the world's most important center of futures trading thanks to Leo's initiative, his
subsequent role in guiding the Chicago Mercantile Exchange
on its expansionary path, and his many contributions to informed public discussion of a wide range of important issues.

---

*"The Case for Flexible Exchanges Rates," in Milton Friedman, *Essays in Positive Eco-
nomics* (Chicago: University of Chicago Press, 1953), pp. 157–203; and "A Proposal for
Resolving the U.S. Balance of Payments Problem: Confidential Memorandum to
President-elect Richard Nixon," in Leo Melamed, ed., *The Merits of Flexible Exchange
Rates: An Anthology* (Fairfax, Va.: George Mason University Press, 1988), pp. 429-438.

# Author's Note

It is imperative to publicly thank my dear friend, esteemed mentor, distinguished teacher, and singular beacon of economic thought, Milton Friedman, for his warm and extremely generous words of praise about my accomplishments in futures. I am humbled and forever indebted to him for taking the time to read this material and offer his historical perspective. I also cannot help but reiterate what I have privately and publicly stated on numerous occasions: *Without Milton Friedman's support, without his intellectual blessing, without his assistance in opening doors and without his consistent and unwavering belief in our mission, I could never have had the courage or tenacity to achieve what I did.*

It was difficult to select the material for this book from the more than 20 years of writings and speeches. The material chosen, however, is fully representative of the task that I undertook in 1972 and provides a historical backdrop to a most exciting and revolutionary period in world markets. As stated in my 1983 piece *The Future of Futures:*

> Our markets experienced a metamorphosis of such dramatic proportions that it defies comprehension. Our markets, which since time immemorial were the unique and exclusive domain of agriculture, seemingly overnight became an integral mechanism of finance. Our markets, which for more than 100 years were strictly limited to tangible and storable products, suddenly shed these fundamental requirements and embraced live animals, foreign exchange and government securities. Our markets, whose defined boundaries precluded entry into the sphere reserved for securities, brazenly transgressed the dividing line by inventing instruments that blurred the age-old distinction. Our markets, whose birth-right necessitated a system of physical

delivery, broke their genetic code and engendered products without a delivery. Our markets, which only yesterday were viewed with scorn and considered barely at the edge of respectability, are today an indispensable member of the financial family.

With due apologies to the reader, I forewarn that some of my words, quotations, references and themes are repetitive. The reason is straightforward. Like every preacher, my mission was to explain and to teach. Much of teaching is accomplished by repetition of the lessons—over and over again. This is true whether the subject is simple arithmetic or the theory of relativity. In each instance, my message was delivered before a different audience, within a different forum, and often in a different country and culture. To them the words were always new and often unique. Moreover, each piece selected for this book—aside from its occasional similar theme—also contains a new idea, a new subject, or a new explanation. In their cumulative aggregate, the selections provide a record of the historical march of our markets from existence as a distant and shunned cousin of the financial community to acceptance within the inner sanctum of the orthodox financial world.

Indeed, the phenomenal success of financial futures during the past two decades has few equals in the business arena and exemplifies the power of an idea whose time had come. Statistics dramatize the story. In 1971, on the eve of the birth of financial futures, 14.6 million contracts traded on U.S. futures exchanges; there were no foreign exchanges of any consequence. Twenty years later, in 1991, the total transactions of futures and options on U.S. futures exchanges was 325 million contracts, an astounding increase of over 2100 percent, with agricultural contracts representing a mere 19 percent of the total. In the same year, the burgeoning number of new foreign financial exchanges traded an equally impressive 230 million contracts.

The success of these markets was no single-handed effort; it included an army of talented and devoted people, far too many to enumerate. Still, it is impossible to comment on this unique history without at least naming those select few who, in addition to Milton Friedman, stood with me at the forefront of this movement from its very inception.

First and foremost, at the Chicago Mercantile Exchange (CME), the past president, Everette B. Harris, whom I love dearly. Harris fearlessly undertook the chore at hand, grasped the magnitude of the concept, fervently believed that it could done (he liked to say "we didn't know it couldn't be done"), and personally knew many of the people we had to convince. Dr. Mark Powers, the chief economist, who instantly embraced the idea and whose fertile and quick mind understood how to successfully design the foreign currency and U.S. T-bill contract specifications. Ronald Frost, the CME publicist, who gave the idea its initial national exposure. Lee A. Freeman, followed by Jerrold E. Salzman, who effectively fought the legal battles on behalf of the exchange. Finally, some close personal friends: Barry J. Lind, whose outstanding talents I leaned on in innumerable ways throughout the years and who was particularly instrumental in building the solid financial base on which the CME was structured; Brian P. Monieson, who furnished invaluable expertise with respect to the market's use and application of financial instruments; and Henry G. Jarecki who from the moment of the IMM's birth has provided an international perspective and valued practical advice as well as intellectual stimulus.

At the Chicago Board of Trade, it is mandatory to mention still another close friend and former chairman, Leslie Rosenthal, who was the chairman of the CBOT Financial Instrument Committee in 1975 and a driving force in that exchange's decision to also initiate trading in financial instruments. Similarly, it is essential to underscore the brilliant work of Dr. Richard L. Sandor who is principally credited with designing the U.S. Treasury bond futures contract, one of the most successful futures instruments ever devised.

Although the International Monetary Market (IMM) was a CME offspring, it began life as a separate corporate entity. I had the distinct privilege of serving as chairman of the IMM Board from its inception until its merger with the CME in 1976.* This Board had the formidable challenge of proving the merit of the IMM's revolutionary idea as well as the

---

*The initial IMM Board included John T. Geldermann, First Vice Chairman; Carl E. Anderson, Second Vice Chairman; Robert J. O'Brien, Secretary; Laurence M. Rosenberg, Treasurer; A. Robert Abboud; Lloyd F. Arnold; Richard E. Boerke; William E. Goldstandt; Henry G. Jarecki; Daniel R. Jesser; Marlowe King; Barry J. Lind; Donald L. Minucciani; William C. Muno; Fredrick W. Schantz; Dr. Beryl W. Sprinkel; and Michael Weinberg, Jr.

responsibility of promoting its untested contracts of trade. The members of this body served with distinction and honor and offered our new marketplace a priceless commodity—credibility.

The Governors and Directors of the CME and IMM Boards changed over the years, making it difficult to name all those who served. But it must be emphasized that each of them shouldered the burden and contributed to the result. It is incumbent on me, however, to single out the CME chairmen with whom I shared responsibilities and who stood at my side during the two decades in which the modern futures market was built: Michael Weinberg, Jr., Brian P. Monieson, Laurence M. Rosenberg, John T. Geldermann, and of exceptional note the current chairman, John F. Sandner, who in the later years was an unwavering disciple, companion, and comrade-in-arms.

Of special mention also are the exchange presidents with whom I worked: At the CME, in addition to Everette B. Harris, there is my good friend, Clayton Yeutter, whose tireless efforts on behalf of our markets were difficult to match, and whose exceptional talents eventually catapulted him to Washington, D.C. to serve our nation under President Reagan as United States Representative of Trade, and under President Bush as Secretary of Agriculture and Counsellor for Domestic Policy; and my colleague William J. Brodsky who was recruited from the American Stock Exchange and who brought to the Merc his organizational skills and special expertise in securities markets. At the CBOT, Warren E. Lebeck and Robert K. Wilmouth, presently the president of the National Futures Association. Finally, the CBOT's current Chief Executive Officer, my colleague and close friend, Thomas R. Donovan, who is the CBOT'S staunchest champion and has become the futures industry's strongest advocate. The cumulative product of these officials helped make our successful history possible.

With due respect to all our efforts, before financial futures would become respectable, they needed to become *establishment*. In other words, risk management had to become an orthodox discipline of business, accepted by the commercial world. This is a relatively new concept. It came into being in the course of the past two decades in concert with the development of financial futures and options, and a vast array of other innovative financial instruments, techniques, and information technologies. This process occurred quickly and successfully due primarily to the profound efforts and influence of the U.S. academic community.

Of exceptional note in this intellectual endeavor is the contribution of my esteemed and dear friend Merton H. Miller, the Robert R. McCormick Distinguished Service Professor of the Graduate School of Business, University of Chicago. His outstanding academic research and writings with respect to the genre of risk management was in some measure responsible for his selection in 1990 as the recipient of the Nobel Prize in Economics.

L.M.

# Acknowledgments

I am forever indebted to Chicago Mercantile Exchange executive staff and professional counsel, who, over the years, provided invaluable assistance, advice, and ideas in preparation of this material. Of special note are legal counsel Jerrold E. Salzman, Gerald D. Beyer, and Charles M. Seeger, as well as senior staff T. Eric Kilcollin, C. Dayle Henington, Barbara A. Richards, and Joseph T. Whalen. Above and beyond the foregoing was the assistance of Alysann Posner without whose untiring efforts and advice this book would not have been possible.

# Contents

LEO MELAMED ON
# THE MARKETS

# THE SOUL OF
# THE TRADER

*From the moment I entered the futures scene and opened the door to this arcane world of shouting and gesticulations, I was bewitched. The tumult; the color; the frenzy of activity; the people rushing about, shouting at the top of their voices; and acting out their mysterious incantations instantly inflamed my young and unworldly soul, awakened some unknown and uncontrollable passions from deep within, and caused me to irrevocably conclude that this, whatever it was, was for me. And so it came to pass. Although I finished law school and even successfully practiced law for some six or seven years, my heart, mind, and soul never left the world of futures or the floor of the Chicago Mercantile Exchange (CMI).*

*Whether it was an innate understanding of the laws that dictate supply and demand, or whether it was the consequence of a newborn passion to consume everything written on markets and economics, I had little problem quickly understanding the nature of futures or appreciating the beauty of the free market process. I also had an abundance of teachers—those hard-bitten professionals who prowled the floor of the Exchange. Many of these early characters, who acted and looked more like persona found in a Dickens' novel of the 1850s than at a financial institution a century later, took a liking to this young law student, some even taking him under their wings.*

*These members of the Chicago Mercantile Exchange were my mentors, my teachers, my friends. They came from every walk of life; they were from every part of America; they were of every type and every kind. I learned to understand them; I grasped what motivated them; I discovered what they hoped for and what they feared; and I got to see their soul. Later, they became the soldiers I depended on in our mission to glorify our markets.*

*From the beginning I recorded a little of what I learned. It was all so fascinating and so much of it unrecorded. All but the last two articles in this chapter were written before the formal introduction of financial futures. The thoughts offered were based on trading experience in agricultural markets. However, the rules and philosophies espoused for those markets and what I learned about those traders is equally true and applicable to financial instruments and its traders.*

# Be a Lover, Not a Fighter

*This age-old credo was learned the hard way—it usually is. It came to me as a revelation after years of fighting the market. Unfortunately, it is a rule we traders often forget. Rest assured, the market will remind us.*

> **Presented at a Chicago Mercantile Exchange Traders Seminar, Chicago, Illinois, March 20, 1969**

*B**e a Lover, Not a Fighter:* This motto is prominently displayed on a plaque in my office. The thought behind the words is as old as trading itself. It represents a credo that every good trader knows and abides—forgetting it can prove fatal. There are many ways to say it. When you violate this doctrine in stock trading, it is known as "fighting the tape."

Fighting a market is a professional trader's greatest enemy. It prejudices his* reasoning process, it warps his logic, it clouds his mind, it disrupts his market "feel," it destroys his ability to participate in other market opportunities, it becomes debilitating, and ultimately it can take all his money. All professionals get caught in this nightmare from time to time. The winners remedy the condition as soon as they detect it.

Ask any stock or futures trader what it means to fight a market and he will know exactly what you mean. He may not always find the right words for a satisfactory definition, he may not always be able to explain how he can determine when it happens or why, but he knows precisely what it is and he knows most emphatically that it is a road to disaster.

---

*The conventional use of the pronoun "he" in this book is purely for ease of reading; the material herein applies impartially to men and women unless the context specifically states otherwise.

When you fight the market, you rationalize that your position is correct even when the market screams that it is not, when all the facts contradict your opinion, when your instincts tell you to get out. On rare occasions, such stubborn trading can turn in your favor. When that happens, it is a doomsday event. You will apply the same procedure the next time, and the next time you will go broke. Clearly, there are some exceptions to this rule—as there are with every rule. Some traders have been very successful fighting the market. But for each exception, thousands more fail.

How do you know when you are fighting the market? There are no specific rules—and each trader has his own dictate or guidepost to serve as an early warning system. Some intuitively know when it is time to get out before it becomes a fight; others get out of their positions as soon as a losing position causes them a sleepless night; still others never go home with a losing position. Whatever the system, whatever the rule, you must have it in your arsenal of futures' trading weapons.

The rule does not require that a futures trader discard an opinion or liquidate a position after his first loss or even after a series of losses. Quite the contrary. No professional can expect every market play to show a profit. Nor is an immediate losing position the sign of a wrong position. Indeed, conviction about a position in the market is an important ingredient to success. Conviction is especially important when you are not immediately proven correct. However, every professional trader knows the difference between conviction and obsession. The difference is critical. In every market play of consequence, there is a point at which that difference divides winners from losers. Losers fight a market, winners do not.

Somewhere between an immediate losing position and an eventual wrong position lies an imaginary line that, when crossed, turns a losing position into fighting the market. Experience will help in establishing the necessary guidepost. But until a trader develops this early warning sense, he should ask himself the following questions whenever he has a losing position:

> *Would I take the same position today at this new price level if I did not have a previous position in the market?* If the answer is *no*, you should not maintain your present position.

*Is the loss one that I am afraid, or cannot afford, to take?* If the answer is *yes*, you are in the market for the wrong reasons—you are in the market not because you think you are right, but because the loss will be too much for your emotional equilibrium or finances to bear.

*Am I still in the position because I hope to make back the money I lost?* Hoping and wishing are not reasons to maintain a losing position.

*Has the position twisted my reasoning and calculations?*

*Do the figures still logically add up to what I originally expected or am I rationalizing?*

*Am I so prejudiced by my position that I refuse to discuss or hear a contrary opinion?*

*And, if I hear one, can I still logically refute it?*

*Do I have a point at which time I will take my loss and get out?*

*Is a further loss on this position worth the potential profit?*

An honest appraisal of the answers to these questions can help the trader determine whether he has crossed that crucial line. Once he has crossed it, the trader will be lost in a quagmire of hope and desperation. He will no longer be rational with respect to the position; he will never honestly know his rationale for remaining with the position—whether he truly believes in it, or whether he is simply "married" to it. The ultimate test will come on the day the trader liquidates his position. Inevitably, this will be near or at the end of that particular market move.

Sometimes results are catastrophic, not only because of the money lost and the inability to capitalize on the market play when it finally arrives but because market fighters often liquidate their positions at the very bottom (or top) of a market and then reverse their market opinion in a fit of desperation. They then go for a bundle in the other direction. Such are the unfortunate fates of the fighters.

How much better and more fun it is to be a lover. A trader who is a lover is a trend player—the trend is his friend. He seeks out the trend of the market and romances it. He loves the market whether it is bull or bear; he follows wherever it leads. If it's in an uptrend, he's bullish or he leaves it alone; if it's in a downtrend, he's bearish or he stays out. He does not try to pick reversals or outsmart the world, he merely wants to follow the market's direction. When a lover increases his position, his original position is profitable and the market shows continued promise. Clearly, lovers also have losing positions, but they never allow them to become a fight with the market. Unlike the fighter, the lover never closes his eyes with righteous indignation, *I will be right*. Unlike the fighter, the lover seldom blames a loss on the market. He may be wrong, but never the market.

It is rare for a lover to catch the bottom of a market, nor will he often get out at the top. At the bottom, he is most likely still short; at the top, he is still long. As soon as he suspects the market is changing direction, he gets out—even if this means reinstating the same position at a less advantageous price or missing a further move. Lovers often liquidate positions long before the market reaches its ultimate level. To take a little out of the middle is a lover's delight. While lovers do not earn as much as they potentially could, year after year they go home with a profit. Maybe the real difference between lovers and fighters is that lovers never want to be right, they just want to make money. In the long run, only the lovers do.

# The Art of
# Futures Trading

*In the 1960s—long before financial futures, and even longer before these markets were an established arena of finance and received serious attention from academia—very little had been written about the art of futures trading. It was generally considered an arcane, esoteric, and wild world for reckless speculators and gamblers.*

*It was a revelation to discover firsthand the truth about trading: to learn that the rules for good trading techniques were quite the opposite of conventional wisdom; that successful futures trading required a business approach, discipline, and the ability to manage money; and that luck was of minimal value, the rules of chance did not apply, and that a trader's psychological makeup was the most critical component of success.*

> **Presented at the Financial Editors Seminar, Chicago, Illinois, November 10, 1969**

To many, futures trading is a blessing.
To many, it is a curse.
To the majority, it is an enigma.

W hy this divergence of opinion? Why this love–hate relationship? Perhaps because futures trading today represents one of the last frontiers of the business world. A frontier where the courageous trader must rely solely on his own ingenuity and common sense, where he must be brave and willing to meet formidable personal challenges, where the challenges demand intelligence, fortitude, character, and adventuresome spirit, and where the reward justifies the risks.

7

Personal futures trading is one of the last remaining spheres where an individual can still pyramid a sizable fortune from a modest investment. Little wonder so many try, though so many fail. Little wonder many of those who fail blame the challenge rather than their own inadequacies. Little wonder those who succeed become obsessed with the adventure. And little wonder so few know about it, for as with any frontier, the unknown is awesome, complicated, and frightening. And as with most things of consequence, the challenge is formidable and fraught with risk.

For these reasons, many myths have developed about trading futures: You must be on the in; you have to be lucky; it's only for the pros; you have to be a gambler; there's no rhyme or reason to it. These myths are false. Often these myths are used as excuses and alibis by those who have failed at futures trading for a variety of reasons, some of them rather personal. Perhaps they lacked the ability to concentrate or did not possess sufficient analytical skills; perhaps they lacked a well-adjusted personality, a mature temperament, or business discipline. Others fail because they lack adequate capital; but capital, although important, is not usually the central reason individuals fail at trading.

Take the element of luck. Futures trading is one of the few areas where luck is of minimal importance. While luck never hurts (and on occasion—as in all things—it can play an important role) luck, in general, is not a factor. Luck can go both ways and usually evens out. And good luck can also have an adverse effect. For example, a trader who is lucky in his early trading experience either has learned nothing or has learned the opposite of what he should. In the long run, an early streak of good luck will do him in.

In the final analysis, success at trading futures is determined by the person's ability to decipher and analyze salient facts and statistics in order to reach a logical opinion about the intermediate or ultimate price of a given product. In short, it depends on the ability to correctly measure supply and demand.

If that sounds simple, it isn't! It is a most difficult task. Implicit in the challenge are some exacting requirements: knowing the significant economic components that can affect the price of a given product; keeping abreast of current facts and statistics; comprehending these facts and their effects on supply and demand; correctly prorating the importance of the various components as they apply to a given price structure—a ratio that changes from year to year, sometimes from week to week, as well as from commodity to commodity; understanding the different price idiosyncrasies of different commodities; adjusting for all unknown variables; and finally, having the courage to apply your conclusions to the market.

It is this last requirement—the courage to apply your conclusions to the market—that proves to be the Waterloo for most futures traders. It is the point where your personality meets its most formidable challenge and you learn the type of trader you really are. Indeed, a trader's psychological makeup is the most critical component in his success in futures trading.

While special education and professional training will help, they are not mandatory. Tips or inside information are of small consequence. What is necessary is an orderly thought process, a businesslike approach, a well-balanced personality, a willingness to study the significant factors, and a working knowledge of the past history. And, of course, patience. The trader needs patience to learn from trading experiences, patience to learn from past mistakes, and patience for confidence and trading ability to grow. These are not simple requisites, and yet they are not impossible or so complicated as to warrant the taboos or prohibitions that so many have placed on this challenging field.

The rules of odds or probabilities—the normal tools of a good gambler—are not required for futures trading and can be a distinct disadvantage. Successful professional futures traders, as a rule, are not gamblers in the classic sense; most of the time, when gamblers try their skill at futures, they lose. The reasons for this are quite simple. Futures prices are dictated by the laws of economics, whereas successful gambling is a consequence of the rules of chance. These two regimes are light years apart. Rules of chance, over the long haul, cannot be applied successfully to trading. A good bet based on odds in other areas of life may be the worst possible trade in futures. A bad chance based on probabilities may in fact be a terrific futures position. For instance, in a bear market of long duration, pure odds will favor a rally; unfortunately, if an oversupply continues to dictate lower prices, those who buy the market on the basis of probabilities will lose money.

I have often heard the statement, "I had to liquidate my long position because the market was up ten days in a row." Those traders are applying the rule of probabilities to trading. While that may sometimes turn out to be a correct decision, it is far from the right reason. The long position may have been a better position on the eleventh day than it was on the first; maybe, on the eleventh day the world finally recognized what the trader's instincts had told him ten days before. Thus, the rule of probabilities cannot be the controlling factor for a market decision.

Successful futures traders are good businessmen and good money managers. Though traders risk their capital, those who are successful follow conservative and disciplined business practices. Thus, money management is every bit as important as being correct in the market. Unfortunately, this principle has somehow been lost by the public, and futures exchanges are instead often likened to gambling casinos.

I am often asked how much money is needed to begin trading. It is not really a question about the *amount* of capital required, rather it is a question of the *type* of capital. While I would not recommend it, you can begin trading futures with as little as a couple of thousand dollars—the minimum margin requirement—if a brokerage firm will accept your account.* The amount of capital available to begin trading will determine the trader's latitude in the learning process. With a small amount, he has little room for error. With a larger sum, he has more time to learn. More important than the amount of money is that it not be *necessary* money. The trader should not speculate with capital needed for daily subsistence; that is, the money required for food and shelter, for school or clothing, or for any of the other normal demands of life. The capital recommended for futures trading is "risk capital": money that, if lost, would not materially affect the trader's living standards. While this precondition excludes a great many from futures trading, it still leaves the possibility open to a good many others.

Will a large sum of risk capital provide a better chance at success than a small sum? Yes, to the degree that it will provide

---

*The rules pertaining to the amount of capital required for futures trading have changed considerably since this essay was written in 1969. Inflation, the type of products available, and volatility of prices have affected the amount of margin capital required.

more room to learn. However, more capital may produce a false sense of security, which in the long run will impair your ability to succeed. Whether you begin with a large or small pool of risk capital, you must adjust the size of your futures position accordingly: With a small sum, you should begin trading on a very small scale; conversely, with a large sum, you may want to begin with larger positions. In either case you must pace yourself so that there will be some risk capital remaining after you have learned to trade. It will do you little good to face all the dangers and learn all the lessons if, after you graduate, you have no cash left to put your knowledge to work.

Since it takes years of study and firsthand application to become thoroughly familiar with all the principles, rules, variations, and exceptions involved for successful futures trading, it would be impossible to discuss these in depth. However, the following are three of the most salient principles.

First, spend time educating yourself about the product you plan to trade; that is, the various statistics and other factors that affect the supply–demand equation and therefore the price of the product. Implicit in this requirement is the corollary that you cannot rely solely on another's opinion. For example, if you use a broker, never take his word as gospel. While you should listen to what he has to say because he is an expert, you would be foolish to rely solely on his information or interpretation of the facts. This will also require that you fully understand the broker's jargon and reasoning, which again requires some personal education.

The second most important principle is not to overtrade. This cannot be defined in terms of money or in terms of the number of trades per week, month, or year. It will depend on your proximity to the market—how closely you can monitor price movement, the amount of time spent studying the product, and the objectives of your trading plan. Overtrading will overexpose you to risk and danger, as well as to unnecessary commissions. Consequently, you must accept that you cannot participate in every market move, nor should you want to. The most successful trader who is not daily on the trading floor of the exchange will pick his spots carefully. Futures prices have trends as well as seasonal movements. Concentrate on these rather than the daily fluctuations, which are best left to the professionals. A successful trader who chooses his moves judiciously needs to be correct only 30 to 40 percent of the time. On the other hand, a non-member trader attempting to trade daily must maintain a profitable track record 60 to 70 percent of the time to come out ahead.

The third principle is to follow a predetermined trading plan; a set of rules or established guidelines that you believe are valid, that have withstood the test of time, and that will guide your decisions. There is not one special formula or one set of trading rules. There are many. If you are not a professional trader, it will require a great deal of study to determine which rules make the most sense to you and best fit your temperament and your primary vocation. Whichever they are, once you choose your trading rules, adhere to them. This will require discipline and will test your emotional qualities. Unless you abide by a set of sound trading practices, you will be subject to the whim of every market idiosyncracy and fall easy prey to the stresses of a given moment. As an extension of this principle, I would caution you not to allow successful speculation to go to your head and cause you to discard your rules. Conversely, if at first you are unsuccessful or suffer a series of defeats, do not despair and discard a sound set of trading principles.

Futures markets represent financial democracy. They offer an open marketplace for investment and speculation where everyone has a right to an opinion. Some opinions are more qualified than others. How qualified you become depends on you alone. This frontier is still open to a multitude of Americans who have the heart and spirit to learn what it takes. It is one field where the victorious have the satisfaction of knowing they have no one to thank for success except their own intellect, fortitude, and capability. And the reward can certainly justify the effort and risk involved.

# A Technical Approach to Trading

*At the time this address was delivered, trading on the basis of technical analysis was nowhere near as prevalent or accepted as it is today. Conventional wisdom considered such trading techniques mystical and not to be utilized for serious market application.*

*However, the concept of chart analysis—that is the extent of what was available in the genre of technical analysis—appealed to me. The logic that dictated the basic precepts in charting seemed to make sense. Thus I read whatever was available on the subject and became an ardent devotee of the technical approach to markets. And over time, as futures markets grew, technical analysis reached a dimension, complexity, and sophistication never dreamed of when this was written. Yet it is noteworthy how much of what I then learned is still valid.*

*Most importantly, I learned that a technician who ignores market fundamentals is nowhere near as successful as a trader who studiously applies both regimes to his trading methodology.*

Presented at the Seminar on Investing, New York, New York, April 1970

There are two approaches to trading: the *fundamental* approach—a market opinion based on analysis of economic factors of supply and demand; and the *technical* approach—a market opinion based on an interpretation of charting or other technical analysis. The two approaches are eons apart: One approach depends solely on technical interpretation and is devoid of all economic facts; the other approach depends on statistics and economic facts and ignores technical analysis.

13

Chartists are quite certain that they have the surest way to successful trading. They do not bother with supply–demand statistics, government reports, or any other factual economic considerations in reaching their market opinion. Such factual knowledge gets in their way. In their opinion, fundamentalists must depend on too many variables to be successful traders. The charts, they claim, say it all. They adhere to the Confucius concept of trading—one look at the charts is worth a thousand statistics.

Fundamentalists, on the other hand, believe that only cold hard analysis of the facts can lead to a valid market opinion. They consider technical analysis akin to voodoo. Such market opinions, in their view, are nothing more than gibberish, without rhyme or reason. To them, using charts to ascertain the market's direction is a throwback to the days when people sought their future in the stars or read tarot cards to divine their destiny. No two chartists, they claim, will offer the same interpretation of the charts because technical analysis can only tell you where a market has been, not where it is going.

So what is the truth about the technique of charting? Does it have merit or is it voodoo? In my opinion, a technical approach to trading markets, while far from perfect, has great value. Chart analysis is an important market tool. However, as with most things, it cannot be taken on blind faith. A trader's market opinion should not be based exclusively on technical analysis.

Since this subject matter requires months and even years of study and necessitates firsthand application as part of its course, it would be most difficult to explain comprehensively in this essay even a small portion of charting theory and technical analysis. Instead, I will seek to achieve three goals: explode some popular myths and misconceptions about technical trading; offer an insight into the professional chartist's mind and methodology; and entice you to do some further study about this most effective tool for trading futures.

The most popular misconception is that a magic formula exists for trading. There is no such thing. While charting and technical trading may seem to be magical or hocus pocus to the uninitiated (especially if its application turns out correct and produces a winning trade), behind every charting principle or technical theory lies a perfectly logical explanation and rationale. Charting should be approached in the manner a scientist approaches an unknown phenomenon. If charting works, one should inquire why.

To understand the logic behind charting, you must begin by recognizing that a chart represents a graphic picture of past market behavior. This is true regardless of the chart methodology utilized—bar, point and figure, reversal, and so on. Those graphic representations achieved are the consequence of market participants taking a position in the market. Thus, the chart represents a giant up-to-the-minute opinion poll, recording every single bit of information—fundamental and technical—utilized by each and every market participant in making a market decision.

For example, on a daily bar chart, each line represents one day's market movement, showing its high, its low, and its close. But these lines depict more than simply daily price movement. They also represent the trades made by those involved in the market each day—and by extension—over a given period of time. In other words, those lines provide a graphic picture of the cumulative opinions of everyone in the market.

How can a picture of past market behavior then help predict future market direction? Quite simply. Since the chart represents the cumulative beliefs of all participants in the market, it also represents a graphic description of the cumulative psychology of the market participants. Since the predictability of human behavior is well documented, the chart can be utilized to predict the next move by those same participants who created the graphic picture in the first place.

Another myth about charting by unbelievers is that no two chartists will interpret the same pattern the same way. This is simply not true! Except for highly unusual circumstances, most qualified chartists will not differ on a basic interpretation of a given pattern. When two chartists differ on a basic interpretation of a pattern, it is because one or both of them do not know what they are talking about; one or both of them is mistaken; or the pattern does not have sufficient elements to warrant a decisive interpretation.

The knowledge and experience required to identify a chart pattern is relatively simple to attain. There are many books on the subject. There are also but a limited number of important chart formations such as the head and shoulder; double tops and bottoms; the rounded formation; coils, flags or triangles; descending and ascending formations; and broadening formations. These can easily be studied and understood. However, interpreting these patterns during actual market action is not so easy. In fact, achieving the level of expertise necessary to make a theoretical interpretation about a chart pattern provides the trader with no more than about 25 percent of the expertise necessary for technical chart trading.

The professional technician does not rely with finality on his initial interpretation of a chart pattern. Most patterns are not so definite as to provide this luxury. There is as much art as there is science to technical trading. Patterns are often subject to imaginative interpretation, to feel, and to experience. A head and shoulder, for instance, can take a protracted time to form. You have to see it in your mind's eye. It may have a stunted right or left shoulder, its head may be outside the expected graphic dimensions, or it may differ from the classic examples in a hundred ways that require expert interpretation. Moreover, there are exceptions to all the general rules about patterns; in fact, there are more exceptions than there are general rules.

The other 75 percent of chart expertise is in the ability to make on-going diagnosis. It comprises the experience, feel, and knowledge it takes to determine whether your initial interpretation of a pattern remains valid as the market explains itself in the movements that follow. In this sense, the professional chartist is very much like a physician who examines, listens, interprets, and analyzes his findings. Are the heartbeats in keeping with his interpretation? Is the pulse within the expected parameters? Are the patient's symptoms in keeping with the diagnosis? Or, are there danger signals indicating that the initial opinion might be in error?

The foregoing requires understanding of a complex set of guidelines by which the trader can judge whether a given pattern is confirming the indicated interpretation or not. In a live market situation where the pattern is in formation, questions about the validity of your initial interpretation, whether the pattern instead fits one of the many other chart possibilities, whether the pattern is perhaps an exception to the general rule and so on, are much more difficult to answer than when they are asked about a fully formed pattern shown in a chart book.

The answers to these questions spell the difference between success and failure in technical trading.

Despite the prevalent myth about the purity of technical versus fundamental application in today's trading environment, it is quite rare to find a pure technician or a pure fundamentalist. Rather, in today's futures trading, there are but varying degrees of both. The most successful chartist will keep an eye on fundamentals while the best fundamentalist will keep abreast of technical analysis. A professional chartist will want to know something of the salient market fundamentals to determine whether they conform to his chart interpretation. Do incoming statistics and reports correlate with the theory the chart is projecting? If not, perhaps the chart interpretation is faulty. Similarly, the most able fundamentalist will check with a technical expert to determine whether the pattern conforms to his interpretation of the economic dictates. For a fundamentalist, technical analysis is especially critical in timing his intended market position.

On a personal note, I can testify that my greatest trading successes occur when my chart interpretation coincides with my fundamental opinion. Consequently, although I advocate a technical approach to commodity trading, I do not advise trading without a basic understanding of the fundamentals. If your chart interpretation is in conflict with your best understanding or conclusion about market fundamentals, stay out of the market; conversely, if both your chart and fundamental analysis coincide, it is time to take a stronger position in the market.

The paramount advantage of a technical approach to the market is that it is often easier than a fundamental approach. A fundamentalist must keep abreast of and correctly analyze all the factors influencing the supply and demand of a given product. This myriad of information can be quite difficult to follow with precision, especially if you are not a full-time professional trader. Consequently, the fundamental picture can often be unclear or can be subject to a variety of interpretations. With a technical approach, in theory at least, the chart provides all the information you need to trade. The chart says it all: No statistical information is required; no new reports need be awaited.

Futures are volatile. And it is this volatility that gives the professional technician an overwhelming advantage. Because his chart is constantly in touch with the ever-changing panorama, because he has at his disposal all the necessary guidelines to determine the degree his market position is in danger (which it always is), he will theoretically be well ahead of the fundamentalist in detecting a danger signal and responding to its dictates.

Of course, the professional technician should know how much leeway to give before he must react, which signals are valid and which are not, and how much credence to give to each. He must also learn when to pyramid his position and when not. The same guidelines that guard him and warn him of exceptions to the general rule will also advise him that his interpretation was correct and that he is safe to press his investment.

The professional also knows that although general technical principles apply to every futures market, there are specific differences between commodities. Each commodity has its own unique characteristics. Additionally, the professional must recognize that even within a specific commodity, these guidelines will vary depending on the time period of the pattern as it relates to the contract's life.

Not only must the professional technician know the guidelines, he must adhere to them as if it were his religion. He knows that only through strict observance of his charting principles, coupled with his understanding of the fundamentals, will he survive the fast-moving idiosyncracies of futures markets. He will accept that these rules will sometimes force him out of a position that could have earned him much more had he stayed. But he will be satisfied in the knowledge that by adhering to his time-proven principles, he will be trading futures for a long time. And, although he may not make as much as another fellow on every given play, he will still be trading when the other fellow is selling shoestrings for a living.

My advice to the would-be professional is that after you have learned your basics in charting, spend a considerable period of time with charts. Read them, reread them, memorize them, sleep with them, and mentally or physically record the rules that will become evident by careful and exhaustive study. If you think this may take years, you have grasped the enormity of the project.

# The Psychology of a Successful Trader

*Living as a pit trader day after day teaches you many things about the people who inhabit this arena. You learn to distinguish the good traders from the bad, the successful techniques from the unsuccessful, and the good habits from the faulty. You also learn to distinguish the lovers from the fighters, the winners from losers, the serious from the frivolous, the cerebral from the superficial, and the friend from the foe. But above all, you learn that the psychological makeup of the trader is the single most critical element of success.*

**Presented before a group of would-be futures traders,
Chicago, Illinois, October 10, 1970**

"*Do you think I can become a successful futures trader?*" I have been asked this question countless times. It is a difficult question with no certain answer. Obviously, the question is not whether someone can make an occasional profitable transaction; mere chance alone will cause that to happen. The question is whether the person is likely to be consistently successful over the long term. My usual response is a bit of a hedge: "Only you and you alone are best qualified to ascertain the answer."

It would be wonderful if there were a test to determine the issue. Alas, none exists. Seemingly well-qualified people fail at trading while the least likely sometimes succeed. Clearly, many traders make money speculating in futures—sometimes big money—yet many others are losers. What makes the difference? Unfortunately, the only real test of trading potential is the market itself. It is extremely difficult to evaluate a

19

prospective trader's potential before observing his actions and reactions to real market situations.

What are the requirements for success in futures trading? At least four important requisites come to mind that materially influence ultimate success as a futures trader—whether on or off the trading floor. The first three I will simply enumerate without further discussion, the fourth is cardinal and requires thorough comprehension:

1. Approach futures trading as a business enterprise, applying orthodox business rules, judgment, and money management. Futures trading is not a game nor a gamble toward which you can apply rules of chance or probabilities. Futures markets are governed by the fundamental rules of economics.

2. Adopt a predetermined trading plan; a set of rules and established guidelines that are known to be valid and have withstood the test of time. If your philosophy is based on a technical approach to the market, know your rules and religiously adhere to them. If your philosophy is based on a fundamental approach to the market, know the components that will affect supply and demand and honor their dictates.

3. Utilize only *risk capital*—money that, if lost, would not materially alter your standard of living.

However, while the foregoing are very important, it is the fourth requisite that divides the winners from the losers in futures trading. It concerns your psychological makeup. The type of person you are—the way you react under pressure, your ability to make quick decisions, to think logically, the strength of your character, the emotional quotient of your personality, your philosophical approach toward money—will determine your probable chances of success or failure in trading. In futures trading, more so than perhaps in any other field of endeavor, your psychological makeup is critical. Here is what I mean:

After you have established a position in the market, will your judgment be influenced by emotion? Will you be unbiased in your interpretations of facts and market action? Are you likely to mistake an emotional decision for a logical one?

Will you be foolishly swayed by the actions of others? Conversely, will you stubbornly refuse to listen to good advice? If you find you are wrong, can you admit error in the face of defeat? Remember, ultimately you will have to face the truth *openly*—your broker will always know, your family and friends will eventually learn, and floor traders usually know how other traders have fared.

Will you have the strength to remain in the market at a loss when you are certain your calculations are correct? Conversely, when you know you are wrong, will you have the courage to liquidate your losing position quickly to minimize the loss? The old saw about "running away to fight some other day" is nowhere more applicable than to futures. Will your trading be dictated by cold factual interpretation of statistics, instincts, and experience, and not by ego, fear, or stubbornness? Or will inertia, fear to act, or hope for a favorable market turn take over?

Do you have the temperament to allow profits to pyramid when you are right, irrespective of their impressive sums? Conversely, will you know to take your profit quickly, even though the market *may* do better if you wait? Will you know when to do one and not the other? Will you learn from your mistakes, or are you prone to repeating them time and again? Can you take defeat after defeat without succumbing to a defeatist attitude? Will you have the patience necessary to learn the different types of markets, market situations, and how to react to each of them? After a heavy loss, can you face the market the following day without looking back on yesterday? Or, are you more likely to brood about a previous trade and allow it to affect your next attempt?

These questions relate to personality and character. The answers to them spell the difference between a successful futures trader and a loser. But this should come as no surprise. Isn't a person's psychological makeup equally important to success or failure in most fields of endeavor? Of course it is. But there is a difference.

In futures trading, your personality and emotions are stripped of the customary buffers that offer comfort and assistance in most other areas of life. Moreover, in trading, emotional problems are enormously magnified because you are dealing with money—your money! Here, your personality, your emotions, and your character are tested as nowhere else. The normal tranquilizers we consciously or unconsciously lean on in other fields of endeavor are not available in this field. Here, you cannot adjourn the meeting to think things over; you cannot temporarily turn to a different subject; you cannot postpone a decision to consult with an expert or friend; nor can you take time out to relax. The market continues on with or without you; the moment of decision cannot wait. Your emotions and your psychological makeup must not interfere with your ability to make a prudent decision the instant it must be made.

I am reminded of one of the ads written by the Chicago Mercantile Exchange's advertising agency to profile the typical trader: *"Was Toulouse-Lautrec too short to trade commodities? No. Too temperamental. Lautrec was a highly emotional man given to impulsive changes of opinion. Such a personality is ill-suited to futures trading."* Truer words were never spoken.

Thus, in answer to the original question posed, there is much to being a successful futures trader. There are many rules to be applied and many lessons to be learned. There must be a willingness and ability to learn, to comprehend fundamentals and statistics, to grasp technical applications, to develop an inner trading sense, to accept defeat and live with victory, and much more. But most of all, there must be present a multitude of inborn characteristics relating to the trader's personality, psychology, emotional equilibrium, courage, and patience. Alas, such characteristics are generally hidden from view.

# On Tips and Tipping

*One of the most prevalent myths about futures trading is that to succeed a person had to be on the "in"—that tips are the key to success. It was imperative for someone to debunk this myth.*

Presented at a trading seminar, Chicago, Illinois, December 1970

TIP: Alleged inside information—often garbled and rarely useful.

TIPSTER: The person providing the alleged inside information—well intentioned but often a fool.

TIPEE: The person to whom the alleged inside information is passed—well advised to ignore it.

Tips in the stock market are as common as stocks themselves. They increase or decrease with the amount of public attention the market is receiving and the extent of participation by the general public. A good market analyst can fairly accurately predict a peak in a bull market rally by measuring the volume of tips floating around. The more people participating in the market, the more tips, tipsters, and tipees. And the more tips, the more likely the market is nearing its top. Conversely, there are very few tips during a bear market, or when the market is nearing its bottom.

Tipsters are not malicious people. They are not out to give you a bad tip or cause you to lose money. As a matter of fact, more often than not, their intent is benevolent. Tipsters may be motivated by a variety of sincere reasons: They may be your friend, they may want to befriend you, they may owe you a favor, they may have a psychological need for promoting their image of knowledgeability, and on rare occasions they may even have a malicious ulterior motive. The truth of the matter is that however good their intentions, tipsters themselves are often fools. In most cases, they are recently converted tipees, having acquired their information from some other tipster. And they are no more erudite than the previous tipster or next tippee because they have probably acted on the information without ever investigating its source or veracity.

Brokers are the worst offenders. Because they are considered experts, because they have ready access to many tipees, because they have learned to use impressive language, because they have access to information considered tipworthy, they are one of the largest sources of tips. Brokers do not tip maliciously. Although one of their motivations is to make commissions, they do not as a rule create or pass a false tip to generate transactions. After all, since they do better if their customers make money, it follows that their intentions are usually good. But, alas, brokers are no more than human beings. For the most part, they too are driven by greed like so many others and are therefore susceptible to the get-rich-quick syndrome. They too, quite often, cannot determine the veracity of a tip. After all, most tips are based on hidden knowledge and by definition cannot be fully checked. In other words, brokers themselves get embroiled in the belief that their tip has value.

Clearly, there are occasions when the original information tipped had merit. A tip may have started life with a worthwhile rationale about a given stock. However, as in the game of telephone, the tip, in its travels from tipee to tipee becomes garbled or misunderstood; eventually, it gets way too far from its source for its accuracy to be checked. Usually, by the time any of us get a tip, we have no way of knowing whether we are receiving the original information or a distorted version. And even if the tip had merit, there is no way to ascertain how many others acted on it before it reached us and to what extent the price of the stock already discounted the value of the tip.

Many shrewd professional stock players capitalize on tips —not on the tip's inherent value but on its purchasing power. They take a ride on the tip's ability to produce buyers and cause a rise in the stock's price. To capitalize on the tip, these professionals act early in the tip's journey and exit before the tip's value is gone. Unfortunately, the nonprofessional cannot be this agile and is usually left holding the bag.

The negative aspects of tips as they relate to stocks is even more the case with respect to futures. The inherent differences between the two markets are such that there is almost no reason for a tip to exist in the futures market. In the stock market, there is always the possibility that something important occurred that will affect the earnings of a company and thereby its stock price. Moreover, it is possible that such information has somehow leaked out. In the futures market, however, such situations are virtually nonexistent. For instance, it would be impossible to have inside information on the amount of beans or hogs that will be consumed during the coming year, or the size of a crop to be produced, or future weather conditions. Such information can be estimated, such conclusions can be derived through analysis, but in such cases, they are nothing more than predictions and certainly cannot be regarded as tips.

To underscore the difference between tips in securities markets and those in futures, let's examine several types of common tips.

## THE NEW INVENTION TIP

Suppose it were possible to invent a new method of producing more cattle or wheat. Although this may sound like a tip with significance (assuming it is correct), it cannot be expected to affect current crops. If such a tip were to be of any value, it would only be with respect to crops much farther into the future than the currently traded contracts—normally those do not trade more than a year forward. In addition, to ascertain its effect on production, there would have to be an extended period of experimentation with the new invention. By the time the facts were conclusive, it would be no secret and would have no value as a tip in the futures market.

## THE HEALTH EFFECT TIP

A discovery by a doctor or research group that use of a given commodity will prevent cancer, or restore hair, and so on, would certainly have an impact on the given commodity market. But such discoveries are rare. Few people would act on tips about such earthshaking discoveries if they were offered as frequently as their counterparts in the securities market. Not only must you consider that the tip itself may be false or garbled, but—even more so than in stocks—there is no way to determine how many people knew of the discovery before you. Chances are good that you are not getting this tip early enough in its life to capitalize on it in the market. Consequently, such futures markets tips are rare, highly unlikely, and not worth acting on.

## THE SPECIAL SALES AND EXPORT TIPS

An example of this situation could have occurred recently when the United States government agreed to export large quantities of wheat to Russia. If there was inside information, it was quite valuable. However, for every real special sale in the past 10 years, there have probably been 1,000 false rumors or tips about such situations. Which one do you think you would have access to? Can you afford to act on all the false tips in order to catch a true one every once in a thousand times?

These three examples illustrate how the usual form of securities tips are generally inapplicable to commodity markets. One type of tip, however, is somewhat unique to futures and is the source of most so-called commodities tips. It relates to government reports and can be the source of great profit opportunities.

The United States Department of Agriculture (USDA), as well as other government agencies, compiles information and statistics which are released in daily, weekly, monthly, or quarterly reports. The daily reports contain relatively minor information and can be discounted as they relate to tips. However, the weekly, monthly, and quarterly reports often have significant information that can have a substantial impact on markets and their prices. A valid tip on such reports can sometimes be of enormous value.

The security precautions surrounding government reports are formidable. The likelihood of an actual leak of an important USDA report is negligible. Still, rumors of such tips are heard year after year. Greed makes people want to believe they have received special information. However, usually when a tipster tells you he has it on good authority that the price of pork bellies is going to increase because the hog report is bullish, or that a soybeans report will be bearish, he is no more than giving you his or someone else's opinion on the content of the USDA report. That is not a tip based on leaked information.

Quite often, just prior to the release of an important government report, a given brokerage firm does a great deal of buying or selling in a commodity. The word gets out that they know the content of the government's report. Invariably, irrespective of whether the brokerage firm turns out to be correct about the ultimate direction of the market, their knowledge was based on their own research and analysis, not on a tip. Obviously, every brokerage firm can and will attempt to compile the same statistics on which the government bases its reports. The better equipped the brokerage firm, the better its prediction. But it is an informed prediction and no more. Thus, although government reports can be a source of futures market tips, there is no reason to believe that leaks occur except perhaps on the rarest occasion. Any tips you may receive about government reports are most likely someone's opinion about the report.

Unfortunately, most people are susceptible to the idea that someone else knows more than they do. This is particularly true about markets as complex and arcane as futures and particularly if the tipster has some reasonable-sounding rationale about how the information reached him. Everyone wants to make money on a sure thing. Because greed makes people want to believe in them, tips exist and tipees act on them. It will probably always be so.

# Market Liquidity and the Technique of Spreading

*The use of futures markets for the purposes of tax straddles—a technique to defer federal taxation—became one of the most controversial issues facing the American futures industry during the period 1977 through 1981. The issue added to the generally negative image of futures markets and lent credence to the mindless impression that much of the business transacted on futures exchanges was without a commercial purpose.*

*Senator Patrick Moynihan (D-NY) popularized the tax straddle issue by exclaiming that until that moment he had thought that "a butterfly straddle must refer to a highly pleasurable erotic activity popular during the Ming Dynasty." The Economic Recovery Tax Act of 1981 changed the law and instituted end-of-the-year valuations that prevented tax deferral through futures markets. As industry experts predicted, the new tax law was highly detrimental to agricultural futures.*

*As a consequence of this controversy, it became a prevalent belief that the age-old futures technique of spreading (straddling) was utilized primarily for tax purposes. That was blatantly false. However, members of Congress and their staffs who were wrestling with this issue, knew precious little about futures markets. There were but a few primers around and virtually nothing about spreading. The following explanation provided an elementary lesson about the technique of spreading for those who were learning about our markets for the first time.*

> **Presented to members of Congress and their staff as an elementary lesson about the technique of spreading in conjunction with the tax straddle issue, Washington D.C., May 1977**

To explain spreading as a trading technique—its importance to the liquidity and viability of futures markets—it is necessary first to understand the sources that give rise to market liquidity and to explain something of the other traditional futures market trading techniques.

The success of any market—especially a futures market—is largely dependent on its liquidity; that is, the constancy and quantity of bids and offers flowing to that market. In markets, it is axiomatic that the more bids and offers compete with each other, the narrower the spread between the bid and the offer. And the narrower the spread between the bid and offer, the more liquid and efficient the market. Conversely stated, an illiquid market is one where the spread between bid and offer is wide. In such a market there are large price gaps between sales.

The difference between a liquid and illiquid market is critical. Liquid markets are a sure sign that the market is necessary and successfully utilized by the commercial world. The more liquid a market, the less impact a buy or sell order will have on the price. A commercial hedger cannot be certain of the prospective *basis* for his hedge unless he can, with some degree of certainty, be assured of the price level at which his order will be executed. Similarly, a speculator must know that he can buy or sell a given futures market without his own order substantially affecting the price structure. Illiquid markets are generally shunned by both the commercial user and the speculator. Traders know it is no trick to get *into* a market, it is the ability to get *out* that counts. Illiquid markets can become traps from which it is difficult to liquidate a position. Ultimately, illiquid markets dry up and cease to exist.

Bids and offers—the source of liquidity—are the result of orders flowing to the market. This is true whether the orders come in written form, over electronic equipment, or whether they originate in the mind of the member in the "pits" or on the floor of the exchange. This is true whether the orders are at a certain price (price orders), or whether they are to be executed at the going market price (market orders) or in any other form. In every case, orders are the underlying source of bids or offers. Broadly speaking, orders flowing to a futures market stem from two general categories: orders originating *off* the floor of an exchange; and orders originating from members *on* the floor of an exchange.

As a general rule, the more active the floor participation, the more liquid the market. Analysis undertaken at the Chicago

Board of Trade (CBOT) and at the Chicago Mercantile Exchange (CME)—whose combined transaction volume represents approximately 75 percent of this nation's futures business—indicates that between 40 and 60 percent of daily transactions originate on the floor of the exchanges. Less active exchanges have a much lower percentage of floor-originating daily transactions as a percentage of their total volume.

In any discussion of liquidity, it is thus imperative to understand the methodologies that generate on-the-floor order flow. The primary source of on-the-floor order flow comes from exchange member traders who act for their own account; a secondary source of on-the-floor order flow comes from exchange member order-fillers, brokers who from time to time also act for their own account. Together, these exchange members (locals) are the source of a significant proportion of the daily liquidity and are highly meaningful to the success of any market.

There are only a few basic techniques for trading futures markets; they are used interchangeably by participants whether they are off or on the floors of the exchanges. (In practice, however, there is a marked difference in the application of these techniques between the two categories.) These techniques are broadly defined in the following manner: *scalpers* (market-makers), *position traders,* and *spreaders* (spreads are sometimes called straddles, which take many forms including Senator Moynihan's butterfly spread). It must be underscored, however, that there is no exclusivity in this regard; market participants may from time to time interchangeably utilize all the different market techniques.

Scalpers in futures are the equivalent to market-makers in the securities world. However, unlike market-makers in securities, scalpers are under no obligation to make a market in futures, yet that is exactly their function. Their motivation is profit. The scalper is a trader who is constantly bidding as well as offering a market. His trading procedure is geared toward making small profits on each transaction. Thus, he attempts to limit his risk—and at the same time his profit potential—on each transaction by his immediate willingness to offset an assumed position as soon as it becomes profitable. Similarly, he will attempt to immediately offset a losing position. His methodology is based primarily on volume rather than a large profit potential on any given transaction.

There are many types of scalpers. Some operate along classical lines by buying and selling between the smallest increment allowed by contract specifications. Others attempt to profit by buying and selling between larger daily market gyrations. Most scalpers fall somewhere between these two methods or combine the two. In every case, the scalper attempts to flow with the immediate market movement: being among the first to sell as the market begins to fall, and the first to buy when the market starts to rise.

In most cases, the scalper liquidates a portion or his entire position as soon as the minor market movement has ended or as soon as he finds that his purchase or sale is in danger of turning into a loss. Thus, a scalper will institute and liquidate a small position many times during one day. Scalpers seldom leave the pit during trading. As a general rule, most scalpers will keep only a very small—if any—open position overnight. Their methodology generally does not allow for the risk exposure associated with an open overnight position.

Scalpers are predominantly on-the-floor member participants since it is very difficult and far too costly for an off-the-floor participant to conduct this type of market trading. As an obvious consequence of this methodology, the scalper is a constant and continuous source of bids and offers and the primary provider of market liquidity.

Position traders are market participants who take either a long or short position in the market and intend to stay with the position for an undetermined length of time. Their theory is to stay with their position until either the market reaches their price level objective, or the market moves against them to a point that they must liquidate the position. They may stay in positions for as little as one day or as long as several months. It is not time, but rather price level or market economics, that dictates when to assume and when to liquidate positions.

Hedgers and commercial users are predominantly position traders. By definition, their futures position is linked to a nonfutures commercial transaction; therefore, they will maintain their futures position until their price-hedge purpose has been satisfied, or until market economics dictate a different posture. Generally speaking, commercial users are off-the-floor participants.

Similarly, many speculators—both on and off the floor—are position traders. Their market decision is not based on a tangential commercial transaction as with hedgers. They will stay in a position until market conditions have altered considerably, their price level has been reached, or they changed their opinion. Position traders are an important segment of futures market business. They provide the market with stability since their positions account for a major portion of the open interest* of futures contracts. However, by definition, position traders do not often move in and out of the market and therefore do not provide as much market liquidity as market makers.

The technique of a futures market spreader is quite different from a scalper or a position trader. A spreader trades the differential† between two or more contract months in a given commodity rather than the price of any given contract. In other words, the spreader will go *long* a quantity of one contract month and simultaneously go *short* an equal quantity of another month of the same commodity. Thus, his profit potential is not based on whether the price of the commodity goes up or down, but on the narrowing or widening of the differential between the contract months that make up his spread position.

The professional spreader is an artist. His aptitude, agility, and ability to detect the slightest market shift are extraordinary. He is constantly active, moving as a buyer of one month to a seller of another, and immediately back again. In fact, many spreaders perform this activity among three or four contract months at the same time. The object is to pick up even the smallest increment of profit in the shift of the differential(s). The spreader is always alert to a new offer or bid in one given month that could be spread profitably into another month. He is quick to react to any sudden down-draft or up-draft in the market so that he can *unwind* one side of his spread for that small moment of market movement and *hook* it up again as soon as the price movement has stopped.

The vast majority of spreaders apply this technique as a consequence of an accumulated open spread position. A

---

*Open interest (or open commitment) is the total of open long and short positions in a given futures contract. This figure is published daily by every exchange.

†The differential is the difference between the price of one futures contract month and that of another contract month of the same commodity. It can also be the price difference between related markets.

spreader will usually have a theory—based on his analysis of market economics or dynamics—that a certain differential in a given commodity future will, over a period of time, narrow or widen. Thus, he accumulates a spread position commensurate with his opinion and may stay with it for an extended period. This spread position becomes his inventory to which he applies his daily spread transactions. Although often at the end of the trading session, his inventory may not have changed very much during the course of the day, he has constantly traded the spread in question. In other words, during the course of each trading session, a spreader constantly offsets and reinstates a portion of his preestablished spread inventory in an attempt to produce a daily profit as well as to better the overall position.

The techniques of daily spreading against a preestablished inventory represent the principal difference between off-the-floor spreaders and on-the-floor spreaders. Those off the floor rarely attempt this procedure (too difficult and costly); those on the floor almost always do. Consequently, there is a significant difference between the two categories when calculating their respective contribution to liquidity. The on-the-floor group contributes significantly more to daily liquidity than does the off-the-floor group. However, the combined categories are an extremely important component in the open commitment of futures contracts and a major factor in providing market thickness and stability to the price structure. In fact, it is highly doubtful whether any agricultural futures market could function effectively without a large pool of participating spread traders.

Spreading is also carried on—although to a lesser extent—on an intermarket basis. That is, traders also trade the differential between related commodities; for example, going *long* corn and *short* wheat, or *short* hogs and *long* cattle. The theory for this type of transaction is based almost entirely on economic analysis. Both commercial users and speculators make exhaustive studies of the price relationships among related commodities (sometimes of three or four different commodities) and then institute spread positions on the basis of their analysis, or on the basis of the dictates of their commercial transactions. Again, such spreading activities contribute materially to market stability.

Spreaders are critically important in providing bids and offers in *forward* contract months (contracts further out into time) without which commercial agricultural hedging would be impaired. It is a fundamental fact in futures markets that the largest transaction activity occurs in the *nearby* contract months of every commodity. Most speculative orders flow to those contract months that have only a few months of life remaining.* As a general rule, the further out into time a futures contract month is located, the less the trading activity. As a consequence, *back* contract months have much less liquidity than *nearby* contract months. However, commercial hedgers primarily place their hedges in *back* contract months. They could not effectively do so without spreaders.

Indeed, spreaders are sometimes the only source of large quantities of bids and offers in *back* contract months of agricultural products. Commercial hedgers depend on spreaders to provide bids or offers of sufficient size to withstand the impact of the intended hedge transaction. The spreader does so as part of his market technique—buying or selling the *forward* month and simultaneously doing the reverse in the *nearby* month. The hedger is more than happy to offer the spreader a favorable price structure in order to provide the incentive for the spreader to act, for otherwise the hedge may not be placed at all. The importance of the spreader to this function cannot be underestimated. It is a role that no one else is consistently willing to assume.

Spreading is of such importance to the viability of every market that it is one of the central considerations when designing a trading pit. Whenever possible, trading pits are specifically designed to facilitate the spreaders' need to quickly move from one contract month to another. In most successful markets, the pit is essentially circular with a specific area of trading for each contract month at designated places around the circle. In such a configuration, the spreader—standing inside the pit—can hear the bids and

---

*Futures, unlike most securities, have a definite life. Most futures contracts, when first listed, have less than two years of existence. After the contract month reaches maturity, deliveries of the actual product may occur and the contract month ceases to exist. The nearby months are those that will reach maturity within a few months; the forward or back contract months are those that are further out into time.

offers in all the contract months and quickly move to buy and sell in two or more of them.

Spreading is such a significant element in futures markets that an active market may have many spread transactions consummated by and between spreaders or spread orders. On any given day, spread traders or brokers with spread orders will execute their spread orders directly with another spread trader or spread broker. In such cases, two spreaders are intent on making the exact opposite spread transaction; they or their customers each have a different need, opinion, or theory as to which direction the spread differential is headed.

As a result of the different applications, theories, commercial needs, and different opinions, there is almost always an active spread market in every successful futures contract, wherein spreaders seek out their opposites by calling out the differential at which they are willing to do a spread trade. Indeed, it is customary for a trader or broker to enter a pit and inquire about the going spread to buy one given month and sell another or vice versa. If it is a successful market, there is always an available differential for either side of a spread.

There is an erroneous assumption among some unschooled market observers that spreading is virtually a riskless procedure. This is untrue. Naturally, as a general rule, when a given market goes up or down, all the contract months of that market tend to move in the same direction; thus, spreads do carry less risk than an outright long or short position. However, the degree of movement for one contract month may be quite different than for another. As a consequence, the differential between two or more futures contract months in any given commodity is constantly in flux.

There are many reasons for this changing relationship between contract months. In the first place, the differential is consistently subject to different views and applications of market participants. More important, the differential is constantly affected by supply and demand statistics, prospective anticipations, cyclical considerations, interest rates, general U.S. and world economic conditions, a variety of government reports, technical market dynamics, and a host of other factors.

The contention that a spread position differential is completely safe is blatantly absurd as any simple analysis will show. Moreover, such an assumption would belie the fact that spreading is a highly profitable technique for those market participants who have the talent and degree of sophistication it demands. It is axiomatic that where there is a potential for reward, there is also risk.

Actually, there are probably more different theoretical views on spread differentials than there are on whether the market price will go up or down. A variety of market applications are also possible with the spread technique that are not as efficient through position trading. For instance, when a trader desires to accumulate a large outright long or short position in a *back* month, he often cannot easily do so because of lack of liquidity in the *forward* contract. In such a case, the trader can sometimes find another trader seeking to execute a spread transaction where one of the contract months involved is of interest to the first trader. In such a case, the first trader will make the spread transaction and then liquidate the *nearby* contract month in which he has no interest, ending up with an outright long or short position in the distant contract month he wanted in the first place.

Although a simultaneous buy-and-sell transaction is the technique used by the majority of spread traders, this is not the only form of spreading. Spreading is also a function of a delayed and separate futures transaction. Sometimes a trader who has maintained a long or short position in a given contract month will subsequently establish the opposite position in another month of the same commodity thereby creating a spread position. In that case, the trader's motivation may be twofold: By establishing the spread, he reduces the market risk for his original position; and second, he hopes to enhance his profit on the basis of the spread differential he established. Such delayed spreading techniques are often also undertaken when the original trade is at a loss and the trader does not yet wish to liquidate the position. In such cases, the trader believes the original position will eventually prove profitable, but until a more favorable market trend develops, he wants to limit his exposure by assuming an opposite position on another contract month. His intention is, at some future date, to liquidate the secondary position and reassume his original outright long or short posture.

Often such delayed spreads are also motivated by tax considerations. For instance, if an original long market position has earned a substantial profit and if the position has been in existence for several months—in the absence of tax considerations—the trader might liquidate it whenever he feels the market has reached the desired profit potential. However, because of tax considerations, it sometimes behooves the trader instead to institute a spread by selling an equivalent quantity of the same commodity in another contract month. Although the trader now exposes his accumulated profit to the risk of an adverse differential movement, he may thereby establish a long-term capital gain in the original position. In other words, the delayed spread gives the trader the ability to stay with his long position for the 6-month tax period necessary at a reduced market risk.

Unfortunately, the so-called *tax spread* is often mistaken with a similar non-tax-motivated spread transaction. It is almost impossible to differentiate one spread from another. In fact, many spread positions—originally placed as part of a participant's normal market methodology—may later be motivated by tax considerations and utilized according to the dictates of prudent tax consequence.

In theory, a "tax spread" is a spread motivated *solely* by tax considerations. In practice, such a transaction is highly unlikely since in every situation the market participant will also want to place the spread in a manner that will afford him the potential for a profitable spread differential. By definition, therefore, all spread transactions include a profit motivation. Conversely, tax spreads are subject to the same differential risks as any other spread position. Motivation aside, it should be understood that a tax spread is placed in the market with the same rules and in accordance with the same procedural requirements as all other spread transactions.

While it is not the objective of this analysis to dwell on tax spreads, it should be noted that their inherent tax considerations are essentially no different than tax considerations in other fields of endeavor. Similar business decisions legitimately occur in every walk of life and within virtually every form of commerce. Moreover, tax implications are always a critical element and integral consideration for every businessman in every field, and with respect to every commercial venture or transaction. Most important, the idea that the majority of futures spread transactions are tax motivated is pure nonsense.

Spreading is a futures technique as old as the markets themselves, and is one of the largest contributing sources of bids and offers to the market. Indeed, it can be argued that spreaders are the backbone of agricultural futures market liquidity. Without the activities of spreaders, agricultural commercial hedgers cannot effectively place their hedges in forward contract months of futures markets—to the ultimate detriment of U.S. agriculture.

# Our American
# Free Markets

*Here was a unique opportunity to speak about a characteristic of free markets, particularly futures markets, which is rarely mentioned in assessments of their intrinsic values: their unyielding force on behalf of human rights.*

*Indeed, it is an eye-opening experience to visit the floors of the futures exchanges, their administrative departments, and the back offices of their member firms. Only then does one gain insight into the free market's disregard of age-old prejudices and traditional inequalities that continue to plague other spheres of our society.*

Presented at the American Jewish Committee (AJC) Human Rights Dinner, Chicago, Illinois, June 17, 1991, at which Mr. Melamed was awarded the AJC Human Rights Medallion. Congressman Dan Rostenkowski was the guest speaker

We hear much these days about the sins of the marketplace. We hear much about the sins of market-makers: their greed, their lack of integrity, their misconduct. No doubt some of what we hear is true and that is most unfortunate. We must be vigilant in our efforts to do better. But these regrettable sins of the free marketplace do not represent the whole story, nor do they even represent a significant portion of the story. For lost in all this negative rhetoric is something so fundamentally important about free markets, something so priceless, something so valuable, that lest we occasionally stop to remind ourselves, we might allow irreparable injury to occur. We might someday, in a thoughtless moment of sanctimonious folly, allow someone or something to take from us the most precious gift we possess: the markets of America and the unyielding force on behalf of human rights that these markets represent.

In *Free to Choose*, Nobel laureate Milton Friedman asserts that the United States is the result of two separate but interdependent miracles: an economic miracle and a political miracle. He explains that each miracle resulted from the implementation of a separate set of revolutionary ideas and that both sets of ideas—by a curious coincidence—were formulated in documents published in the same year, 1776.

One set of ideas was embodied in Adam Smith's *The Wealth of Nations*, a masterpiece of economic thought. It established that an economic system could succeed only in an environment that permits individuals freely to pursue their own objectives for purely personal gain. As a consequence of such pursuits, the individual, when taken in mass, will be led by an invisible hand to promote an overall social good.

The second set of ideas, drafted by Thomas Jefferson, was embodied in the *Declaration of Independence*. It proclaimed a new nation—the first in history to be established based on a set of self-evident truths: *that all men are created equal, that they are endowed by their Creator with certain unalienable Rights; that among these are Life, Liberty, and the pursuit of Happiness.*

The success of our nation, asserts Friedman, is a consequence of the combination of these two basic ideals: economic freedom coupled with political freedom. The ideals are inexorably intertwined. One without the other cannot work.

History is replete with examples of sovereign powers that ignored these truths. Indeed, we need only be mindful of the desperate events unfolding today in the Soviet Union to bear witness to the unmitigated failure of communism, a dictatorial political system embedded in an economic structure based on government central planning. As Friedman suggests, the Soviet experiment not only proves that economic freedom is an essential requisite for political freedom, it is unequivocal proof of the opposite as well: The combination of economic and political power in the same hands is a sure road to tyranny.

When we move from the macroeconomic stage to the practical arena of everyday life, we find that there is yet another dimension to Adam Smith's free market postulates that is also entwined with Thomas Jefferson's political freedom ideals.

The lofty principles published in 1776, when applied to the practical world of 1991, offer some startling, albeit expected, results: Successful markets are the quintessential example of human rights and equality.

Did you ever hear any rational person say: *"I won't buy those lower priced wares I need, simply because you—the seller—are a Jew"*? If you did, it was not for long. Those who conducted their business practices in this fashion were soon left in the historical scrap heap of economic malfunction. Did you ever hear any rational person say: *"I will not sell my wares to your higher bid simply because you are Polish or because you are Afro-American, Irish, or Chinese."* Not in the markets I know. Ask Lee Iacocca whether Americans refused to buy Japanese cars simply because they were not made by Americans!

The financial markets I know are color blind. They know no distinction between race, they know nothing about ethnic origin, and they are indifferent to gender. Price and quality are what matters. In the financial markets I know, the trophy goes not to the Catholic or to the Jew, not to the white or black, not to the male or female, but to the one who understands the economic principles of supply and demand. Family background or origin, physical infirmities, and gender are meaningless when measured against an individual's ability to determine the customer's needs and how to market a product. Little else matters. The market rewards you when you are right and punishes you when you are wrong no matter who your father was, no matter what he did for a living, and no matter where he came from.

No other private sector establishment, entity, or apparatus is more free of human prejudice and less concerned with race or religion than the American free market structures. The principles embodied in Adam Smith's *Wealth of Nations* and the precepts set forth in Thomas Jefferson's Declaration of Independence have produced the miracle we know as the United States of America.

Not only have those principles triumphed over centrally planned economic systems, they have brought the practical world of our markets to the leading edge of human rights and equality. This is especially evident in the financial markets of Chicago. Examine our trading floors and our employees, walk into our trading pits, and review our firms and their personnel. Religious discriminations of past eras are virtually nonexistent; racial barriers still practiced elsewhere are not recognizable here; and ethnic distinctions of consequence in other endeavors are meaningless in our workplace. Did you know that sex discrimination within the infrastructure of American finance was first challenged by our Chicago markets? Did you know that our Chicago markets led the battle against race discrimination in the business world? This was accomplished without fanfare, without marches, and without outside pressures.

While we do not claim utopia, Chicago's financial markets have gone a long way toward becoming the ultimate equalizer of race and religion, ethnic origin, and sexual gender. Here, talent is supreme, hard work is rewarded, integrity is prized, and excellence is absolute. Indeed, with respect to human rights, the financial markets of Chicago practice what the United States Constitution preaches.

Is it any wonder Carl Sandburg immortalized our city's distinguished market history: *Hog Butcher for the World/Stacker of Wheat.* Is it any wonder our good friend Congressman Dan Rostenkowski has stood up to those who threaten our markets' existence or impede their growth. He does it in such a delicate manner. He reads to them a poem by Thomas Babington Macaulay which tells of *Horatius at the Gate,* the lone Roman gatekeeper who valiantly defended the ashes of his fathers and the temples of his gods. Then Congressman Rostenkowski explains the following to our adversaries: *At the end of the day, after all the battles they have faced, they will yet have to face the chairman of the House Ways and Means Committee, who, like Horatius, will stand to protect the temples of Chicago—our markets.*

And like Horatius, whenever we hear a blanket condemnation of the free market system, let us too rise up zealously in its defense. At stake is the very essence of the American miracle. At stake is our very freedom. And while there are failings within the markets, and regrettably, while there are sins by some within the system, these negatives are insignificant when measured against the incalculable and priceless achievements of the American free market system.

# PART II

# THE BIRTH OF A
# MARKET—FINANCIAL
# FUTURES

*The successful birth of financial futures was the result of a convergence of many factors: The right idea at the precisely correct moment in world history; the wherewithal to convince government officials of its merit; the ability to implement the idea and convert it into practical contracts for trade; the designing of a strategy to publicize the concept and convince the financial community of its value, potential, and practicability; a sequence of world events ideally suited to spur the utilization of markets designed to manage the risk of currency and interest rate price movements; and traders who could start the ball rolling.*

*Each of the foregoing components was important. Without any one of them, the idea may have faltered. But what is unequivocally certain is that the last component was the most critical. For without the cadre of Chicago Mercantile Exchange (CME) traders who left the known risks of the cattle, hog, and pork belly pits for the unknown dangers of foreign exchange, the idea could not have been implemented. Similarly, without the unwavering support of the first wave of traders who came to the newly formed International Monetary Market (IMM), betting on a career in a unique and untested arena, the new market surely would have sputtered and could have failed during its critical formative years. Indeed, without the zeal of these members, without their spirit, without their guts, and without their devotion, the revolution we envisioned could not have occurred.*

*It is noteworthy how quickly revolutionary fervor spreads once unleashed. Although the financial futures revolution was initiated by*

43

*the members of the CME, a similar phenomenon followed a year later at the Chicago Board of Trade (CBOT) when the Chicago Board Options Exchange, the first organized market for exchange-traded options, was born. And it happened again a few years later when CBOT traders ventured forth from century old successful grain markets to enter the untested realm of Treasury bond futures.*

*Who were these venturesome traders? What did they know? Why did they do it? Listen to a poem I wrote for the celebration of the tenth anniversary of the International Monetary Market, June 4, 1982:*

### Who Were We?

*We were traders to whom it not matter*
*Whether it was eggs or gold, bellies or*
*The British Pound, turkeys or T-bills.*

*We were babes in the woods, innocents,*
*In a world we did not understand,*
*Too dumb to be scared.*

*We were audacious, brazen, raucous pioneers,*
*Too unworldly to know we could not win.*

*That the odds against us were too high;*
*That the banks would never trust us;*
*That the government would never let us;*
*That Chicago was the wrong place.*

*The traders became our army. They were our secret weapon. Most of the world underestimated the power they represented.*

# A Futures Market
# in Currencies

*At the time of this address, we were less than 30 days from what was to become the dawn of the financial futures revolution. Most of the financial world had ignored the coming event. Others scorned the idea, ridiculing the concept that financial instruments could become the realm of futures trade. The chance to appear before the New York Society of Security Analysts was a welcomed opportunity to preach to the heathens.*

**Presented to the New York Society of Security Analysts, Inc., New York, New York, April 19, 1972**

On the eve of the birth of the International Monetary Market, it is fitting to address the Society of Security Analysts. My mission is to explain why there should be a futures market in currency, how this market will be different from the interbank forward system currently used by the commercial world, and why we believe the IMM will succeed.

Indeed, why is there a need for a futures market in currencies? In other words, might this not merely be the invention of a legalized form of gambling, another unnecessary evil? Certainly that has been suggested by many, on more than one occasion. You might even ask *why a futures market in anything?*

The fact of the matter is that, whether we like it or not, we deal in futures all the time. The housewife who buys more than she immediately needs because a given product is on sale; the butcher who contracts for delivery of pork at an agreed upon price months in advance of his anticipated sales, the weaver who agrees to deliver his cloth at a future date, long before the product is ready; the wholesaler who builds inventory in advance of anticipated demand.

Isn't the investor in real estate speculating in futures? Isn't the farmer doing the same when he plants his crop? Surely a securities analyst is speculating in futures when he gives a buy recommendation on a particular stock on the basis of his projection of future earnings. Doesn't the buyer for a department store take into consideration the same elements that go into a futures market trade? What is the supply, what is the demand, what is the trend? Indeed, there are thousands of everyday examples in business and social life that inherently include the elements of futures trade and futures speculation. Dealing in futures is an ordinary, daily occurrence.

Does this suggest that we are always gambling? I suppose so, in a sense. But only in the sense that we gamble when we cross a busy intersection. Rather, I think what we are doing is applying to our social and business needs those factors that experience has taught us are necessary and prudent in moving successfully through life. We walk on the green light and look both ways before we cross the street. A futures exchange is an extension of this principle. It is a central facility for businessmen who wish to cross the street more safely. It is a mechanism that provides the procedure and prescribes the rules by which certain spheres of commercial activity can shed some risk and implement their business needs in a more prudent and organized fashion.

When the first question posed is approached from this perspective, the question is not *why*, but rather *why not* a futures market in currency? And why did it take so long to come about?

To begin with, an organized exchange cannot establish a market in a given product unless society has an inherent need to transfer risk. In other words, to be viably traded on a futures exchange, the commodity in question must be subject to consistent and substantial price changes that necessitate forward transactions. This also implies that the commodity to be traded at a futures exchange must already sustain an active, albeit, decentralized cash market.

Currency meets the foregoing requirements. Even *before* the decision on December 18, 1971, by the financial ministers of the Group of 10 to substantially widen the permissible band of exchange-rate differentials between the dollar and other currencies from existing parity to plus or minus 2.25 percent, foreign currency was actively traded in the interbank market on a spot and forward basis. The decision by the Group of 10, necessitated by the dictates of reality, officially recognized that currency price fluctuations were going to continue in a consistent and substantial manner. The new rate of parity— and the strong probability of further band expansion or even currency floating, whether by traditional floating methods, crawling pegs or other forms of parity adjustments—dramatically increased the need for importers, exporters, multinational corporations, and financial institutions to utilize the currency interbank market for their international business transactions. You can hardly open the newspaper these days without coming across an item about a loss suffered by a major company as a consequence of currency value changes, or about a corporate comptroller who was relieved of his duties because he neglected to protect his employer from the possibility of currency devaluation or revaluation. Clearly, the basic elements for currency to be listed for trade on a futures exchange are abundantly evident.

The real question is whether a futures exchange should undertake this mission? The answer can be found in a paragraph from Professor Milton Friedman's paper, *The Need for a Futures Market in Currencies*, commissioned by the Chicago Mercantile Exchange in the fall of 1971:

> Changes in the international financial structure will create a great expansion in the demand for foreign cover. It is highly desirable that this demand be met by as broad, as deep, as resilient a futures market in foreign currencies as possible in order to facilitate foreign trade and investment.

This leads us to the second question: How does the futures market differ from the existing interbank market? In terms of a general definition, the interbank market performs the same functions as our intended futures market. Both markets will provide the mechanism for the purchase and sale of currency for delivery on a forward date. Both, then, allow for the transfer of risk. However, the similarity ends with the general definition. The differences begin in application.

The most basic difference is that the interbank market is restricted to the commercial world. A futures market will not succeed unless it draws participation from both the commercial user as well as the speculator. And why not the speculator? Doesn't the individual—speculator or not—have a similar right as a businessman to protect his estate from possible loss by virtue of currency value change? Would it be fair if the individual—speculator or not—were excluded from the stock market, the bond market, or the real estate market? But, more importantly, could these markets work effectively without the individual speculator? The speculator's role in a futures market is imperative. It is the speculator who can provide constant bids and offers in the market. It is the speculator who is willing to accept and offset the risk of the commercial user. It is the speculator who can fuel the necessary liquidity without which the commercial participant cannot effectively use the market. Friedman's requirement for breadth, depth, and resiliency are precisely the features that can be best provided by an organized futures exchange. Or to put it another way, it is our view that a market in currency will become viable only through the interaction of speculative and commercial activity in an open, free, and competitive arena. Such an arena is what we provide.

The second paramount distinction between the interbank and futures market is the nature of the transactions. Futures markets are impersonal. They are not tooled for the specific needs of each separate business transaction, nor is each transaction defined by the buyer's or seller's specific need of that moment. Instead, every transaction is based on the same uniform unit of trade, the same uniform manner of delivery, on the same uniform predetermined forward date. The element of uniformity is unique to organized futures exchanges and is perhaps the quintessential ingredient of their existence. This ingredient makes it possible for every participant to offset an existing market position with any other participant regardless with whom the original transaction was undertaken. Consequently, the exchange becomes the clearinghouse of all the transactions, which allows the exchange to act as the guarantor to the buyer as well as to the seller. No similar capability exists in the interbank market. It is the underpinning of futures markets.

Another difference is in the way transactions are made. In the interbank market, transactions are private, making it necessary to get other quotes to ensure the price you are quoted is fair and competitive. In the futures market, bids and offers are by open outcry in an open and competitive arena.

Less dramatic but also important is a futures exchange's capacity for compiling and disseminating facts, statistics, and information concerning a particular market. There is no other agency, except perhaps the federal government, that can better serve the public and industry concerned. And there is today an overwhelming need for information on the subject of currency. This demand is going to continue and increase. A futures exchange is capable of fulfilling this need in an organized and comprehensive manner.

Futures exchanges can also provide the necessary service and communication mechanisms to make their markets accessible to every segment of commerce, industry, and the public in every corner of the globe. An exchange can and will provide instant access to all participants, enabling them to translate their needs to action in seconds. Consequently, interest in the currency market will expand substantially. When it does, the need for informed advisors will grow and an educational process within the brokerage industry will ensue. While this process is slow and often intangible, it nevertheless is very real and desperately needed. When it happens, it will greatly benefit the interbank market as well.

Finally, a futures exchange will act as a public weather vane and instant barometer of the market. It will offer an up-to-the-minute opinion poll of skilled, unskilled, public, and commercial experts concerning the value, stability, or lack of stability of a given currency. Good news or bad will openly and immediately be reflected in the price of the product. This is a vital element of a competitive marketplace and is integral to the free enterprise system.

The foregoing are but a few of the basic differences between the futures and interbank markets. There are many more, but none of them are such that they prevent coexistence. As a matter of fact, we are certain that if the IMM is successful, it will both complement and supplement the existing spot and forward currency market. The interbank market will learn to depend on the futures market and vice versa.

Will we be successful? The best and honest answer is that only time will tell. We have the will and the fortitude; we have the facilities, the infrastructure, the personnel, the breadth of membership, the communications mechanisms, and (we think) the correct contract specifications. Moreover, while there are many who disagree, in our opinion all indications so far are that we will triumph with this idea. The interest we have generated from commerce and public alike—even before we started trading—has been phenomenal. Even the banking community—which received the idea coolly at first—is taking a second look and in many cases has lent a hand. Several respected bank officials have even joined our board of directors. In addition, we have received help, advice, and encouragement from virtually every segment of the academic and financial world as well as from the federal government. And this is only the beginning.

We realize we have much yet to learn and that much of our knowledge will come after the market has opened. As we learn, our market may change; in fact, it may become dramatically different from what it will be on opening day. It may expand its horizons. Nor do we anticipate instant success. We strongly feel that because the concept is important and correct, our market must be given a minimum test of two or three years before it can be judged.

Finally, why us and why here? Again Milton Friedman answered the query:

> Such a wider market is almost certain to develop in response to the demand. The major question is where. The U.S. is a natural place and it is very much in the interest of the U.S. that it should develop here. Its development here will encourage the growth of other financial activities in this country, providing both additional income from export of services and easing the problem of executing monetary policy.

*Us*—because the Chicago Mercantile Exchange is a large and established futures institution with the expertise to take on such a mission; *us*—because the Chicago Mercantile Exchange has created a unique and separate futures entity to trade exclusively in financial instruments. We believe in the future of the International Monetary Market. We are ready to do everything that is necessary and to give it the full measure of our ability toward its success.

# Chicago's Future
# in Futures

*The primary requirement for success of the IMM was the unwavering support of our members. Thus, the results of our first year were critical. To our relief, we were able to point proudly to our achievements and talk bravely about the new era the IMM represented. The 1973 Annual Report to the IMM membership reflected this belief. In it, I unabashedly stated to IMM members, "The new era will afford us the opportunity to expand our potential into other areas within the monetary frame of reference. That was the essence of the philosophy that fostered the IMM. Our new market was specifically designed to encompass as many viable trading vehicles in the world of finance as practicable. We must be willing and ready to explore all possibilities."*

*The results of our first year also gave us courage to explain to our immediate community what was happening at the Chicago Mercantile Exchange. This was no idle task. Success of our ambitious IMM plans—in great measure— depended on the support of Chicago's establishment and its leadership. It was imperative that we spend time at Chicago's two prominent academic institutions: the University of Chicago and Northwestern University.*

*The theme delivered here was central to the message we reserved for Chicago. Our city was special, its citizens were innovators, and its institutions vibrant. Of particular importance were the futures markets of Chicago. They were inventive, successful, and expanding. What's more, they represented an economic engine that could lead our city to greatness.*

*The message was productive. We once had occasion to make an important IMM request of Chicago's well known Mayor, Richard J. Daley. "But what will the IMM do for Chicago?" the Mayor inquired. "Mr. Mayor," I responded unabashedly, "if I am right about financial futures, the IMM will move the center of gravity of U.S. finance a couple of feet westward from New York." The Mayor laughed and instantly granted our request.*

---

Presented at the 23rd Annual Fall Management Conference,
Northwestern University, Evanston, Illinois, November 7, 1973

---

51

Much of what happens is by accident;
Much of what happens is by design;
Much of what happens is a combination of both.

A city lives or dies, prospers or fails as a result of both accident and design but particularly as a result of what its inhabitants do with what they have. Let us read from the *Book of Genesis:*

> After two whole years, Pharaoh dreamed that he was standing by the Nile, and behold, there came up out of the Nile, seven cows, sleek and fat, and they fed in the reed grass.
>
> And behold, seven other cows, gaunt and thin, came up out of the Nile after them and stood by the other cows on the bank of the Nile, and the gaunt and thin cows ate up the seven sleek and fat cows, and the Pharaoh awoke.
>
> And he fell asleep and dreamed a second time; and behold, seven ears of grain, plump and good, were growing on one stalk.
>
> And behold, after them sprouted seven ears, thin and blighted by the east wind.
>
> And the thin ears swallowed up the seven plump and full ears. And the Pharaoh awoke, and behold, it was a dream.

And after Pharaoh summoned Joseph to interpret the dream, Joseph said to Pharaoh:

> There will come seven years of great plenty throughout all the land of Egypt, but after them, there will arise seven years of famine.

And Joseph proposed:

> Let them gather all the food of these good years that are coming, and lay up grain under the authority of Pharaoh for food in the cities, and let them keep it.
>
> That food shall be a reserve for the land against the seven years of famine that are to befall the land of Egypt, so that the land may not perish through famine.

Ergo, the concept of a futures market was born. Joseph's idea saved the day. Egypt would place forward buy hedges during the period of oversupply to provide for their needs during the period of undersupply. Alas, Joseph and the Pharaoh did not go far enough. They failed to grasp the full magnitude of Joseph's innovation. They missed their chance to open the First Nile Board of Trade. Indeed, it would take centuries before the concept would fully crystallize and be utilized to the full scope of its potential. Indeed, it required the resourcefulness, wisdom, and vision of Chicagoans to put Joseph's concept to work.

Was it an accident that happened in Chicago? Was it some grand design? Or was it a combination of both? We could discuss these questions at length. We could examine them philosophically or logically. But they are of no great concern to us now. What is important is that it happened here. As a result, today Chicago is the capital of the world's futures markets.

In the first 10 months of this year, 903,000 hog contracts were traded at the Chicago Mercantile Exchange (CME) equaling 144.5 million hogs with a monetary value of $11.2 billion. During the same period, 1.2 million wheat contracts were traded at the Chicago Board of Trade (CBOT) equaling 181.6 million tons of wheat with a monetary value of $23 billion.

A city grows by adjusting to changes and bending with the constant flux of time. To survive, it must fit and meet the needs of the present. In Chicago, the stockyards are gone. But, in 1972 at the Chicago Mercantile Exchange, approximately 1.4 million cattle contracts were traded, the equivalent of 48 million head of cattle amounting to a value of approximately $20 billion. We no longer store grain in Chicago. But, in the first 10 months of this year, the Chicago Board of Trade recorded approximately 7 million transactions of wheat, corn, and soybeans, the monetary value of which is upward of $170 billion.

Need we explain the significance of these markets? Need we spell out their benefits to our city, country, or the world? Suffice it to say that futures markets are now an integral part of the agricultural structure of this country. Suffice it to say that the benefits are of such scope and magnitude that a person would be hard-pressed to enumerate and evaluate them all. Suffice it to say that futures markets provide our nation with a unique economic tool that cannot be duplicated in any other form. Suffice it to say that its users are diverse and everywhere. Futures serve as an insurer, act to discover prices, function as a stabilizer of prices, operate to level out supply, provide a consensus prediction, stimulate competition, perform as an educational institution, catalog and disseminate statistics, work for both the consumer and producer, aid in the marketing of food products, and, at the same time, offer speculators the opportunity to test their ability against the wiles of the price gods.

Suffice it to say that U.S. commodity futures exchanges are part and parcel of the most successful system of agriculture and marketing in the world—a system whose productivity has more than trebled in the past 20 years; a system that is the marvel and model for the rest of the world. Indeed, it is with a great deal of pride that we in Chicago can boast of having the two exchanges that account for over 80 percent of this nation's futures business.

Can we fully evaluate what this means for Chicago? Can we fully assess what $66.1 billion worth of transactions on the CME in 1972 and $123 billion worth at the CBOT means to the financial infrastructure of our city? Can we fully estimate the value of the daily margin deposits to our city banks? The CME alone currently deposits $100 million per day. We estimate that the cash deposits of the Chicago Board of Trade, the Chicago Mercantile Exchange, and the International Monetary Market (IMM) to Chicago banks on any given business day amount to approximately $400 million. And margin deposits are but a portion of the total deposits held in Chicago by the member firms of these markets. Can we calculate the economic thrust generated by these deposits? The financial services? I leave that to the bankers. Moreover, these figures will easily be doubled in 1973.

As a matter of fact, there are those who estimate that by 1980, the futures business in the United States will have increased fivefold. This would mean that the Chicago Mercantile Exchange, the Chicago Board of Trade and the International Monetary Market should be generating about $2 billion in margin deposits at Chicago's banks. If this estimate is extreme, remember that an increase of only $1^1/_2$ times present levels—a considerable slowdown of our present rate of growth—would still account for $1 billion in daily margin money deposits for Chicago banks. A sizable figure by anyone's standards.

What is abundantly clear is that Chicago's futures markets are an important and integral part of our nation's agriculture, while also a significant financial engine in this city's infrastructure. Of equal import is that in this field of business,

Chicago is second to none. So can we rest on our laurels? Should we be satisfied with the growth of our Chicago markets during the past decade? Volume on the CME alone has risen by nearly 1700 percent since 1963. An observer might conclude that we could take a well-deserved rest and enjoy our successes. If we did, it would not be the way of Chicago.

It was with good reason that Nelson Algren called Chicago the "City on the Make." Chicago has a restless soul. It is forever probing new vistas, new frontiers. This spirit has made us great and leads us to an even greater destiny. This is the essence of our future. And when Treasury Secretary Shultz visited Chicago several months ago, he made a remarkable statement. He stated he was proud of his Chicago heritage because most of the important new ideas emerging during the past two or three decades were either born in Chicago or were conceived by Chicagoans.

Chicago's futures markets are true to this tradition. Not satisfied with their phenomenal growth, they gave birth in 1972 to two new and highly innovative concepts that may prove to be of revolutionary significance in the growth of Chicago as a world financial center. The Chicago Board of Trade inaugurated its Chicago Board Options Exchange; and the Chicago Mercantile Exchange, its International Monetary Market.

I will dwell on the latter because I know of it firsthand. I fervently believed in the idea for a futures market in foreign currency. I convinced our Board members and our membership that it was a concept on which we could build the International Monetary Market and the future of the CME.

Having done so we were faced with the formidable task of translating the idea into practicable application. To implement it, we needed a helping hand from yet another Chicagoan, Professor Milton Friedman. It was Professor Friedman who gave us the courage to believe we were onto something big and worthwhile. And it was his unquestionable prestige and credentials that opened doors for us in Washington and enabled us to state with confidence that a futures exchange for foreign currency was a necessity whose time had come.

Listen to what he wrote in his position paper on this subject upon the fall of Bretton Woods:*

---

*Commissioned by the Chicago Mercantile Exchange, "The Need for a Futures Market in Currencies," was written by Professor Milton Friedman in 1971.

Admitting that there is now a spot and forward market in London, Zurich and New York, but it has neither the breadth, nor the depth, nor the resilience that is needed. A really satisfactory futures market cannot depend solely on hedging transactions by persons involved in foreign trade or investment. . . . The market needs speculators who are willing to take open positions as well as hedgers. The larger the volume of speculative activity, the better the market and the easier it will be for persons involved in foreign trade and investment to hedge at lower costs and at market prices that move only gradually and are not significantly affected by even large commercial transactions.

The changes in the international financial structure will create a great expansion in the demand for foreign cover. It is highly desirable that this demand be met by as broad, as deep, as resilient a futures market in foreign currencies as possible in order to facilitate foreign trade and investment. Such a wider market is almost certain to develop in response to the demand. The major open question is where. The U.S. is a natural place and it is very much in the interest of the U.S. that it should develop here. Its development here will encourage the growth of other financial activities in this country, providing both additional income from the export of services, and easing the problem of executing monetary policy.

You must fully comprehend the magnitude of our undertaking to assess and evaluate its progress and success. What we did was revolutionary. What we did was journey into uncharted waters. What we did was enter an arena that was the private and sacred shrine of the banking community. What we did was design an economic tool that previously had been used exclusively in agriculture. What we undertook was to explain the meaning of Bretton Woods and the significance of its breakdown. What we undertook was to teach the American public about a investment vehicle heretofore unknown on the American shore.

We knew it would be a long and hard lesson about a new order that we ourselves were to learn as we went along. Because we were dealing with a new commodity, there were no rules, no frame of reference. Predictably, our market has already experienced a number of significant changes. It has been subjected to modifications brought about by our own daily dealings with this new vehicle of finance, previously the sole possession of the gnomes of Zurich, London, and Frankfurt.

Why, we asked, should this be so? By what right should European centuries-old markets be the sole determinants of the value of the dollar? Why should there not be an equally resilient market on the American shore? And why should such a market not serve both the business community as well as the public at large? As a matter of fact, the market we had in mind would work effectively only when there was a real interaction between speculative and commercial interests. Such a market would act as an alternative to the interbank market. Such a market would force foreign exchange rates to become more competitive and realistic. Such a market could become liquid much farther out into time.

In the beginning, New York banks and bankers considered the project too ridiculous to consider seriously. Today, the New York banks look at our venture in an entirely different light. Today, for instance, both the Chase Manhattan and the City National Bank of New York participate directly in our market. In Chicago, we were accepted from the very inception. Not only were we assisted by all the major Chicago banks, but the Continental Illinois National Bank became our foreign exchange delivery agent and the First National Bank of Chicago became a clearing member. Moreover Mr. A. Robert Abboud, then Executive Vice President of the First National Bank, and Dr. Beryl Sprinkel, then chief economist of the Harris Trust & Savings Bank became members of our Board of Directors.

To us it was obvious. If we were right about the need for such a market, then it belonged in Chicago—the capital of futures markets. It would be a long, long time before our market fully blossomed, but from the start we were certain the result would be worth the effort. What spurred us on was the magnificent potential of the concept. Finance was, after all, limitless in its application.

To date, the evidence continues to mount that our idea is in synch with the new world monetary standard. Indeed, when the IMM began, all we sought was a world in which rates would annually fluctuate up or down against the dollar by as much as $2^{1}/_{4}$ percent. We soon learned that such would be its daily rate of fluctuation. Today, barely 18 months after the IMM's opening, we have every reason to be proud of its achievement and are certain of its immense potential. In our first year, there were 142,928 IMM transactions amounting to a value of $21 billion. In the first 10 months of 1973, there were already 249,345 IMM transactions.

Accordingly, we believe the IMM to be a grand project with an unlimited potential—a project that is in the national interest and vital to Chicago. To put it simply, just as London for centuries demonstrated the value and power of acting as the world center of financial services, so can the IMM act as the force to make Chicago a financial center for the world.

# The "Sleazy" Speculator

*In spreading the word about the new currency futures market at the IMM, I was conscious that some of the concepts we espoused were either foreign to Americans or contrary to orthodox teachings. While I attempted to explain all the principles of the revolutionary market we were nurturing and the rationale for its creation, I often found it more productive to concentrate on one or two of the most critical issues.*

*In my opinion it was imperative to focus on two of the fundamental components of our marketplace: First, few understood or even heard of the Bretton Woods Agreement—the IMF's official system of fixed exchange rates. What was it, who created it, why was it being replaced, and what relationship did it have to the IMM? Second, the role of the speculator in markets was totally misunderstood and viewed with suspicion by the vast majority of the American public.*

*The very foundation of the IMM was based on the logic that Bretton Woods was not returning, that global realities demanded a floating system of exchange rates, and that the new financial order would foster a futures market in foreign exchange in which speculators were necessary participants.*

Presented at the University of Chicago Law School, Chicago, Illinois, November 27, 1974

For a number of years during the past decade, the Bank of England fought to maintain the value of the British pound at levels not commensurate with reality. They did this with continuous and tortured intervention in the marketplace. Finally, in November 1967, the Bank again surrendered to the inevitable by devaluating pound sterling from $2.80 to $2.60. From that point forward, it became fashionable in official British government press releases to blame the devaluation on the pressures caused by speculators. Other

59

governments joined the charade. We were given to understand that speculators were *persona non grata*, enemies of the state, and that if their activities were not curtailed, they would surely bring down the currency system of the civilized world.

Consequently, the lowly image of the speculator became even lowlier. Speculation, never an occupation to be proud of, took on obscene proportions. And of all the speculators, the very worst of the breed were those who dabbled in currency—those sleazy-looking characters who lurked about the financial centers of London, Zurich, and Frankfurt selling a pound here and a dollar there, buying a yen or a Deutsche mark, going short francs when it pleased them—for no other purpose than personal greed. We envisioned these despicable characters gleefully laughing up their proverbial sleeves whenever they earned a profit at the expense of the Central Banks, and jumping for joy whenever they caused a devaluation or revaluation. Speculators, those unpatriotic, irresponsible, no-good louts, became the rallying symbol of the Central Bankers, the patriotic, responsible good guys who fought bravely for law, order, and fixed values for their currencies.

When on Saturday, January 19, 1974, the government of France floated the French franc, the sad news was out. The good guys had lost. France, the last embittered proponent of fixed exchange rates, had given up the battle. But by then, many of us had taken a closer look at this drama. By then we had ample opportunity to read the economic analyses of such critics as Milton Friedman, Otmar Emminger, Fritz Machlup, Robert Aliber, and George Shultz. They were among the very first who were brave enough to advise that all was not quite as we were given to understand; later their ranks swelled.

First we learned that the bad guys—the speculators—were often corporate treasurers of respected multinational firms, or bankers, or finance ministers of nations, or highly regarded financiers. By establishment rules, how could these guys be so bad? We also learned, quite to our amazement, that their motivations were not always personal gain. Quite often, these market participants were acting to prevent or minimize a loss on behalf of the enterprise they represented—be it a bank, corporation, or nation. Indeed, their actions were based on what they perceived to be prudent business judgment. To our surprise, we learned that they considered the well-being of the interests they represented every bit as important as world monetary order is to Central Bankers. A shocking discovery, indeed! But the most startling revelation came when a growing number of highly respected economists openly dared to suggest that speculators were acting rationally and that the Central Banks were unwilling to face reality; that those who represented themselves as the good guys were reading from a script that was now outdated. How was such a turnabout possible?

Under the foreign exchange system designed in 1946 known as the Bretton Woods Agreement, the countries within the International Monetary Fund (IMF) agreed that their currencies would have fixed parities in terms of both gold and dollars. The dollar, in turn, was not to have a fixed parity. It was to be freely convertible into gold for official holders of dollars at the fixed price of $35 an ounce. The maximum range of permitted deviation from ascribed parities was 2 percent (1 percent on each side of the parities). In practice, the range of fluctuations in relation to the dollar was actually 1.5 percent.

The Bretton Woods system worked quite well for a time; in fact, longer than expected. It would still be a good system today had nothing changed after 1946, or if all the changes had occurred equally to all nations. Alas, that was not the case. Ultimately, the rate of exchange of one nation's currency for another nation's currency is determined by the forces of supply and demand for the given currency. The factors that influence supply and demand are based on the economic and political— but primarily the economic—conditions of a nation. Would it be surprising to learn that the economic conditions of the IMF nations changed since 1946, that they were drastic changes, and that these changes were not equally proportioned among the nations? We all know what has happened since the end of World War II with respect to the relative economic conditions of the United States, Great Britain, West Germany, and Japan. In fact, the world has changed in its entirety. It has grown smaller while various nations within its structure have grown larger. We also know that world economic and political conditions are in constant and sometimes dramatic flux.

The Bretton Woods script, which was inflexible and insensitive to major change, was not written for the new and changing world conditions. Today, technological advancements have made it possible to know immediately of every economic or political change occurring within every nation, such that the reaction time to such information is dramatically reduced. The effects of all such internal changes can now be felt in terms of days, weeks, and months rather than years. At the same time, the growth of private industrial complexes are of such a magnitude that they now play as large—or larger—a role than the Central Banks in determining currency supply and demand.

These realities were officially ignored by the nations within the IMF for a very long time. Finally it became so unmanageable that the Central Bankers had to come to grips with the truth. It became impossible for a government to maintain its currency at the official rate when economic and political logic dictated a higher or lower value. It was an exercise in futility for a single or a combination of Central Banks to support a given currency at the established rate when all the world's so-called speculators responded to reality by selling or buying against the fictitious rate. The unceasing pressure toward the real value of a currency almost bankrupted IMF member nations in their attempts to abide by an outdated agreement. It was particularly difficult for the United States to maintain the agreement since the American dollar was the parity mechanism for all other IMF currencies.

Finally, the United States—which had suffered dearly as a consequence of maintaining unrealistic dollar values—forced everyone's hand. On August 15, 1971, President Nixon closed the gold window and aborted the Bretton Woods system. The era of fixed rates had ended and the financial world would never be the same. The shock waves of that decision are still felt today and will continue to be felt for years to come.

The Chicago Mercantile Exchange watched the events leading to this momentous event with more interest than that of an idle bystander. We envisioned what was coming, we saw the opportunity, and we saw a necessity in the making. With the demise of Bretton Woods, we believed a new era was dawning, not only with respect to flexible exchange rates, but in the very essence of American psychology. For we recognized that the United States was no longer alone in the financial world and that this would offer futures exchanges an important opportunity.

We recognized that Americans would soon understand that the United States economy is very much dependent on the economies of other nations; that our economic strength is affected by such factors as balance of trade, interest rates, and rate of inflation; that our nation alone could not determine the value of its currency; that the value of the dollar was not absolute, but relative to the value of other currencies. Indeed, we foresaw a rude awakening for many Americans and that this would have special relevance to our exchange. We believed that when the phrase *balance of trade* became a topic of concern for all informed Americans rather than a subject limited to economists, it would result in dramatic changes in the financial fabric of this nation. In other words, it seemed reasonable to assume that many people would soon seek investment and speculative opportunities in arenas involved with international finance. We saw this as a trend that would grow for decades, and one that would demand investment instruments of an international monetary nature.

Thus the philosophy of the International Monetary Market (IMM) was born: To organize a futures exchange for the express purpose of dealing in financial instruments. Our first financial instruments were to be foreign currencies. Later we planned to add other instruments of finance.

Even under the fixed regime of Bretton Woods, exchange rates fluctuated. In other words, there would be no changes in a given currency value until pent-up forces compelled the world system to catch up with reality. Suddenly one morning you were advised that the British pound was devalued by 8 percent, or that the Japanese yen was revalued by 12 percent. That is the way of a fixed market: an abrupt and violent eruption in price, a sudden inordinate change in value, followed by the fictitious and temporary peace of a fixed new parity. Fixed order then chaos; chaos then fixed order. Such a world offered no chance for a futures market. Futures markets can exist only when prices are allowed to respond freely to the continual changes brought about by the forces of supply and demand.

The Chicago Mercantile Exchange had to wait for such a day to introduce currency futures at the IMM. But while we waited, we did some homework. Approximately one year before the Smithsonian Agreement, and with the fervent belief that the era of fixed exchange rates was doomed, we asked Professor Milton Friedman two critical questions: Will the new financial order include exchange rate flexibility? If so, will there be a need for a futures market in currency? His unqualified affirmative response to both queries gave us the courage to proceed. In his position paper on this subject which he wrote at our behest in September 1971, Professor Friedman asserted:

> Changes in the international financial structure will create a great expansion in the demand for foreign cover. It is highly desirable that this demand be met by as broad, as deep, as resilient a futures market in foreign currencies as possible in order to facilitate foreign trade and investment.

> Such a wider market is almost certain to develop in response to the demand. The major open question is where. The U.S. is a natural place and it is very much in the interests of the U.S. that it should develop here.

He was not alone in his opinion. Many other notable economists concurred and encouraged us. But Professor Friedman's opinion meant more to us than all the others combined. Without his credentials on our side, our idea would not have had the credibility we thought necessary.

The Smithsonian Agreement on December 20, 1971, brought official flexibility to the world currency system and was the first step in the desired direction. The agreement provided that currency rates would be allowed to fluctuate 2.25 percent higher or lower than a predetermined parity. It was obvious to us that this new system was also too rigid to last. Nevertheless, it officially provided a 4.5 percent range for currency fluctuations, sufficient flexibility to justify the need for a futures market in foreign currency.

Two days after the Smithsonian announcement, the Chicago Mercantile Exchange announced the birth of the International Monetary Market. We were about to become singular pioneers in the frontier of flexible exchange rates. On May 16, 1972, the IMM listed futures contracts in British pounds, Canadian dollar, Deutsche marks, Italian lira, Japanese yen, Mexican pesos, and Swiss francs.*

As everyone knows there is no such thing as a little bit pregnant. The world quickly realized that if flexible exchange

---

*Since then, the Dutch guilder and French franc have been added, and the Italian lira has been delisted.

rates were better than fixed, floating exchange rates would be even better. Thus, at a much quicker pace than even Friedman predicted, one nation after another was forced to admit that the world of today demands a system where exchange rates are determined to the largest extent by free market forces rather than by government edict or government manipulation. In other words, the official world recognized what Milton Friedman had preached, that currency rates between nations must be allowed to adjust freely on a day-to-day basis. In other words, they must float.

Today, all the major currencies float against the dollar. The common market nations, however, have set a range for parity between their own respective currencies known as the *tunnel;* their currencies fluctuate against each other like a snake in the tunnel; and the tunnel itself floats against the dollar. The snake in the tunnel concept has experienced some problems and, from time to time, there have been adjustments to the agreed parities. It cannot be assumed with certainty that this system will continue to exist. However, irrespective of the tunnel or the snake, the IMM was clearly on the right track, and the world followed.

Was the IMM the first or only futures market for foreign currencies? Of course not. To begin with, there has always been a forward market in currency conducted by the world's major banks. The interbank market is a highly active and viable market that conducts billions of dollars of transactions on a daily basis. But, just as its name implies, the market operates on a bank-to-bank basis. In this sense, it is limited exclusively to banks that act for themselves and their clients. To fully understand the IMM, we must examine the characteristics that distinguish it from its interbank counterpart.

The first and most telling difference is that the IMM is an open market—one that is open both to hedgers as well as speculators—while the interbank market is not. Those who do not have a commercial reason to trade foreign exchange are excluded from this avenue of investment in the interbank market. To us, speculators are as welcome as hedgers. Our philosophy is never to differentiate between a commercial or private motivation for making a trade. Both reasons, we believe, are driven by the same or similar motivation. In a free society, everyone ought to have this right.

Indeed, this very feature spells the quintessential difference between a competitive market and one that is monopolistic. We believe that no forward market can achieve Friedman's desired broad, deep, and resilient level of efficiency without the participation of speculators. A market that is limited to commercial transactions must, by definition, remain narrow. Commercially motivated transactions usually tend to move in the same direction at the same time. Thus, in times of stress when commercial elements want to sell, there are few buyers, and vice versa.

The impact is lessened when speculators are involved. For example, when speculators establish short positions, they can be buyers at a time when commercial interests wish to sell, and vice versa. It works that way in all open futures markets. Speculators provide a market with liquidity. Liquidity gives a market breadth, depth, and resiliency which, in turn, lowers the cost of hedging.

There are also some important technical differences. The IMM is conducted on the floor of an exchange. Its participant brokers include approximately 80 brokerage firms and its members include the five major Chicago banks and many commercial concerns. Orders for trading in currencies are placed through these firms, allowing easy accessibility to the market no matter where the orders originated. This means continuous availability of market quotations and currency rates. The rates are determined as at an auction—bids and offers are made by open outcry in an open and competitive fashion. The exchange itself does not engage in trading. We believe that an open and competitive auction mechanism will, in the long run, produce the lowest market rates. That has been the historic result of every successful commodity traded on any futures exchange.

Our currency contract sizes and specifications are uniform and impersonal. Contracts are bought or sold only in units of prescribed sizes, and delivery can be taken only on specified dates. Because futures contracts are standardized, a position can be offset by making the opposite trade. No position is locked in until maturity as in the interbank market. We are developing a market for 18 months forward. The current bank market operates mostly for 30, 60, or 90 days forward. The majority of its business is in *spot* transactions. The IMM does not conduct a spot market in currency. The user of our market does not need a compensating bank balance, but he does require margin. Margin is small, ranging between 1.5 and 5 percent of the value of the contract. He also will pay a $45 round-turn commission.

These are the major visible differences between the IMM and the interbank market. But it is important to note that the IMM was not created to act as a competitor to the banks. Its primary function is to act as an additional tool in the world of international trade.

In the past, businessmen have had several alternative means for protecting themselves against the vagaries of exchange rate changes: Hold assets in strong currencies; hold liabilities in weak currencies; employ leads and lags in payments and receipts; buy spot currency and hold until needed or borrow spot currency for future payment; or hedge in the forward bank market. Since May 1972 when the IMM opened for trading, they have one more alternative: They can call their local broker and hedge with a futures contract traded on an organized exchange.

Is there a need for such an additional tool? Emphatically so. There are two additional reasons for the birth of the IMM that cannot yet be measured and may be more important than all the others.

First, the new world order, which subjects individuals or corporations that conduct business overseas not only to normal business risks but also to changes in currency rates, demands a broad foreign exchange market. This need will grow in geometric proportion. It requires a market of wider scope and much easier access than the present interbank market.

There is an equally critical need for information and education in the use of foreign exchange. American enterprise must learn how to utilize foreign currency hedging as a marketing tool. An organized exchange can fill this need better than any other institution except the federal government. In the two and one-half years of our existence, we have produced and published more statistics and practical information on the use of foreign exchange than was published in the previous decade. And through the far-reaching facilities of our brokerage firms, we can disseminate this information and material in a manner that would be hard to equal. We have organized study courses, we have offered a multitude of lectures, we have held symposia and conferences, we have instituted courses at the college and university level, we have published tape cassettes, we have produced a 30-minute movie—and this does not begin to enumerate the continuous flow of printed material we have made available. Moreover, this is only the beginning.

We believe the IMM to be in synch with the new world monetary order. Whether we have floating rates, snakes in tunnels, worms in tubes, crawling pegs, or whatever, there will be more flexibility in exchange rates. The fixed rate system of the past will be impossible to reinstate. And therein lies the economic justification for the International Monetary Market. The IMM was organized to provide hedge services to commercial interests who need protection from changes in exchange rates, and to provide opportunities for speculators to participate in the price discovery process. In short, it is an invention created by the necessity of our times.

# The Birth of LIFFE

*The creation of the London International Financial Futures Exchange (LIFFE), aside from offering an endless possibility of puns, was an enormous compliment to the concept of financial futures and a valuable boost to its short history. Indeed, many of us in the U.S. futures industry encouraged the process in Great Britain and gave our time, advice, and assistance to the Bank of England and the organizers of this endeavor, principally John Barkshire.*

*Consequently, it was no accident that LIFFE was modeled after the IMM. In fact, Barkshire and I, who became good friends, both believed that one day there would be a system of mutual offset between our two exchanges similar to the system the IMM was working toward with the SIMEX. While this did not materialize, we nevertheless recognized the value of new financial futures markets around the globe: that they would validate the concept, spread the gospel, and in turn, create users and uses for all futures markets.*

Presented at the World Financial Futures Conference, London, England, September 14–15, 1982

The opening of the London International Financial Futures Exchange (LIFFE) underscores the internationalization of financial futures markets. It embodies a dual achievement: the realization of a dream for this center of finance and a clear signal that the idea of financial futures—born in Chicago—responds to a global necessity. The stage is now set in London. For those who labored these past years, the creative process is over; the many hours, the frustrations, the plans, negotiations, and the myriad of problems are now behind you. The one critical question remaining is whether LIFFE will succeed.

The financial futures community in Chicago shares your pride and your excitement. We are acutely aware of the difficult

69

process you have just completed, and we understand your anxieties only too well. After all, it was just 10 years ago that we at the Chicago Mercantile Exchange (CME) suffered similar formative pains in our creation of the International Monetary Market (IMM)—a move destined to vault a group of pork belly and cattle traders into the center of world finance and an effort that resulted in revolutionizing our industry.

In one major respect, the work of LIFFE creators was much simpler than ours. At the birth of the IMM and the conceptual introduction of financial futures, it was necessary first to convince the world financial community that financial futures were a necessary adjunct to the management of risk. It took years of late nights and early mornings, an incalculable amount of traveling, unceasing gospel spreading, arm twisting, and ear bending. LIFFE has a much easier task before it than did the IMM a decade ago. Financial futures are now an accepted fact of life on our shore and undoubtedly receives a favorable appraisal here. That will not guarantee your success but at least it will make your work easier since you do not have justify your existence.

The world entered the 1980s after enduring a decade of greater financial turmoil than ever before experienced. Inflation, energy costs, changing values between currencies, volatile interest rate movements, and extreme swings of commodity prices combined to create a business climate fraught with danger and one demanding new programs and mechanisms for the management of risk. It represented the emergence of a new economic order, one bound to stay with us for the foreseeable future and one for which financial futures are ideally suited. Indeed, if we had not already done so, we would need to invent financial futures all over again.

Success, however, cannot be assured simply because the idea is right. Success is the result of hard work. We expect to be here 10 years from now to share with you the pride of equal success of your new market.

Allow me now to offer a brief historical sketch of the growth of our Chicago markets these past 10 years in order to suggest a goal for your market. During that decade, the IMM set the industry standard for growth in volume and contract diversity. The autumn of 1982 has not yet even fully arrived and already it is clear that financial futures volume at the CME will smash all previous annual records. In the first eight months of this year, IMM financial futures volume totaled 12.6 million contracts, a 40 percent increase over the same period in 1981 and just 2 million contracts shy of the record-breaking 1981 total.

So far this year, nearly 6 million contracts have traded in our short-term interest rate futures complex of Treasury bills, Certificates of Deposit, and Eurodollars, while currency futures topped 5.7 million contracts. In both cases, volume is almost two thirds above the 1981 pace. And figures show our new contracts performing even better. The Standard and Poor's (S&P) 500 stock index futures contract pierced the one-million-contract level in August, after just four months of trading. It is a statistic of such wonderment that it is difficult even for us who experienced it to believe it. Additionally, in May, just 10 months after opening, the Certificates of Deposit futures contract likewise topped one million contracts. These are the first two contracts in the history of the Chicago Mercantile Exchange to trade one million contracts in less than four years' time.

Furthermore, yearly volume records have been broken in the Canadian dollar, Japanese yen, and Swiss franc futures. Swiss francs, our second most active contract in August with a record monthly volume of more than 313,000 contracts, has traded nearly 1.8 million contracts on the IMM so far this year. These transaction statistics in a wide array of futures instruments have justifiably propelled the IMM to its place as the number one financial futures market in the world.

As a direct consequence of this success, there has been a meteoric rise in exchange membership prices over the years. IMM seats were originally sold to the public for $10,000; they are now well over $250,000. And the IMM growth helped to push the full CME seats to a high of $380,000—the highest seat price ever attained on any futures exchange. The high membership values and the willingness of individuals and institutions to pay the price for them is strong evidence of the widespread confidence in the stability, integrity, and future of the International Monetary Market.

The overriding strategy that has been central to our success has been the effort to diversify the exchange. Calculated and exhaustive research efforts have preceded each new contract introduction. At each juncture we sought to balance user demand for diverse and sophisticated contracts on the one hand with the necessity for liquid markets and manageable overall exchange operations on the other. The IMM has consistently attempted to strike a correct balance between those who implored for more futures instruments and those who cautioned us not to overextend our capabilities. Indeed, those capabilities were stretched to the limit recently when, in just 10 months, we introduced an unprecedented series of new financial futures contracts: the 90-day domestic Certificate of Deposit—the first futures contract based on private short-term debt instruments—introduced July 1981; the 90-day Eurodollar time deposit contract—which, in my opinion has the potential of becoming the most successful futures instrument ever devised—introduced December 1981; and the revolutionary S&P 500 Stock Index contract—which we believe will become the bellwether for equity futures—introduced April 1982. That all these contracts have proved successful is something of a minor miracle.

It is incumbent to underscore that the opening of the Eurodollar futures contract represents an important milestone in the history of futures. This contract initiates the revolutionary concept of cash settlement, a dramatic departure from the age-old physical delivery procedure of futures markets. Cash settlement paved the way for the S&P 500 stock index futures contract as well as for other potential futures concepts and instruments never before thought feasible.

Another predominant consideration at the CME in the development of new contracts is floor liquidity. Liquidity demands that we have on hand a pool of skilled, professional traders and brokers. This subject was and continues to be of similar concern to the organizers of LIFFE. To this end, I am proud to have pioneered a divisional concept at the CME. The creation of the IMM division a decade ago served to infuse our institution with new members. We have since applied similar programs to achieve similar results. During the past year, the CME adopted two separate plans to expand the trading floor population. The first was the Membership Rights program, which expanded the number of floor brokers and traders by 25 percent while maintaining the value of existing memberships. At the close of 1981, we again unveiled the creation of a new division—the Index and Options Market (IOM). The IOM division is designed to provide a marketplace for contracts based on indices and options on futures contracts. We anticipate that more than 1,200 members will become floor participants of this new market.

The diversity and growth at the IMM is only half the story. Of equal importance has been the resulting elevation of our markets and market professionals to a position of integrity and credibility. Initially, when we proposed the idea of futures contracts based on money, many New York bankers laughed at us. Yet these same bankers are now vying for spots on Chicago's trading floors. Some have even applied for and received approval to become futures commissions merchants (FCMs) so that they can act on behalf of clients in futures contracts on currencies, interest rates, and stock indexes. These include such respected financial institutions as Morgan Guaranty Trust, Continental Illinois National Bank, Bankers Trust, First National Bank of Chicago, the Republic National Bank of New York, and others who are waiting in the wings. This is compelling evidence of our raised stature in most traditional investment circles. It is a trend that has spread to Europe and is very visible here where banks from around the world intend to be members of LIFFE.

What has become evident to banks and other financial institutions is that financial futures are an essential risk management mechanism and that their presence on the trading floor is a necessary adjunct to their business. This result was achieved because the futures industry has been successful in responding to the needs of the business world.

The IMM Treasury bill futures contract and the Chicago Board of Trade's Treasury bond futures contract are excellent examples of responding to a market demand. These contracts have more than lived up to their roles as hedging and price discovery mechanisms and have become integral parts of the immense U.S. government securities market. Indeed, the hedging and price discovery aspects of Treasury bond and bill futures permanently altered the old-fashioned negative view about futures markets held by many. Similarly, the introduction of stock index futures is already changing the trading habits and techniques of institutional equity managers.

I hasten to add, the CME is not the only exchange introducing successful new contracts. Early in May, the Chicago Board of Trade began trading a 10-year Treasury note contract that was heralded with the largest ever first-day volume—33,502 contracts. Though volume has been at lower levels on a day-to-day basis since then, open interest has grown as participation in this important intermediate range interest rate contract broadens.

There is ample evidence of the increased professionalism and sophistication of the financial futures industry outside the exchanges. Major American universities—Columbia University in New York, Chicago's Loyola University, and the University of Illinois—have established institutes for the academic study of futures markets. In addition, a pool of talented legal experts specializing in futures has emerged as well as a law bulletin and an academic journal discussing current issues of importance in the expanding futures industry. But the best example of the professionalism that now surrounds the futures industry is the emergence of an industry-sponsored organization designed to ensure the industry's strength and integrity—the National Futures Association (NFA).

Federally sanctioned and authorized by the Commodity Futures Trading Commission, the NFA is designed to play many regulatory roles: It will audit the financial condition of FCMs outside the purview of exchange surveillance; it will regulate sales practices of futures firms; it will arbitrate disputes between customers and FCMs; it will eliminate duplication between government and exchange regulatory programs; and it will lessen the cost of federal regulation of the futures industry by funding itself. NFA membership will be drawn from all sectors of the industry: exchanges, FCMs, commodity trading advisors, pool operators, and banks. Consequently, the NFA will become a national unifying body and the industry's focal point.

Finally, the IMM, from its inception, recognized that the financial futures concept was of a global nature. Thus in January 1980, we opened an IMM office here in London—the first of its kind by an American exchange. The London office has proved to be most instrumental in the education process for our markets. We are now taking direct steps to develop a market link with the Singapore International Monetary Exchange (SIMEX).

That is the IMM's record of its first 10 years. Impressive, I hope you will agree—and a goal for LIFFE. Most important: Today's global environment makes LIFFE's creation mandatory. Your success will be beneficial to us and all markets. It will foster growth, better understanding, more participants, and deeper breadth for all futures markets. We wish you success and offer our continuing assistance. Our purpose is common.

# The Future of Futures

*To predict the future is both dangerous and difficult. This is especially true for those of us in the futures industry. Still, we are often asked to do so and we must make the attempt. It is gratifying to find that at least some of the time our predictions have been not far from the mark.*

*The following address was presented at a time when many, both from within and outside our industry, were lamenting the proliferation of new contracts. Proliferation, they said, represented a dangerous trend that would ultimately crush our industry. It was an old theme by those who distrusted the market's inherent ability to determine which products are necessary and which are not. These naysayers proposed a legislative solution to the perceived problem. Fortunately, we repulsed this onslaught.*

**Presented at the New School for Social Research, New York, New York, October 28, 1983**

"I*t is the present that matters. . . . Those who talk about the future are scoundrels.*" These sentiments, espoused by the French novelist, Louis Celine, a bit of a scoundrel himself, epitomize a mind-set embraced by many. Indeed, while it is true that the present matters, to someone who represents an industry so intertwined with the future that it has the audacity to call itself *futures*, it is a rather disheartening contemplation. Instead, equally true and perhaps even a bit more profound is John Galsworthy's declaration: "*If you do not think about the future, you cannot have one.*"

Galsworthy's admonition is of particular significance to us within the futures industry—an industry whose dynamics are in constant flux and whose evolutionary changes are dramatic. In our industry, perhaps more than any other, there is abundant evidence that those who fail to contemplate and prepare for the next step in our expansionary journey will be swiftly left behind and faced with the impossible task of catching up. Our historical scrap heap is replete with examples of those who forgot this truth. For in our industry, to think about the future of futures is the quintessential element for survival.

With so much at stake, how can we prepare for that exclusive domain of providence? How can we predict the unpredictable? How can we harness this elusive prize, so affected by consequences over which we have no control? What are the guidelines? Which crystal ball should we use?

The philosophers tell us that the future is simply a consequence of the past and therefore we should look backward for guidance. As Patrick Henry put it: "I have but one lamp by which my feet are guided, and that is the lamp of experience . . . I know no way of judging the future, but by the past."

History does repeat itself and past reference can be an excellent preview of coming events. But can such conventional wisdom be valid in our case; can our past be a guidepost to our future? The answer is disconcerting. In the span of 20 years, less than a blink from a historical perspective, futures markets experienced a metamorphosis of such dramatic proportions that it defies comprehension. Our recent revolutionary experience represents a phenomenon with few equals in the business arena. And most of the significant changes occurred in the past decade.

Our markets, which since time immemorial were the unique and exclusive domain of agriculture, seemingly overnight became an integral mechanism of finance. Our markets, which for more than 100 years were strictly limited to tangible and storable products, suddenly shed these fundamental requirements and embraced live animals, foreign exchange, and government securities. Our markets, whose defined boundaries precluded entry into the sphere reserved for securities, brazenly transgressed the dividing line by inventing instruments that blurred the age-old distinction. Our markets, whose birthright necessitated a system of physical delivery, broke their genetic code and engendered products without a delivery. Our markets, whose universe was so insignificant that in 1962 they could generate only 5 million transactions, experienced a 2,200 percent increase a decade later. Our markets, which only yesterday were viewed with scorn and considered barely at the edge of respectability, are today an indispensable member of the financial family. Our markets, whose merits for decades were recognized by users of but a handful in the United States, are suddenly the attraction for a multitude of financial centers around the globe.

Can we in all honesty expect that our markets will, in the next 20 years, equal or even approach the futures revolution of the past two decades? It is doubtful at best. I therefore caution that Patrick Henry's formula for forecasting the future by virtue of the past may not be quite applicable to our industry.

The next 20 years should be an era of enhancement, entrenchment, and maturation of our markets. The conceptual breakthroughs and inventions of the futures revolution desperately demand time for our markets to explore their new territories, to fortify their new bases, and for their new identities to mature. Thus, if the futures revolution of the past two decades can be defined as representing a horizontal advancement, the next two decades will be of vertical dimension, capitalizing on the conquests of the 1960s and 1970s. The new directions we have assumed and the new inventions we have produced deserve and will receive our full attention. Indeed, it would be an unconscionable disservice to the labors of the past if we did not now spend the time to explore and exploit their full potential.

Cash delivery unshackled futures from their most burdensome constraint, one that represented an insurmountable wall around their existence. Cash settlement in lieu of physical delivery enabled us to contemplate and explore the market applicability of concepts and intangibles never before possible for futures trade. This unlimited potential will no doubt challenge the minds of even the most provocative market innovators.

Allow me to state for the record that this new era would most likely never have transpired without the existence and courage of the Commodity Futures Trading Commission (CFTC). The concept of cash delivery—so simple and universally accepted a methodology for settlement of contractual obligations (one that is commonplace in every other field of business or walk of life)—was obstinately and irrationally barred to us and would have remained so were it not for the CFTC. It was only by virtue of the public faith placed in the wisdom of a congressionally ordained entity that the issue of cash delivery had a chance to be resolved in our favor. It is to the CFTC's everlasting credit that this was accomplished and unquestionably will be recorded as one of its paramount achievements.

The first wave of index futures is but a sample of what lies ahead. Indexes have become the ubiquitous tools of management in every form of enterprise; they run the gamut from the private to the public sector, from finance to agriculture, from the very specific to the very general. Currently contract markets are discussing or developing indexes on corporate and municipal bonds, insurance and freight rates, consumer prices, agriculture and components of agriculture, real estate, retail new car sales, and others too numerous to mention. In some cases, the index proposed is already in existence and compatible with the mechanics of futures; in others, refinement is needed; in still others, the index must yet be created. However they are chosen or constructed, there is little doubt that in the coming years many will be tested.

Options on indexes will also be attempted. Obviously, not all indexes will take to options; some will do better than the traditional futures vehicle while others will function best in parallel fashion. Still, the specter of options on futures exchanges goes far beyond the index markets. The very nature of the option mechanism is so different from the traditional futures contract, it spells yet another new dimension for our market potential. In similar fashion to indexes, options will run the gamut from agriculture to finance, and from the specific to the general. Options will offer market applications never before possible and will attract participants who never envisioned using a futures broker.

Our new markets will not be limited to index and options. The futures industry thrives on change and responds quickly to new opportunities. As a need becomes apparent, our markets will have the foresight and competitive motivation to respond, just as energy futures resulted from a sudden crisis in the world oil supplies and as currency futures were spawned by the breakdown of the Bretton Woods Agreement. And each new invention will spur yet another idea.

Not all new contracts will succeed. There are bound to be failures along the way as there have been in the past. That is the price of success and competition. We should ignore those who fret about proliferation. The marketplace itself is the only and best determinant of which ideas are viable and which are not. Those products that are flawed will fail quickly enough; those that are redundant will find it most difficult to compete; those that do not answer a specific need will find few users. The market should make this determination rather than some regulator or industry committee. The dynamics of our industry are such that it must continue to explore, experiment, and invent in order to respond to a current or prospective need—either real or imagined.

In the coming years, futures will continue to produce new contracts of trade that will represent extensions of inventions and advances already achieved. The new era will also harvest the fruit of past labors that produced the new stature and astonishing growth in transaction volume of today's futures, two highly significant achievements. The initial volume surge resulting from the first series of index contracts is but a preview of the quantum leap in transactions for our markets. The eventual exponential result will catapult futures to a level of prominence never before contemplated.

The transaction increases will not necessarily be uniform or across the board. Instead, we should expect the expansion process to be selective, favoring one sector at a time, then moving to another and back again. Nor should we expect each successive year to consistently beat the previous year's record. There is bound to come a period of relative price stability or world depression during which the need for futures is diminished with an attendant drop in transaction volume. Such periods will no doubt find doomsayers who will gleefully insist that our industry is finished. These voices will quickly be stilled during the next period of uncertainty or price upheaval that will surely follow. This leads to the inevitable conclusion that those exchanges having the most diversified product mix will be best placed for continued prosperity. Those contract markets with but a limited product base must bear this in mind or face the consequences.

It is also imperative to underscore the value of our agricultural roots. Our nation's international role as a primary food producer is not about to diminish, nor will the world's demand for these products. Similarly, the cyclical supply of these markets is not likely to change. One era of oversupply and low futures volume will surely be followed by its opposite. Consequently, agricultural futures—similar to their financial counterparts—will experience periods of prominence and their necessity both as a hedging mechanism and as an investment tool will continue.

And with the expected transaction explosion will come its consequential counterpart—prestige. This represents the culmination of a process that began just 10 years ago with the introduction of financial futures. Since their inception, our markets have gained more acceptance and respectability than during the first 100 years of their existence. The coming era will, at long last, witness attainment by futures markets of stature-parity with the most-revered temples of finance.

Unfortunately, success on this scale will also bring commensurate problems and dangers. The federal bureaucracy will increase its internal struggle for jurisdictional control. There will be congressional demands for stronger enforcement policies, stronger regulations, and stronger federal agencies. As the definition between futures and securities markets continues to blur, the SEC and CFTC will argue over our turfdom and their composition and division of authority may dramatically change. Alas, there will also be scandals and failures, and surely there will be new legislation.

Our external successes combined with internal pressures will also change our infrastructure. Exchanges will become more alike as rules and practices of trade become stricter and more standardized. A tougher and higher qualification standard will be established for members—both brokers and traders. Although the present auction execution system will survive for the foreseeable future, it will become more mechanized and subject to new technologies. Our present system of separate clearing entities may ultimately vanish and be replaced by a central clearinghouse for all the exchanges. A comprehensive mechanism for financial integrity will be established to adequately protect all member firms and perhaps even a national insurance program for their customers. To this end, the National Futures Association (NFA) will play a central role as it becomes an additional source of industry strength, unification, and oversight.

The present trend of complementary arrangements between different exchanges—both futures and securities—will continue. We should also expect mergers between some markets. Surely, most of the New York markets will one day unify. Similarly, mergers and acquisitions of member firms will continue, resulting in a reduced family of clearing members who are members of every contract market.

During the coming era, our futures markets will complete their long international journey as different world centers of futures trade join the ranks of their North American counterparts. Clearly, LIFFE should remain the dominant European market, while Southeast Asia will most likely be represented by markets in Singapore, Sydney, and Hong Kong. Someday, of course, futures will come to Japan. Most important, we will finally realize futures trading on a 24-hour basis. Not only will futures participants include institutions and investors from every corner of the globe, ultimately most of our markets will have a single offset system.

Thus, the future of futures is promising, secure, and challenging. If the next era is less dramatic than its predecessor, blame it on the successes of the past. At the same time, we are grateful that the futures revolution we started and successfully consummated gave us new scope, dimension, strength, and extraordinary potential.

These predictions carry the same qualification as do all my market prognostications: They are only good till canceled—normally valid for a full 30 seconds.

# Financial Futures
# and the Banks

*To be invited in 1985 to speak at the prestigious annual International Monetary Conference attended by banks, bankers, and high government officials from every part of the world was not simply a great honor, it was clear evidence of the first important step toward admittance of financial futures into the mainstream of finance and banking. Besides representing another important milestone in our journey toward recognition and acceptance, this event provided a welcome opportunity to sell our wares. It was not a time to be shy or timid.*

Presented at the International Monetary Conference, Hong Kong,
June 2, 1985

As the representative of the United States futures industry, I am deeply honored to participate in the International Monetary Conference. This is the first time the futures industry has been included in your prestigious agenda. That is not surprising since our history in your domain has been quite brief. Before financial contracts were initiated on our exchanges, futures markets were not every banker's cup of tea. Financial futures, which began with foreign currency contracts on the International Monetary Market (IMM) of the Chicago Mercantile Exchange, were introduced just 13 years ago. From a banking point of view, our life span has been quite short.

The attention our markets have received and the recognition you have accorded them in recent years are the result of their explosive growth. Prior to 1972, futures were a predominately U.S. experience in which 12 agriculturally based exchanges traded a grand total of 18 million contracts. A dozen years later, on just the IMM, there were 14 million transactions in foreign currencies alone. The 1984 total U.S. futures volume was a staggering 159 million contracts comprising over 70 percent financial instruments and representing transaction values of trillions of dollars. Although the concept of financial futures and options is still principally a U.S. success, it is sought after by many financial centers the world over. Indeed, similar markets have been instituted or are contemplated in London, Paris, Singapore, Hong Kong, Sydney, Montreal, Toronto, and now Tokyo.

I would like to underscore the obvious dramatic changes occurring in banking that relate directly to the prosperity of our futures markets. First, the value of being financially liquid cannot be overstated. In business, you would like to have funding as far out as possible. Our markets are responsive to this necessity. Second, the ability to stay financially secure in the present volatile environment depends greatly on how well you can hedge your risks. Our markets address this necessity. Third, for banks to compete in today's world, they must achieve full service competence for their clientele. To do so, banks are today required to create prices and price structures for strategies that were once comparatively exotic financial arrangements. The markets of futures and options provide mechanisms that assist banks in achieving these capabilities.

The explosive growth of futures trading over the past several years is attributable primarily to a clear recognition of financial futures as an effective risk management tool. It is therefore imperative to understand the salient features of these new market instruments and how they differ from more traditional market mechanisms.

Compared with relevant cash or forward markets, futures provide more reliable price information. For instance, forward markets are usually fragmented among alternative delivery dates and locations and price information is not easily uncovered especially by the nonprofessional public. On the other hand, futures contracts specify a homogeneous variety of products and designate a single delivery date for settlement. This standardization permits third party transfers of contracts and reduces the search cost of locating buyers and sellers. Futures quotations are easily obtained. Moreover, the futures market quotes a combined price for the spot commodity plus the carrying cost (usually the inherent interest charge). This combined price cannot be directly inferred from spot market quotations.

The most important aspect of standardization is the liquidity that emerges by virtue of the increased participation of hedgers and speculators. This liquidity results in a substantially lower transaction cost and permits execution of commercial transactions in a more efficient and profitable manner. To experience firsthand the effect of liquidity or the lack of it and the resulting impact on prices, examine the bid/ask spreads in the currency markets after the futures markets close for the day. The bid/ask spreads can be half as wide while futures are trading as they are when our markets are closed. Moreover, any trader will tell you the size of trades possible at prevailing spreads is considerably larger during futures trade than afterward.

Futures tend to simplify complex transactions and do not consume valuable credit lines with other banks. Consider the comparatively simple problem of quoting a forward/forward rate to a client. For instance, suppose your client would like to borrow money in September and pay it back three months later. If you quote a fixed rate today, you are exposed to interest rate risk. To cover that risk without using futures, you must do two trades in the forward market: lend to September and borrow from December. With futures, on the other hand, one trade will suffice: sell the 3-month Eurodollar futures contract for settlement in September. To unwind the coverage before September, the only way out in the forward market is to do two more trades, leaving the bank with four forward positions on the books. With the futures markets, simply buy September Eurodollar futures to offset your position and you are out of the market with nothing on the books.

Another striking advantage of futures stems from the manner in which futures contracts are cleared. Once a trade has been matched and confirmed by both sides of the transaction, the futures exchange stands between the two clearing members representing the traders. As a result, even though a buyer of futures contracts may buy from a wide array of different sellers, that buyer only has to deal with his broker. And the broker, in turn, only needs to deal with the exchange—either directly or through his clearing firm. The economies of this arrangement should be clear. In the forward markets, you must know the creditworthiness at all times of each of your many trading partners. In futures markets, you must still be concerned with creditworthiness, but you can focus your attention on just two organizations: the firm representing you as your broker and the exchange's clearing house.

One critical aspect of futures that is too little appreciated is called *mark-to-market* whereby all gains and losses on open positions are settled in cash at the end of every business day. This daily settling of gains and losses is an effective management tool. We are acquainted with the history of banks that have gone bankrupt as the result of trading losses in cash market transactions that were kept secret either from management or from outside auditors and investors—or both. While it is possible to lose substantial amounts of money in futures markets, because the losses must be made good every day, such losses cannot be kept secret and allowed to run. To have to wire funds to cover variation margin calls is an effective way to alert bank comptrollers and management to the activities of bank traders.

Still another dimension of futures is the opportunity provided for global risk management, that is, the opportunity to run the bank's books around the clock. In this regard, our major contribution has been the forging of a trading link with the Singapore International Monetary Exchange (SIMEX) that permits mutual offset. One of the great strengths of futures is the ability to offset a position—allowing a sale to completely liquidate an earlier purchase (or vice versa), leaving no trace of either trade on your books. Through our trading link with SIMEX, we have now extended this feature to two broad time zones—the United States and Asia. With mutual offset, a position opened on the IMM can be completely offset by taking an equal and opposite position on the SIMEX.

To illustrate how banks can put futures and options to their best use, consider again the problem of liquidity. Your treasury managers naturally are torn between two goals. The first is to insulate the bank from unwanted exposure to interest rate risk. The second is to obtain the longest possible funding for the bank. Without futures, the two objectives are conflicting. With futures, however, both goals can be attained because interest rate risk can be separated from sources of funding. Your bank can, for example, get five-year funding and if the risk of that position is considered too great, you can buy whatever futures you need to offset the position. And as I noted before, futures are especially good for this purpose because you do not have to use up valuable credit lines.

Options on interest rates promise to make your lives easier still. Most banks are willing to take a position on interest rates, but rarely is it true that you have an absolute conviction with regard to the direction of interest rates. Rather, the more common case is one in which you have a strong feeling that is shrouded in a considerable amount of uncertainty. For these cases, options are the ideal instrument. For a known cost, the bank can take as large a position as it likes on the direction of interest rates and at the same time avoid the disastrous losses that accompany a bad guess. And because options share with futures the property that they do not bloat your balance sheet, your treasury manager will have a great deal more flexibility with regard to market timing. He does not have to concern himself with the implications of a change in policy on the availability of credit lines.

Futures and options can help banks compete in providing financial services. Consider, for example, a case in which you want to lead a major loan syndication for a client who can also issue commercial paper at favorable interest rates. How do you compete? The answer lies in the complex nature of your client's business. The commercial paper market—similar to other securities markets—is best equipped to deal with standardized instruments with standard terms and indentures. For most of your clients, however, these terms rarely fit their requirements. As a bank, therefore, you are in a position to establish financing arrangements with features that are desirable to your clients but would make conventional forms of commercial paper unsalable. For example, banks can establish a takedown schedule for a construction project that provides for guaranteed or capped interest rates. You can accomplish this without putting the bank at risk by using interest rate futures or options.

The features of exchange-traded futures and options make them ideally suited for use by banks. Our futures and options contracts are highly standardized and mature or expire only four times a year. As a result, trading is focused on just a few contracts and each is extremely liquid. To use the markets effectively, however, requires skill and understanding. And to adopt such standardized instruments to the specialized needs of the commercial world requires still more expertise. This is where banks are finding their niche. They are in a position to know their clients' special financing needs and can adapt the highly liquid but specialized futures and options markets to closely fit those needs. Consequently, banks will stand between the futures and options markets and their clients. For providing this service, banks will be rewarded handsomely while banks that do not provide this service will not be rewarded at all.

The rapid growth of financial futures and options can be attributed to the simple fact they answer a need. In a world plagued by risk that demands a hedge and risk transfer mechanism; in a world where liquidity is the single most important element toward success; in a world where full service is the unmistakable essence of competitive pressures, futures and options are neither a foolish caprice nor an exotic luxury. They are a mandatory and practical tool in a banker's arsenal of expertise with which to stay competitive and strong.

# Homecoming

*I was honored to be the guest of honor at the opening of the NIKKEI 225 Stock Index contract at the Osaka Securities Exchange. That Japan had moved so quickly in developing a futures contract in stock indices and in achieving government approval for its trade was the most telling evidence that financial futures had made their permanent mark on this financial community.*

*It was confirmation that our strategy of spreading financial futures knowledge to the Far East had succeeded and that globalization would ultimately result in Japan's opening its financial markets to the world. In the near term, it meant a growing flow of financial futures business from Japan to Chicago, for as the futures learning curve of this community rose, so would its use of the financial futures markets.*

*Another interesting aspect of the Japanese creation of stock index futures was its similarity to U.S. financial history with respect to the rivalry between Tokyo and Osaka. Just as the New York Stock Exchange sought to wrest control of this product line from Chicago by instituting futures trade on the New York Stock Exchange Composite Index, so did the Tokyo Stock Exchange attempt to undo Osaka by creating the Tokyo Price Index (TOPIX) contract. The CME bet on the NIKKEI and Osaka, Chicago's sister city.*

---

**Presented at the Nihon Keizai Shimbun/Osaka Securities Exchange Seminar on the NIKKEI 225 Stock Index, Osaka, Japan, September 2, 1988**

---

There is an old American saying: "What goes around, comes around." No doubt there is a Japanese equivalent, for no culture or language has a monopoly on aphorisms. The wise man who first coined this saying might have had this day and age in mind. Futures markets, having moved from country to country around the globe, are about to return to the land of their origin—Japan. It was in Osaka, the Kitchen of the Nation, during the Edo period (1600–1867) that feudal clans established warehouses to store and sell the rice paid to them as land-tax by their villagers. To protect themselves from wide price fluctuations from harvest to harvest, these merchants in 1730 established the first organized futures exchange. It enabled them to hedge the inherent price risk of rice and helped Osaka become the largest commercial Japanese city of that era.

It is apropos that futures markets return to Japan particularly at this time in its history. Today, Japan is the principal source of capital for the world, with the world's largest banks, largest insurance companies, and largest brokerage firms. Its companies have the highest market value of any industrial country, and its Tokyo Stock Exchange (TSE) is the largest in the world in terms of capitalization. In this financial environment, it would be shortsighted for Japan not to afford its financial institutions and investment community with the same financial tools for risk management available in all other major centers of finance.

After wandering around the globe for 200 years, futures markets will return to Japan in a somewhat different form from that invented by their ancestors. Instead of an agricultural base, today's futures have a financial foundation. Instead of rice as the instrument of trade, stocks will be traded by virtue of an index. Instead of handwritten tickets, computerized screens will serve as the transaction medium. What will be the same as it was two centuries before is their underlying purpose: to provide a secure market for hedging the inherent forward risk of commercial users.

On the eve of this homecoming, it is important to mention briefly some of the noteworthy milestones encountered by futures markets in their journey around the world, to underscore the lessons we learned, and to attempt to peer over the horizon at what lies ahead.

The most important transformation of futures markets occurred less than two decades ago on the American shore. For it was in Chicago in 1972 that the nature and destiny of futures dramatically changed. It was there that the International Monetary Market (IMM) was born at the Chicago Mercantile Exchange (CME), initiating the era of financial futures. Indeed, with the introduction of currency futures, the

IMM revolutionized the long agricultural history of futures markets and gave it at once new direction and limitless potential. The event is considered so signal in the annals of finance that the University of Chicago has called it "the most important financial innovation of the last 20 years."

The financial revolution that began with currencies quickly extended to interest rates and fostered the idea of cash settlement. A decade later, cash settlement became the gateway to index products—most importantly, stock index futures. Today the CME's S&P 500 futures contract, the most successful stock index futures contract in the world, is an indispensable tool for U.S. portfolio managers, a fact not overlooked by the Japanese government.

Indeed, in May of this year, the Japanese *Diet* wisely recognized that a market for the hedging of risk endemic to large portfolios of stock is an idea whose time has come. As a result, two markets will be created. In the city that gave birth to futures, the Osaka Securities Exchange will commence futures trading in the NIKKEI 225 stock index contract. In Tokyo, the Tokyo Stock Exchange will trade its new TOPIX index contract.

For the Chicago Mercantile Exchange, this occasion is of special significance. Not only did we launch financial futures, not only were we instrumental in developing cash-settled stock index futures, but we were first to recognize the potential of the Japanese stock market in the sphere of global equities. In 1985, we forged an agreement with the Nihon Keizai Shimbun (NKS)—your country's giant communications organization—to work jointly toward the development of the NIKKEI 225 index as a futures instrument. To us it was axiomatic. The NIKKEI 225 stock index has a long history as the primary indicator of the performance of the Japanese stock market. It has been so since 1949 when the Tokyo Stock Exchange reopened after World War II. The NIKKEI has become the accepted world benchmark for measuring the performance of Japanese stock portfolios. Toward our mutual goal, NKS and the CME encouraged the Singapore International Monetary Exchange (SIMEX) to begin futures trading in the NIKKEI 225 and assisted its inauguration on September 3, 1986. We rejoiced when on May 6, 1987, the Osaka Securities Exchange introduced the OSF 50 and became the first Japanese exchange to launch stock index futures in this country. Significantly, the

OSF 50 was specifically designed to correlate closely with the movements of the NIKKEI 225.

The Far Eastern time zone is of special significance. Where once American equity markets were the world's largest, today that distinction belongs to Japan with 40% of the world's market share. Thus, until the SIMEX began trading the NIKKEI 225 futures contract, a critical component of equity investment was missing: There existed no means by which portfolio managers could effectively and efficiently hedge risk in large portfolios of Japanese stock. Beginning this fall, money managers will have that capability in Japan as well. That Japan will have two stock index futures markets—the NIKKEI 225 and the TOPIX—will provide a healthy competitive environment and foster arbitrage between the two markets. Since the indexes are weighted differently—the TOPIX is capitalization-weighted and the NIKKEI 225 is a price average—there will be a continuous ebb and flow of the price differential between the two contracts. Such price differentials create an important trading opportunity that will provide additional liquidity to both markets.

The launching of stock index futures in Japan is much more than a historic economic event for this country. It is symbolic of the absolute acceptance of futures markets as an indispensable tool for modern risk management. Indeed, even as some individuals cast doubts on the benefits of stock index futures, and still others openly criticized them, the Japanese *Diet* correctly recognized that all such negativism was unfounded and nonsensical. A decade ago, the presence of large banks and a stock exchange was the accepted benchmark for a city to be considered a financial center. Today the global investor's growing dependence on equity indexes and other financial contracts necessitates that a true financial center must have a futures exchange as well. If not, today's free flowing capital funds will move to the center that does.

The trend is ubiquitous and worldwide. Osaka and Tokyo join a global family of futures markets. While the axis of futures markets is in Chicago, other major world financial centers have opened or plan to open futures exchanges. In the Asian time zone, there is the Hong Kong Futures Exchange (HKFE) and the SIMEX; yen bond futures on the Tokyo Stock Exchange have become one of the most actively traded futures contracts in the world. In your neighboring Southern Hemisphere is the thriving and successful Sydney Futures Exchange (SFE) as well as the New Zealand Futures Exchange (NZFE). In Europe, LIFFE—the London International Financial Futures Exchange—was the original pioneer; now in France, Le MATIF's French Government Bond futures contract has become the third largest in the world. Amsterdam has the European Options Exchange (EOE), Stockholm has the Sweden Options and Futures Exchange, and Geneva has the Swiss Options and Financial Futures Exchange (SOFFEX). Helsinki has recently opened the Finnish Options Exchange, and Dublin has big plans to open one or more futures exchanges. In Germany, there are plans to open a futures market in Frankfurt. Elsewhere in North America is the Toronto Futures Exchange where activity in the Toronto 35 index is thriving. In South America, there is the *Bolsa Brasileira de Futuros* in Rio de Janeiro and the *Bolsa de Mercadorias* in São Paulo.

Finally, since it is obvious that the most momentous influence on our markets is globalization, it is safe to assume that its effects will dramatically direct the destiny of our markets. Indeed, a recent Coopers & Lybrand study *Opportunity and Risk in the 24-Hour Global Marketplace* concluded:

> The global financial marketplace is a reality for many of the world's leading banks, insurers, money managers and securities firms—and 24-hour-a-day access to this marketplace is believed to be inevitable. Prompted by a growing economic need for enhanced access to capital sources and supported by deregulation and advances in technology, the global market has been irrevocably established.

The Chicago Mercantile Exchange understood this reality when four years ago, it instituted the mutual-offset trading link with SIMEX. It was the first successful attempt to link the trading capability of two different markets in two different time zones and served as a model for other exchanges to follow. This experiment brought the world one step closer to the 24-hour trading day and proved that world markets can be safely and efficiently linked. Other market links followed. In December 1984, the Boston Stock Exchange and the Montreal Exchange established a computerized linkage enabling Canadian users to direct trading orders to the Boston floor. In September 1985, the American Stock Exchange and the Toronto Stock Exchange instituted a two-way trading link for dually listed securities. Recently, NASDAQ has forged a link with the International Stock Exchange's SEAQ quotation system. An additional NASDAQ link is now operational with Singapore's stock exchange.

Recently, the CME has chosen a dramatically different response to the demands of globalization. Indeed, our response has been described as a revolutionary milestone in the development of futures trading. We have entered into a joint venture with Reuters Holdings PLC—the world's foremost communications organization—to develop a global automated electronic transaction system.

The CME is convinced this concept embodies the manner in which the world of tomorrow will function. We have invited every center of finance to participate. We particularly invite the Japanese financial community to join with us as partners in the development of this bold and comprehensive plan for the future. In the spirit of friendship and kinship, we welcome you to our global community of futures. And while the ultimate benefits of futures markets for Japan can be measured only over the span of many years, there is an immediate cause for celebration: What began here in the 17th century has returned home.

# PART III

# FUTURES—THEIR ROLE AND POTENTIAL

*I crisscrossed the United States dozens of times during the months leading to the birth of the IMM and hundreds of times during the years thereafter in an unending effort to explain our new concept, its rationale, its role, and its potential. I was like an evangelist spreading the gospel of a new religion, obsessed with the idea and its promise. I accepted every opportunity to be heard.*

*To say I was cognizant of the scope of our revolution and the immense potential it represented may sound like a case of hyperbole based on hindsight, but the record gives some license to this claim. Although at the time it may have amounted to nothing short of audacious bravado, I dared state in the* first IMM Annual Report:

> *The opening of the International Monetary Market on May 16, 1972, was as revolutionary a step as the establishment of the first organized commodity exchange when that event occurred. . . . We believe that the IMM is larger in scope than currency futures alone, and accordingly, we hope to bring to our threshold many other contracts and commodities that relate directly to monetary matters and that would complement the economics of money futures.*

*Easier said than done. It took the better part of a full decade to prove the case for financial futures. It required an unwavering belief in the idea and an untiring fervor to communicate our message. It took the ability and devotion of countless members, elected officers, and exchange officials. It took the talent and ardor of thousands of professionals and amateurs alike. In the course of this process we encountered the entire gamut of establishment officialdom. We met with officials at the highest levels of our government as well as those from foreign lands; we met with senators and congressmen; we met with domestic and international bureaucrats; we met with market officials of every kind, from every market sector, and from every part of the globe; we met with academicians, professors, writers, economists, and journalists; we met with businessmen, corporate executives, bankers, money managers, foreign exchange traders, broker-dealers, security analysts, block traders, insurance company officials, and pension and mutual fund managers; and in an interminable and unceasing sequence of interviews and press briefings, we met with members of the media.*

*We also confronted a host of local, national, and global issues; some directly related to our mission on behalf of futures markets, others merely tangential. Often the matter concerned a current topic that only recently had surfaced to impact our domain; sometimes the subject was perennial and of a nature that continuously affected and influenced the well being of our marketplace. Some issues were important, others relatively meaningless. In each case, the matter demanded our attention, necessitated thought, patience, time, and required a plan of action that conformed with our long range strategies. And regardless of the issue, it entailed another trip, another article, or another speech.*

# The Futures of Chicago

*The support of Chicago's establishment for our futures markets, to a large extent, meant the unwavering support from the city's banking commu-nity. As in most urban centers, the banks held a key role in Chicago's decision-making process. It, therefore, was incumbent on us to educate the banks and bankers on the value of futures markets to the city.*

*Fortunately, we had an excellent story to tell, and our markets were just as important to the banks as the banks were to our future growth. More-over, the relationship between the Chicago banks and futures markets went a long way back. For decades, Chicago banks had benefited from the margin deposits of the exchanges and the business of our clearing mem-bers. And as we grew, so did those deposits. Of special value to the banks was the profitable agricultural hedging and delivery business that was tangential to futures. As a consequence, Chicago banks, more than any other banks in the world, understood futures markets.*

*This historical friendship was of great significance during the formative days of the International Monetary Market (IMM). While New York banks generally ignored our new financial futures, the Chicago banks not only understood how currency futures would function but were very sup-portive. Dr. Beryl W. Sprinkel, then Vice President and Chief Economist of Harris Bank and Trust Co. (and who in 1985 became Chairman of the Council of Economic Advisors under President Reagan), served on the IMM's original Board of Directors. Similarly, A. Robert Abboud, then Vice Chairman, First National Bank of Chicago, was on the IMM's orig-inal Board. The Continental Illinois National Bank & Trust Company of Chicago, Chicago's largest bank at the time, undertook the obligation of becoming the IMM's currency delivery facility. Without a delivery mech-anism, the IMM could not have begun operations.*

Presented at the Conference on Chicago as an International Financial Center Sponsored by the First National Bank of Chicago and the Chicago Association of Commerce and Industry, Chicago, Illinois, July 12, 1976

The futures markets and Chicago have become synonymous—80 percent of all futures are transacted here. Thus it would be difficult to discuss Chicago as an international financial center without including the role of the futures markets. Over the past decade, futures have not only become a major component in the world of business, they have become one of this city's leading industries. The Chicago Board of Trade (CBOT) is unquestionably the world's largest futures exchange; the Chicago Mercantile Exchange (CME), a close second, is recognized worldwide as the innovative leader of futures markets; and the International Monetary Market (IMM) is clearly the fastest growing world market for financial instruments.

Futures markets are an annual $600 billion industry. This statistic is based on the dollar value of every transaction. However, since the vast majority of futures transactions do not terminate in delivery but merely are part of a constant process of risk shifting from trader to trader, the cumulative dollar volume gives an erroneous impression. Still, the figure has value. When you consider that in 1965 the total value of futures traded in the United States was a mere $89 billion, this statistic becomes very significant. In the past decade, U.S. futures transaction volume has grown from 6.4 million contracts traded in 1965 to a 1975 total of 32.2 million contracts, an increase of 400 percent.

The economic impact of this activity on Chicago is profound. Chicago exchanges and its member firms rent in excess of 1 million square feet of office space, the exchanges pay real estate taxes in excess of $2 million annually, the annual payroll of exchange employees is approximately $5 million, and exchange member firms employ nearly 11,000 people with an annual payroll between $125 million and $150 million. In 1975, exchange margin deposits with the major Chicago banks averaged $507 million per day, while the full daily total of member firm and customer funds on deposit in Chicago banks is easily in excess of $1.5 billion.

Although the foregoing statistics are impressive, you must consider their direct ramifications to the Chicago business community in assessing their full value. To grasp the magnitude of just one of the many tangential bank business activities generated by futures, calculate the annual interest paid to

Chicago banks for loans made to futures market users in their hedge operations or in deliveries made on futures contracts. This is but one of the many direct business benefits futures exchanges bring to Chicago. Other examples include investment capital made available by our members to the surrounding community, use by our members of the surrounding service industry, banking services utilized, related manpower employment, employment of attorneys, accountants, and on and on. Indeed, a comprehensive analysis of the direct benefits to this city as a consequence of futures exchanges and members would easily place us in the first tier of industries responsible for the continued prosperity of Chicago.

While the foregoing direct and related business implications are significant, we have yet to assess the financial productivity attracted to Chicago by our industry. Chicago is the benefactor of a host of invisible activity because it is the center of gravity of the futures industry. However, since many of these enterprises are intangible and elusive, it is quite difficult to measure. Still, their benefits are real and meaningful. Consider the business endeavors distinct from futures that are initiated because the client, the firm, the customer, and his capital are already here. For example, a real estate developer, or an insurance company or even a restaurateur might take up shop in Chicago simply because the investors reside here. Then consider the inevitable chain reaction that will result from such new business activities. Think of the jobs that will be created. Moreover, while the foregoing indirect role of futures markets in making Chicago an attractive business center is obvious and important, the direct connection between our markets and Chicago as an international center for finance have yet to be considered.

Agriculture has taken on international dimensions of such magnitude that it represents one of our nation's greatest exportable assets. But American agriculture could not function as effectively or efficiently—if it could function at all—were it not for the existence of futures markets. Agricultural productivity in the United States is the model and envy of the rest of the world, and futures markets are part and parcel of this wondrous complex. Futures markets provide virtually the only available broad-based means of insuring cost and/ or profit for the producer, warehouseman, slaughterer, grain elevator operator, packer, wholesaler, and banker as our nation's commodities move from origin to consumption. This is the primary function of futures and it can be the vital ingredient in the success of any marketing system. The ability of the producer, or those who stand in his place, to transfer risk by way of hedging spells the difference between the U.S. agricultural complex and that of other countries.

The need for price insurance has grown dramatically in direct proportion to the increase in price volatility and the world's growing demand for our products. The unique futures market tool as a hedging mechanism has become indispensable to agriculture. The grain contracts at the Chicago Board of Trade, and the hog and cattle contracts at the Chicago Mercantile Exchange have thus become indivisible from the success of the actual markets in these commodities or their by-products.

Still another highly significant dimension of our exchanges directly impacts Chicago's quest as an international financial center. It is a dimension that will be of more significance to this city's future than any of the components already discussed—our financial futures contracts. Chicago has long been known for its innovative spirit. Appropriately, it was here that the International Monetary Market of the Chicago Mercantile Exchange was born, the first attempt by any major exchange in the world to develop a futures market in financial instruments. Today, less than five years later, this concept has taken root and expanded. It is now well recognized that price insurance can be as beneficial to finance as it is to agriculture. The IMM proudly maintains active futures contracts in foreign currency and gold, while the CBOT has an active silver futures contract.

Recently, spurred by the increased gyrations of interest rates, the IMM initiated trading in U.S. Treasury bill futures and the CBOT began its GNMA contract. Both interest rate markets have already proved that the financial community has enthusiastically accepted the concept. Consider the vast potential of these interest rate markets: the daily dollar amounts of transactions in the United States that relate to fluctuations in interest rates; and the cash volume of Treasury bills and bonds, certificates of deposit, mortgages, prime commercial paper, bankers' acceptances, federal funds, and Eurodollars. If even a small percentage of this cash volume were translated into futures markets transactions, the positive implications to this city's growth as an international financial center would be overwhelming. Indeed, the potential of the Eurodollar market alone is enough to make the IMM the world's center for short-term interest rate activity.

It is clear. Our industry and its members are proud of their contribution to Chicago and are committed to making this city nothing less than a primary center of international finance.

# The Food–Price Crisis

*In a narrow sense, the U.S. food–price crisis of the early 1970s could be viewed as a unique or rare phenomenon of small import to the history of financial markets. The causes of the phenomenon itself are of minor historical relevance. There is, however, a deeper significance. The political reactions and economic reverberations to price rise consequences are profound events and highly indicative of the manner in which the American economic/political system works. It evidences our tenuous trust in free markets in general and futures markets in particular. The same or similar issues as they pertain to financial markets or the American economy consistently recur.*

*The 1992 U.S. debate relating to the American trade gap and protectionism, as well as the Japan bashing syndrome, are consequences of the underlying distrust in some quarters of our market-driven economic order. It has brought to surface some of the identical issues that caused the heated debate of two decades ago, which then resulted in dreadful economic consequences. Simply change the 1973 demand for price controls with today's demand for fair trade and it is déjà vu. The Soviet Union tried to control its economic processes for seven decades. The USSR is now history. Are we, as Santayana suggested, doomed to repeat our past mistakes?*

> Op-Ed piece presented before consumer groups who were blaming futures markets for the price-rise spiral of the early 1970s, Chicago, Illinois, July 1973

Much that has been said and written about the recent food spiral has been distorted, garbled, or simply political rhetoric, while too little of the true cause of the food price rise has surfaced or been properly explained.

For instance, the power of the housewife has been extolled as if it were a new invention comparable to the discovery of the wheel. The truth is that consumer price resistance is a time-honored weapon of the marketplace and is as old as the marketplace itself. It is today what it has been from time immemorial—the check in the balance between supply and demand. Sooner or later, every commodity is liable to face the price resistance level of the consumer, at which point the supply will begin to outweigh the demand.

Aside from health considerations, consumer price resistance is second only to supply in affecting the price of any given commodity. The present boycott is not an extension of Women's Liberation, nor an invention of 1973, nor is it entitled to the reverence attached to it by the press. Such glamorization of an important but normal economic function will undoubtedly add to the polarization between the consumer and the producer. This will reduce the matter to a war between boycott groups and antiboycott groups, thus further distorting the supply and demand picture—a disservice to our economy.

A more serious problem, however, is the irresponsible response of many of our political leaders to the current dilemma. They have all, it seems, hopped aboard a bandwagon of popular sentiment with cries of "the President hasn't done enough," "roll back the prices," and so on. Such talk may make votes, but not sense. Where are the leaders brave enough to explain the true nature of this problem? Where are our officials who would point out that the present crisis was caused by the convergence of a number of significant factors that include severe weather, previously depressed prices and profit squeezes, and an enormously increased demand for meat. Indeed, the percentage of consumer income spent on beef, historically at the 2.5 to 2.6 percent level, rose in January and February of this year to the 3.2 percent range. More revealing yet is that in 1972, each person ate 87 percent more beef than he or she did 20 years ago. This is a result of higher wages, more employment, changed eating habits, and government food programs.

Where are the leaders willing to explain that some of the foregoing factors are of a permanent nature, others cyclical, and still others temporary; that one of the main causes has been the devaluation of the dollar coupled with foreign inflation and increased world affluence; that these effects have created additional funds and disposable income in foreign countries increasing exports of our products; that U.S. food products, such as grain and meat, were some of the biggest bargains available to them; that our government encouraged this result to aid our balance of payments; and, that this cause and its effect is a continuing one because you cannot have your commodity and eat it too!

Finally, and most important, why has so little been written about the fact that our food products are such a bargain? Yes, I said a bargain. Sure, food prices in recent months have risen dramatically and out of proportion with other products. Sure, the price of meat has, in the last year, risen to an extreme. In the past 12 months alone, the price of eggs rose 39 percent, potatoes 33 percent, bacon 22 percent, pork chops 18 percent, hamburger 13 percent, round steak 11 percent, and sirloin steak 9 percent—to cite but a few extreme examples.

The price of farm products cannot be measured in terms of weeks or months or even one year. The rise and fall of farm commodities are affected by a number of complicated factors that cause a constant tug-of-war between supply and demand. At any given moment or during any given year, the price may jump or fall dramatically (drawing exceptional public attention to it), but it is unfair to judge this rise or fall as of that moment or that duration. To judge prices of farm commodities adequately or fairly, you must look at them over a longer period, say 10 or 20 years. Only then can you assess their increase in cost on a basis that has taken into account all the variables, cycles, and adjustments.

How often is it explained that although food prices have risen significantly, they have risen far less than most other important consumer goods? While prices for all consumer items rose by 58 percent and housing prices rose by 64 percent during the past 20 years, prices for our retail food went up only 47 percent since 1952, and the price of food eaten at home, less than 40 percent. In truth, food prices in the past several years have been playing catch-up. Even this 40 percent rise (18 percent less than the rise of other consumer items) is not the full story. Our average food bill, which took 23 percent of our after-tax disposable income in 1952, took only 15.7 percent of the after-tax disposable income in 1972 and is projected even lower for 1973. Moreover, the retail cost of a "market basket" of food, indicative of what the typical household spends annually for

U.S. farm-produced foods, is up no more than 33 percent in the past 20 years.

Much has been written about the reasons for our plentiful food supply, but perhaps not enough. A paramount cause for its success has been a relatively free enterprise system guided mainly by supply, demand, and profit motivation. Price and market controls, ceilings, and five-year plans (as some have suggested) have been tried in every other corner of the globe (and here, too) with disastrous results. We are still the *only* nation that has produced food commodities on a scale that is generally higher than we can consume. The main reason is our free economic order. If we tinker with it, we will surely destroy it.

Instead of facts, we have heard the demands that government put more controls into this system; that we roll back prices; that we install some magic bureaucracy to guide and guard our production machinery, rather than allow it to adjust itself as in the past or as world economic conditions dictate. The old successful way isn't good enough in these modern times, some say, so let's adopt the unsuccessful policies of other nations. That way, we can look forward to the same results they have achieved, *and soon we too will lack the same commodities*. Although controls, ceilings, and such sound like wonderful ideas, a number of elemental things are wrong with them:

> *Price Controls Do Not Affect the Fundamental Cause of the Problem.* Rises in prices can be predominantly attributed to lack of supply, or to put it another way, demand in excess of supply. Increase of supply or decrease of demand are the only real means of reducing price. Controls on prices will in no way affect greater supply or lower demand.

> *Price Controls Are Counterproductive.* For the producer, controls induce the psychology that no matter what he does for his product's quality, he cannot get a better price; no matter how hard he works or how much money he spends to produce more, his potential profit per item will remain the same. Thus controls diminish his incentive to produce more or better quality. For the consumer, controls induce the psychology that no matter how much he buys of the product, the price will not rise—and probably will not

decrease. Therefore, his demand for the product has no reason to diminish; it, in fact, increases. Controls have always, in the final analysis, produced shortages.

*Price Controls Create Political and Public Mass Psychology That Can Be Dangerous.* Just like any pacifier, controls create the impression that the problem is solved. Therefore, the underlying causes of the problem go unattended. Worse, often as not, such psychology leads directly to programs and attitudes that aggravate the basic problem.

*Price Controls Are Inherently Inflationary.* In order to regulate and enforce them, costly new government agencies must be created. Such additional government expenditures can be paid for by higher taxes, but usually are not. Instead, the government pays for it with borrowed or created funds. Such funds add to the inflation spiral that is the basic cause of the problem.

*Price Controls Create Unforeseen Complexities and, in the Long Run, Are Self-Defeating.* No control system has yet been devised that can foresee at the outset all the effects and countereffects on the nation's economy. New rules and interpretations must be constantly added. Controls, can in time, become an incomprehensible morass of rules and exceptions riddled with loopholes and conflicting interpretations. Furthermore, human nature will, in the long run, cause consumers to circumvent or violate control prices to get better quality or more of a given product. In essence, this means that prices continue to rise, albeit unofficially.

*Price Controls Tend to Become "Alive" Once Installed.* Controls are most difficult to do away with. The psychology that created them and the psychology that they in turn create seem to make them independent of their creator. Like opium or any artificial stimulant, once you have had it, you think you cannot live without it, regardless of the harm it causes.

If I have oversimplified these issues, it was for brevity. The facts are there for anyone to draw his own conclusions. It is indeed sad that while we now have meat ceilings in response to the public clamor for a pacifier, should the price of meat recede, it will be attributed to the effectiveness of these controls.

Forgotten will be the fact that any reduction in meat prices will have unquestionably been caused by stiff consumer price resistance, coupled with a continuing increase in meat supplies, and not at all by the artificial magic of the ceiling. Alas, no lesson will have been learned—just the opposite—an erroneous impression will have been created.

Food commodities are our biggest bargain. Their production will not be helped by controls, ceilings, or other artificial means. If our food prices are rising, it is caused by eventualities over which our farmers have little control. Penalizing them will not help. It may be that our food prices will continue to rise. The answer to this problem, as in the past, lies in production, production incentives, and overall national economic management, not in politically inspired rhetoric or artificial price adjustments or controls. Emotionally charged accusations and demands by consumer groups will do nothing except confuse the issues and delay the remedies. Impeding free supply–demand forces will bring disastrous results and lower our standard of living.

# The Birth of the CFTC

*H.R. 13113 is just another number identifying one of the interminable pieces of U.S. House of Representatives' legislation. However, this was no ordinary legislative effort. For U.S. futures markets, it was a momentous occasion because it represented the end of an era and the beginning of a new one—this Bill created the Commodity Futures Trading Commission (CFTC).*

*Many within our industry opposed the idea of a federal agency to regulate futures markets. They cited all the expected reasons in opposition: Federal regulations will suffocate the markets; the federal government will create unnecessary red tape; the growth of federal bureaucracy should be curtailed; federal bureaucracy will impose burdensome costs on our industry; futures markets cannot be equated with securities markets; futures markets expertise can only be found within the markets, and so on. Much of what they said is true.*

*Other industry leaders, however, felt there were compelling reasons for the creation of such an agency, and I, generally speaking, fell into this camp. First of all, in my opinion it was inevitable. Futures markets were growing rapidly, expanding their scope, and becoming prominent; it was naive to believe that our markets would be exempt from federal authority when all other similar market endeavors were federally regulated. In other words, it was to be something akin to a shotgun wedding. Thus I felt that if a federal regulatory agency was unavoidable, it would be best for our industry to accept this fate and partake in its creation.*

*Aside from the foregoing, I was cognizant that a federal agency could also prove beneficial to the growth of our markets. Our plans relating to new financial instrument futures were ambitious and could be greatly assisted with a federal stamp of approval. Indeed, some innovations—such as a market in Treasury bills, or a system of cash settlement—would be impossible to implement unless the federal government embraced them. Moreover, a federal agency could aid the image of futures markets and lend us a measure of credibility.*

*Most of the real work—the endless discussions, the education, the lobbying, and the negotiations—preceded the actual hearings. This was our last opportunity to prevail in some highly significant areas that were proposed in a manner contrary to best interest of futures markets, such as economic justification, margin control, and injunctive powers. And it was the final opportunity to place in the permanent record my personal views on this new federal authority as well as a few words of caution.*

*My testimony also had a most interesting sidelight. I reminded the members of this Senate committee of the success of American agriculture compared with nations that were governed by a centrally planned economic order and where there were no futures markets. I admonished the senators to remember the benefits of futures markets and that there was no Moscow Commodity Exchange, no Peking Duck Exchange, and no Havana Cigar Exchange.*

*Those words gave Mr. Martin Cohen—the CME's advertising executive who was in the audience—an idea for a new advertising campaign. It led to his award-winning advertising theme (and popular CME posters): "How come there's no Moscow Commodity Exchange?" "How come there's no Peking Duck Exchange?" "How come there's no Havana Cigar Exchange?"*

---

**Testimony of Leo Melamed, Chairman, International Monetary Market of the Chicago Mercantile Exchange, before the United States Senate Committee on Agriculture, Nutrition and Forestry, May 14, 1974**

---

Mr. Chairman, I deem it a privilege to come before this Committee and am honored to have an opportunity to speak before you in representation of the Chicago Mercantile Exchange. The position of our Exchange is not in opposition to the creation of a new federal Commodity Commission; nor do we oppose many of the provisions that are under current consideration in the proposed legislation. Indeed, many of the provisions contained in the House Bill, H.R. 13113 were the result of suggestions that we ourselves initiated. Nevertheless, we are strongly opposed to several specific provisions within this legislation and fear that their enactment would be highly injurious to futures markets operation. For the same or similar reasons, we also oppose some of the legislative concepts presently before the Senate. To underscore our point of view, I would like to explain the areas in which we feel legislation should be avoided, and convince you that our goal—as yours—is in the best interests of the public.

Mr. Chairman, there are no commodity exchanges in Moscow; there is no Peking Duck Exchange in China; there is no Havana Cigar Exchange. The farmers of those countries have no need for a mechanism that offers risk transference, price projection, or price protection. In those countries, the governments establish the prices at which farmers can sell their products. Consequently, the farmers' primary risk is entirely removed. Alas, by removing the risk, that system also removes the incentive. The sorry history of such systems is that they have been abysmal failures.

In contrast, during the past 100 years, our nation with its agriculture has proved to be the only one in the world that could continue to produce more food products than we could consume—and of a higher quality and at a lower cost than any other nation. Mr. Chairman, there are many reasons for this remarkable fact. But the central and primary reason is that we have, for the most part, maintained a free enterprise system. This is the pivotal difference between us and them. This is the secret of our success and their failure.

Commodity futures markets, Mr. Chairman, are part and parcel of this successful system as it relates to agriculture. U.S. futures markets have been in existence for more than 100 years and are integrally intertwined with our agriculture and agribusiness complex. It has been proven time and again that these futures markets provide some of the most useful and irreplaceable tools for the producer and the consumer; that the degree of economic benefit from such markets is, in fact, greater than most would realize; and that without these tools and services, our agricultural markets would be severely impaired and far less efficient.

It is our very real concern that in any attempt to better the use of commodity futures markets, we not endanger the very function of such markets. It is our very real concern that, in an attempt to change them for the better, we not inadvertently affect the fundamental operation of this complex mechanism. For if the end result of any new legislation is to impede these contract markets, we impair the free market system as a whole.

Indeed, it is most unfortunate that legislation relating to futures was prompted in large measure by our recent food price spiral. Speculation at our exchanges was erroneously viewed by some as a possible cause of the nation's rising prices. This type of reasoning ignored the fundamental economic and political factors that were underlying the problem, many of which had been festering for more than a decade. It is a reasoning that is analogous to that practiced by ancient monarchs who beheaded the messenger of bad tidings.

To act as a messenger is, in fact, one of the primary functions of futures markets. Futures markets, by their very definition, act to provide us with a glimpse of what is coming. If these markets had failed to predict the reality of higher prices, they would not have functioned properly. As a matter of fact, they did not fail, and moreover, they responded to the emergency far better than might have been anticipated. Those who blamed these markets last year for predicting higher food prices, it would seem, should praise these same markets today for predicting lower prices.

But we accept neither the blame nor the praise. In each case, the markets were acting as a mechanism to transfer risk from the producer to the speculator. In each case, the markets were acting much as a giant computer projecting prices into the future. The markets may not always be correct in their computations, but they represent a moment-to-moment analysis of all involved in the marketplace. A barometer such as this cannot be blamed or given credit for the weather conditions that exist or will occur.

Nor should our markets be castigated because they utilize and are utilized by speculators. Speculators do not affect the eventual outcome of actual supply and demand. But speculators are the essential ingredient for these markets to function. They are willing to shoulder the risk that the farmer undertakes when he first plants his crop or buys his heifers—a risk the farmer wants to shed. It is the risk that Russian, Chinese, and Cuban farmers do not have. Therefore, they need no mechanism for price insurance. That is right; no speculators, no exchanges, and no successful agricultural system.

Therein lies the rub. Should any legislation endanger the liquidity of these markets, should it create the ability of political or arbitrary forces to disrupt their operation, should it place upon markets such requirements that impede their normal processes, should it stifle innovation, it would be a step toward dismantling the free enterprise portion of our nation's agriculture and a giant step toward eventual production quotas. We know where that road leads.

As a matter of fact, our nation has just experienced the horror of price by administrative edict and its inevitable partner—administrative supply allocation. It was just yesterday, it seems, that our Exchange together with other free market institutions and economic experts pleaded that we not adopt a policy of price controls. But, we were then but a frail voice in the storm over inflation. The clamor for immediate relief was too great for Congress and the President to withstand. So our government embraced price controls, and as a result, our nation suffered all the dire consequences attendant to that remedy.

Have we learned any lesson? Are we now ready to accept the proven fact that, especially in agriculture, there is no solution to higher prices other than higher production or lower demand? That higher production cannot be legislated? That lower demand cannot be ordained? That any material government interference with profit incentive is counterproductive? That any government interference with our free enterprise system, which has its own checks and balances, must inevitably lead to disaster? Have we learned this lesson, or are we doomed to make this mistake again and again?

Mr. Chairman, in a similar vein, legislation that gives a federal administrative agency the power to demand economic justification before a new instrument of trade will be approved or the power with which to unduly interfere with the function of our futures markets, will be the same step backward. It will create the ability to inhibit innovation and influence price by administrative action rather than the desired influences of free economic forces. Take, for instance, the issue of margin control. We are vehemently and unequivocally opposed to any legislation that would transfer this authority from the exchanges themselves. Margin is a misnomer with respect to commodities. There is a fundamental difference, both from a conceptual and operational standpoint between margin on securities and margin on commodity futures contracts. Unfortunately, this fact is sometimes not understood.

Securities market margin is a direct measure of the creation of bank credit. It determines the proportion between the amount paid for securities and the amount borrowed for their purchase. There is no such relation in futures markets. In futures markets, margin acts as a surety or security deposit. It is conceptually designed to protect the financial solvency and integrity of the brokerage firm. Our record in this regard is remarkably good, particularly in comparison with the record of securities brokerage firms even though those exchanges have been supervised by the Securities and Exchange Commission (SEC) since 1934.

The function of margin in commodity markets is geared toward protecting the monetary variance between daily fluctuations. The margin required is not measured by the value of the product or contract, but is determined by the volatility of the market and the possible change in daily price movement. It is earnest money to guarantee the sanctity of our contracts.

Everyone who has carefully studied futures markets should reach the same conclusion as did the *Nathan Report* of December 1967. This report was the result of a study on this subject made at the behest of the United States Department of Agriculture (USDA). It concluded that margin on commodity futures markets cannot be utilized for any purpose other than the one presently used without impairing the actual operation of the market itself. That its function is to act as a security deposit and cannot relate to payment on credit toward purchase of the product. And furthermore, that no agency is better equipped or situated to regulate this area than the exchanges themselves.

Were this power transferred to another agency or utilized for any other purpose, such power could easily be applied to create artificial causes for price movement. Mr. Chairman, we would again be on the threshold of price control.

Similarly, legislation that delegates uninhibited injunctive power over these markets to an agency or commission creates the possibility of affecting price by the threat of administrative action. Any such legislation must clearly delineate, without ambiguity, the conditions, causes, and purposes for which such injunctive power is to be utilized. Otherwise, such legislation will prove to be a much greater detriment to our markets than are the ills they attempt to correct.

Mr. Chairman, it is our fundamental belief that the best and most successful manner of regulation is self-regulation. We submit that any legislation that fails to take this principle into account will fail in its primary objectives. We believe that the exchanges not only have the necessary and intimate knowledge of the market operation but also have ready access to the personnel and expertise vital for correct administrative action in matters relating to the intricacies of these markets. It would indeed be a disservice to our nation if the new legislation failed to tap and properly utilize these resources.

We urge that the new legislation, particularly in sensitive areas affecting innovation, price, liquidity, and margin provide a means for the contract markets to first do it right, and for the new agency to intercede only when and if the exchanges have neglected this responsibility.

# Pioneerism Needs No Economic Justification

*The Commodity Futures Trading Commission (CFTC) came into existence by congressional Act in 1974. The debate that preceded this legislation was heated and extensive. Because I believed that the CFTC was inevitable, I felt we could do more good for the futures industry by partaking in the process. Accordingly, I became an official advisor in the congressional proceedings that created this federal agency. It should be noted that the CFTC's internal organizational structure is largely to the credit of Ms. Beverly Splane who became this agency's first Executive Director and later the Executive Vice President of the CME.*

*During the proceedings we never lost sight of the fact that—at best—the new agency was to be a mixed blessing. Thus, while generally supportive of the CFTC Act, we labored to remove certain of the more onerous provisions proposed. We were not always successful. Of particular grave concern to me were the "economic justification" provisions that remained. I believed those provisions were inherently dangerous since they provided the Commission with a means—wittingly or unwittingly—to impede innovation. Innovation was to us the very soul of futures market existence. I like to believe that as a consequence of our influence and continued pressure in this respect, the provisions of Section 5 have never become the detrimental force they might have otherwise been.*

Presented at the Annual Meeting of the American Bar Association, Montreal, Canada, August 13, 1975

Futures trading has become a very important part of the nation's economy. During 1973, the total volume in futures contracts was over $500 billion. This is twice the volume of trading in all stock exchanges in the country. Currently, futures markets perform a vital function for agricultural producers, for manufacturers, for exporters, for consumers, and for others.

With these words, Senator Herman Talmadge, Chairman of the Senate Committee on Agriculture, Nutrition and Forestry introduced to the Senate the final version of the Commodity Futures Trading Commission (CFTC) Act of 1974 thereby creating this new federal agency. Although Senator Talmadge spoke those words in justification of the Act, the uninitiated may have wondered whether the Senator's words were used to justify the legislation or to condemn it.

If, by 1973, futures trading had become so big and so important to the nation's economy *without* the federal government, why was it necessary for the government to now come to its rescue? Weren't there unsuccessful or failing segments of our economy for the Senate to rescue? And if futures had become so important to the well-being of our economy *without* a major congressional act, might not such an Act be detrimental to their further growth and service to the nation?

However, the Commodity Futures Trading Commission Act is now a fact of life and it will be of small purpose to debate its merit or necessity. What is of vital importance is that the Act be administered wisely in order to fulfill what we believe to be its primary purpose: the continued service of the futures industry to our nation's economy.

The Act is probably a better instrument than we had a right to expect. After all, its subject matter—futures markets—is highly complex and technical, while the mechanism is arcane and highly sophisticated. Moreover, the legislators were not market experts or traders. It can be easily understood how errors or omissions could develop. Fortunately, few exist. The major aspects of futures were fully and comprehensively covered.

We are, for instance, especially gratified that the Act placed all contract markets under one roof. We are also pleased that the Act provided the CFTC with strong federal authority in those areas that were in need of regulation. In sum total, therefore, we believe the Act can achieve its intended purposes, that is, to promote the futures industry, ensure fair practices and provide protection to the producer and consumer.

The Act can accomplish these goals because it has breadth and flexibility, ingredients critical to its successful implementation. Without breadth, the CFTC would be too limited in scope to function properly; without flexibility, industry rules would become too rigid for it to succeed. But it is not the words within the Act that will control. Ultimately, as is the case with most legislation, the final determinants of the Act's good or evil will be the commissioners and staff who implement it.

Allow me, therefore, to address CFTC commissioners and staff, present and future, and to focus on one aspect of the Act that is the most critical to the growth of our industry and its continued ability to serve our national interests. The subject is close to my heart. It concerns provisions in the Act that, in my opinion, should not have been included or at least not in the form adopted. It will require much of the CFTC's wisdom and a great deal of its flexibility to apply interpretations to these provisions that will not impede the continued growth of our industry. It is my fervent hope that with these remarks I can leave a legacy of understanding and provide an ounce of prevention in place of a pound of cure.

Section 5 of the Act deals with contract market designation. Its provisions contain requirements that a board of trade must meet before a given instrument can be approved for trade. As a result of historical application of this section and the report of the Senate–House Conference Committee, the CFTC has accepted past interpretations of these requirements to mean that an exchange must demonstrate "economic justification" of a proposed contract prior to approval. In other words, there must be proof of economic purpose before any new futures contract can come into existence.

The foregoing requirement—to which we vehemently object—is further complicated by the provision of paragraph (g), which requires "the board of trade to demonstrate that transactions for future delivery in the commodity for which designation as a contract market is sought will not be contrary to the public interest." In practice, *economic justification* and *public interest*, the two main requisites for designation under Section 5, will merge to act as one.

Futures exchanges have fought in vain against enactment of the foregoing requirements. We will continue to battle against their strict interpretation. Separately, these requirements are dangerous and onerous, and can act as serious impediments to expansion of our markets. In combination, they can become a market straitjacket and the greatest barrier to innovation—the unique and quintessential characteristic of futures markets.

In 1632, Galileo Galilei published his *Dialogue on the Two Principal Systems of the World.* In nonscientific terminology, his work can be described as claiming that Copernicus was right; the earth did, in fact, revolve around the sun. Unfortunately, Galileo's discovery was deemed contrary to the public interest of the times and he was forced to recant. For the next 200 years, the sun continued to revolve obediently around the earth.

In 1957, after spending 250 million dollars on research, design, and development, the Ford Motor Company brought into production the "hottest new automobile of the century," a car that passed every economic justification test that could be devised. Thus, the Edsel was born and died ignominiously two years later. Today, the Edsel is in great demand, not as an automobile, but as a nostalgia relic.

History is replete with great discoveries, inventions, and ideas that failed to meet either the public interest or economic justification test of the day—ideas that were consequently crushed or died aborning, often to be rediscovered and hailed years later. And no doubt there are many suppressed great ideas that remain dormant waiting to be rediscovered. History is equally replete with discoveries, inventions, and ideas that met the public interest and economic justification test of the day with flying colors, only to be subsequently discarded as evil or useless.

Futures market contracts are no different in this respect from other inventions and ideas. The demands of economic justification and public interest seem reasonable and logical enough on the surface. However, a person can never be sure that the criteria used to predetermine the foregoing are the correct standards to apply. Just as beauty is often in the eye of the beholder, so is one man's poison another man's wine.

A predetermined test for economic justification has never by itself been a surefire ingredient to guarantee a successful futures contract. When the Chicago Mercantile Exchange's shrimp futures were instituted, the economic need for such a market was well established. However, the contract never took off the ground and was delisted in less than two years. Examples of such contracts have occurred at every futures exchange in the country.

Would any commissioners be foolish enough to guarantee an exchange the success of a new contract simply because it passed the justification and public interest tests? Futures markets require many ingredients to succeed—some tangible, some intangible. My belief is that 13 components are necessary to ensure a successful contract—12 of which we know, the last one we don't. But it is the 13th element that is the most critical and controlling.

The ultimate and only test for economic justification is the marketplace itself. If justification is indeed lacking, the market will surely fail. No foreordained set of standardized, prepackaged rules or requirements can make that determination. We must have faith in the free market and the competitive arena of ideas and products. A better test has yet to be devised.

In a recent speech, W. Allen Wallis, Chancellor of the University of Rochester, succinctly stated that what concerns him most about government today is the "powerful movement away from limited government and individual freedom toward pervasive government and collective control of all activities. . . ." "It is a shift away," he regrets to say, "from trust in good faith, competence and responsibility toward reliance on detailed prescriptions by government and documentation by individuals of their actions, intentions and motives." Such a shift as it relates to our economy, the chancellor sadly concludes, is resulting in a "dampening of enterprise innovation, initiative and industriousness."

We do not know the exact and detailed prescriptions for economic justification of a futures market. They are not the same for every commodity, nor are they always tangible, nor do they remain constant. Often, the actual economic uses of a futures market are determined, created, or become visible only after the market is in existence.

If futures contracts are forced to show compliance with and evidence of strict and stringent justification prescriptions, there will be few new markets. Strict and automatic justification regulations will, as Chancellor Wallis said, directly stifle any attempt at innovation, any thought of pioneering, and any move toward change.

Not so many years ago, it was an accepted and inexorable truth that to be the product of a successful futures market, the commodity had to be storable. Every existing futures contract until then included this essential prerequisite. To suggest a futures market in a live commodity was unthinkable. Without question an economic justification test of that day would have applied the foregoing principal. Were this the case, the Chicago Mercantile Exchange would not have pioneered its live cattle futures concept. As a result, one of the most successful and most important futures markets in existence today would never have been instituted. As with Galileo's *Dialogue,* the idea would have had to be rediscovered years later.

Even if the commissioners of that day overlooked the issue of storable versus live, the CME revolutionary cattle concept would still have failed to meet the other more standard prescriptions of justification. The CME would have had to bring forth—as is required—sufficient numbers of respectable cattle raisers and feeders to testify that they could and would use such a market for hedging purposes. At the time, the cattle industry was generally opposed to our proposed new market. Their negative bias stemmed from normal resistance to a new concept that would alter entrenched and established modes of operation. Today, the CME's cattle futures contract can boast that up to 50 percent of its open interest comprises cattle hedgers' positions—an extremely high percentage of hedge participation.

But the most striking example is the International Monetary Market (IMM). At the time the idea was conceived, it would have been impossible to pass present-day criteria for economic justification. Indeed, at the time of application for currency futures, the world monetary order would still have been governed by the fixed parity regime of Bretton Woods. Clearly, no futures market could flourish under a fixed-pricing system. And, even later, under the Smithsonian Agreement, when currency rates were permitted to fluctuate 2.25 percent in either direction from fixed parities, it is highly doubtful that our idea would have been approved. Since rates were not permitted to fluctuate significantly, hedging was not a necessity. Who needs a free market within a world system that has a prescribed limitation for price movement? More important, there were precious few bankers or economists who would have supported the necessity for our revolutionary idea. *Futures markets were solely for agricultural products.*

When we pioneered the IMM concept, we believed the fixed exchange rate system was doomed and that sooner or later the world would be forced to accept the idea of floating or flexible exchange rates. We believed that the principles of futures markets that served agriculture all these years could be successfully applied to finance. But we could not prove it at the time. Nor should we have had to. No body of regulators—no matter how well-meaning their purpose—should be allowed to prescribe necessary criteria before a new idea can be tested against the harsh reality of the marketplace.

Today, currency futures are an accepted concept. The IMM would pass any economic justification or public interest test. Today, most economists and bankers would subscribe to the market's necessity, but it might be too late—the IMM might already exist on another shore.

And what about so many other new concepts, new instruments, new ideas yet unborn? Will they be able to meet a fore-ordained system of economic justification? They should not be required to. The CFTC will do this nation a great service if it remembers this fundamental principle of our free market economy.

At the risk of adding one more *ism* to the multitude that already exist, allow me to conclude that *pioneerism*, by definition, needs no economic justification.

# The Fed Study on
# Futures and Options

*Building the image of futures markets is a full-time endeavor. It is a mission that has gone hand-in-hand with our unceasing efforts to create new contracts, to expand market applications, to educate institutional users, and with our overall labors to increase the recognition of our markets.*

*Consider then the importance of the priceless endowment in the form of a favorable official report about futures markets written by four of America's prestigious federal agencies: the Board of Governors of the Federal Reserve System, the U.S. Treasury Department, the Securities and Exchange Commission, and the Commodity Futures Trading Commission.*

*The work,* A Study of the Effects on the Economy of Trading in Futures [and] Options, *was undertaken at the behest of the U.S. Congress and took more than two years to conclude. (I was told it weighed 4 pounds, 4 ounces.) Such a study deserved all the recognition we could engender.*

Published in the *National Journal*, December 21, 1985. The
author wishes to acknowledge the assistance provided by
Galen Burghardt, a former economist at the Federal Reserve
Board, Division of Research and Statistics

From time immemorial, predicting the future has been a hazardous occupation. Good news was universally welcome, but its failure to materialize was shabbily treated. To behead the messenger of bad tidings was not an uncommon reward. Little wonder then that futures and options have since their inception been an area shrouded in mystery, frequently maligned, and more often than not a convenient scapegoat for unpleasant business phenomena. Never mind that there has been little empirical evidence to support many of the fears concerning these markets. Never mind that their protagonists have always responded to antagonistic taunts with seemingly reasonable answers. Never mind that internal market studies have always supported favorable conclusions. Self-serving evidence or rationale is by itself far too feeble a defense to overcome the power of beliefs founded in ignorance.

Consider then the significance of a study about futures and options undertaken at the behest of none other than the U.S. Congress. Consider then the significance of such a study conducted by none other than four federal agencies with lofty credentials and incomparable qualifications. Consider then the value of such a study on the future life of these markets. Would it not, once and for all, shed meaningful light on this dim corner of business activity? Would it not at long last provide credible answers to age-old concerns and nagging doubts? Clearly, this should be its goal.

Such was the mandate of the *Futures Trading Act of 1982* when it directed the Board of Governors of the Federal Reserve System (Fed), the Commodity Futures Trading Commission (CFTC), and the Securities and Exchange Commission (SEC), with assistance of the U.S. Treasury, to address the serious concerns surrounding futures and options and determine their impact on the United States and its business community (see Table 1). Moreover, to ensure the integrity and quality of the result, the Fed was made primary agent for the study and was required to include an analysis of the work product by the other contributors.

The report, *A Study of the Effects on the Economy of Trading in Futures [and] Options,* which took more than two years to complete, deserves special recognition and public attention. It is remarkable in two respects. The first is its scope, which covers almost every conceivable public policy question about futures and options in foreign currencies, interest rates, and stock indexes. The second is its general conclusion that financial futures and option markets seem to be serving a useful social function.

What is especially surprising about the report is the amazing distance the Fed has covered over the past few years. Just seven years ago, the Fed joined with the Treasury in calling for a moratorium on the approval of new futures contracts on Treasury notes and stock indexes. The CFTC obliged them, and the moratorium lasted until the Fed and Treasury could

---

**Table 1**

**What Congress Wanted to Know
(Questions asked of the Fed)**

1. What economic purposes are served by futures and options markets?
2. What effects do futures and options markets have on the formation of real capital in the economy and the liquidity of credit markets?
3. Are the public policy tools currently in place to regulate trading activities in futures and options markets adequate to prevent manipulation of and to guard against other harmful economic effects in these markets, their underlying cash markets and related financial markets?
4. Are there adequate investor protections afforded participants in these markets?

Source: *A Study of the Effects on the Economy of Trading in Futures [and] Options.* Undertaken by the Federal Reserve at the direction of the U.S. Congress in the Futures Trading Act of 1982. Published 1985.

---

complete a joint study that was rather parochial in its regulatory interest. When the Fed/Treasury study was released in the spring of 1979, the CFTC was given a grudging approval to go ahead with its work. But the report then conveyed a high degree of concern that trading in financial futures—Treasury bill, note, and bond futures in particular—could prove harmful to their related cash markets. The Treasury, for example, expressed grave concerns about possible corners and squeezes, because to prevent the ill effects of a corner or squeeze, the Treasury might have to issue more debt of a particular type and maturity than had been planned as part of its normal debt management policy. The Treasury naturally was loath to lose any freedom in conducting its operations.

The present study, although it contains enough "on-the-one-hand-on-the-other-hand" language to make us all wish that economists had only one hand, has none of the former grudging tone of acceptance. The change in tone is all the more remarkable because the authors of the current report were key players in the preparation of the 1979 study. The difference, then, cannot be shrugged off as little more than a change in political philosophy accompanying a change in administration. Rather, the men and women of the Fed have, from their own perspective, grown up with our markets. They have become far better acquainted with these markets: how they work, who uses them, and the tools they represent. They have thus become much more comfortable with what originally appeared to be an enigmatic activity of dubious value.

To fully appreciate the significance of the report's findings, you must first understand the exhaustive nature of the study and the thoroughness by which the Fed examined every aspect of our markets. After conferring with the other agencies, the Fed brought together industry and academic experts to discuss the questions and to get advice on charting a course of study. The course adopted included interviews by the CFTC and SEC staff with more than 100 financial institutions and commercial firms who participate in financial futures and options markets; a broad survey of "public" participants, conducted by Market Facts; a poll of the views of outside experts on various issues raised by the Congress; an extensive survey of about 50 years worth of academic articles written on the subject of futures and options; and the preparation of several original special papers on selected facets of the questions raised by Congress.

The scope of the study covered virtually every issue ever raised about these markets and examined each from every aspect, to wit: the basic economics of futures and options; the development and growth of the markets; the trading conducted and strategies utilized by institutional, commercial, and professional participants; public and noncommercial participation; the effects of these markets on the U.S. economy; market imperfections, unfair trading practices, financial integrity, sales practices and regulations pertaining thereto; legal restrictions on the use of these markets; surveys of market traders; and findings and conclusions.

The result was a massive document which, together with the Fed's separate report on securities and futures margin, represented a most comprehensive and weighty report. Basically, the study found that financial futures and options *do* serve a useful economic purpose by providing a more efficient way to manage risk; that, if anything, the liquidity of related

## Table 2

### What the Fed Determined
### (General conclusions reached by the Joint Study)

1. The new financial futures and options markets serve a useful economic purpose, primarily by providing a means by which risks inherent in economic activity (such as market, interest rate, and exchange rate risks) can be shifted from firms and individuals less willing to bear them to those more willing to do so. This desirable risk transfer function appears likely to spread to additional commercial and financial firms and increase in magnitude as experience is gained with these new markets and legal impediments to their use are modified.

2. Financial futures and options markets appear to have no measurable negative implications for the formation of capital. The new markets for financial futures and options appear to have enhanced liquidity in some of the underlying cash markets on which they are based and do not appear to have reduced the liquidity of any of these markets.

3. Financial futures and options contracts differ in important characteristics. Nonetheless, they have many common elements: both serve similar economic functions, markets for both are closely interrelated with the underlying cash markets on which they are based, participants in both appear to have similar characteristics, and both have similar potential for causing harm if they function improperly. Thus, there is need for close harmonization of federal regulation of these markets.

4. Trading in the functionally similar instruments under the jurisdiction of the SEC or CFTC does not appear to have resulted in significant harm to public customers or to these derivative or related cash markets. Some aberrations have resulted from arbitrage trading in index options and the securities composing the indexes. The potential for such disruptive trading in the index markets requires continued monitoring by the SEC and CFTC.

5. With respect to the issues examined in this study, the agencies believe no additional legislation is needed at this time to establish an appropriate regulatory framework. The SEC and CFTC currently have similar regulations and supervisory procedures in place in some areas requiring government oversight, and both agencies are committed to working cooperatively to establish a compatible framework of regulation capable of dealing effectively with all activities requiring such supervision and regulation.

Source: *A Study of the Effects on the Economy of Trading in Futures [and] Options.*

cash markets such as those for U.S. Treasury securities and common stocks have been improved by the presence of futures and options; and that there appear to be no significant regulatory problems concerning either manipulation or customer protection (see Table 2). The following sections describe some of the specific conclusions.

## ECONOMIC EFFICIENCIES

From interviews with institutional investors, the authors learned that general price risks could be handled far less expensively by buying or selling futures or options than by trading directly in the cash market. In their own words, taken from the report, ". . . it would appear that futures and options make possible greater output per unit of productive resources, just as in the case of any cost saving technological innovation." This means that money managers—including pension fund managers, stock and bond mutual funds, and banks—can produce higher rates of return with our markets for any given level of risk. Or, if greater stress is laid on avoiding risk, the same rate of return can be earned but at a lower level of risk. Either way, pensioners, investors, and bank depositors can be better served.

## CAPITAL ACCUMULATION AND ALLOCATION

The study repudiates the age-old misconception that positions taken in futures or options markets divert investable funds from the rest of the economy and proves that nothing could be further from the truth. Unfortunately, the tenacity of this myth is substantial, making it difficult to eradicate.

## MARKET LIQUIDITY

The study notes, ". . . it appears that financial futures and options markets have, if anything, generally increased cash market liquidity, perhaps most particularly, liquidity in markets for Treasury securities." From the Fed's standpoint, this means that their ". . . ability to conduct open market operations in an orderly manner across a range of maturities in government securities appears to have been enhanced by the new futures and options contracts." It also means that ". . . the Treasury's ability to conduct debt management operations is similarly enhanced."

The study indicates that the public benefits as a result of financial futures. The improved liquidity in the Treasury securities market means interest rates paid by the taxpayer on debt incurred by the federal government is lower than it would be without financial futures markets. And from interviews with investment banking firms, it is clear the ability to hedge corporate bond underwriting results in a lower all-in cost of funds for the private sector as well.

## CASH MARKET PRICE STABILITY

The study finds: "Most formal empirical studies of the impact of futures and options markets on cash market prices and direct studies on the behavior of cash market prices suggest that it is stabilizing, or at least do not establish that it is destabilizing." Even so, the Fed is unwilling to conclude altogether that futures and options are unambiguously good for their related cash markets. The study concludes, instead, that ". . . the role of speculation as a vehicle that generally stabilizes market prices is still in question."

## MARGINS

In a companion piece on federal margin regulation, the Fed has reviewed exhaustively both the theory and evidence on margins and finds the case for federal intervention to be extremely weak. Chairman Volcker, in his cover letter to Congress, went so far as to suggest that ". . . Congress give serious consideration to adopting a new approach toward margin regulation. One such approach might be to repeal existing regulation, effectively turning over responsibility for setting margins to the members of the various securities exchanges and other institutions that make margin loans. . . . Past experience suggests that such entities, independently or through self-regulatory organizations, generally have maintained margins adequate to protect themselves against loss . . ." (Volcker to Helms, January 11, 1985).

Although this alternative was not the Chairman's first choice, it was the first choice of Donald Regan, who was then Secretary of the Treasury and whose reading of the study led him to believe that the federal government could get out of the business of regulating margins altogether.

While the study is to be lauded in most respects, it is noteworthy to record two areas where it is deficient:

## DIFFERENCE BETWEEN FUTURES AND FORWARDS

The study should have done more to distinguish between *futures,* which are standardized contracts traded on commodities exchanges that guarantee both sides of the trade, and *forwards,* which are customized off-exchange arrangements with no guarantor standing in between. While the distinction may seem a bit obscure, the difference is fundamental.

With few exceptions, most financial catastrophes involving trading for future delivery have occurred in the forward market, *not* in the futures market. The problems faced by government securities dealers over the past few years have stemmed from the repo market, an off-exchange market. And banks such as Franklin National in the United States, Herstat Bank in Germany, or Fuji Bank in Tokyo have gotten into trouble from the forward—not the futures—market. The reason for the difference is largely one of accountability. In futures, all gains and losses are settled in cash at the end of every business day: If trades are profitable, money comes in; if trades are losses, money is paid out. With futures, bank traders cannot hide losing positions or unrealized losses from management. Therefore, from the standpoint of control, futures are far superior to forwards. Bank regulators such as the Fed should appreciate this distinction.

## THE REGULATORS' REPORT CARD

As to be expected, the various agencies involved in this study have given themselves high marks. However, I believe they graded themselves a bit too highly in that there are many areas in which both the securities and futures markets are regulated too heavily. And with the sole exception of a brief ray of hope in Chairman Volcker's letter of transmittal for the federal margin study, I find no suggestion in the collected reports that the agencies plan to undo any of the unnecessary regulations they have devised (usually in response to problems more imagined than real).

In conclusion, now that the facts are in, now that the mandate by Congress has been satisfied, how should we view the result and what can we say about the achievement? Will it provide futures and options with an environment within which to prosper, or will it do little in responding to concerns that historically have inhibited their potential? The answers are important and generally positive.

Frankly, for those who are certain our markets are the work of the devil, the Fed report will be discarded as so much rubbish. The results of this study—or any other study—will make little difference to confirmed unbelievers, detractors, or the unenlightened. These naysayers are not easily persuaded by the facts nor do they often bother to examine the evidence. Thus, for the most part, this large body of negative thinking will remain intact, believing as it always has and continuing its attack on our markets unabated.

On the other hand, for those who are charged with the responsibility of legislating or regulating our markets, the Fed study has monumental significance. It offers generally positive answers to virtually every concern posed about futures and options and provides a rationale for their favorable treatment. Indeed, the report gives reason not to impede their continued growth and provides impetus to foster an environment wherein they can expand and continue to serve the business sectors for whom they are intended.

Finally, for those of us whose daily lives are intertwined with futures and options, the Fed study represents a signal milestone. It provides us with concrete and impeccable evidence that much of what we have maintained for years is true: Our financial markets serve a useful and important economic function. Moreover, they do not undermine existing cash market structures, nor impede the formation of capital. On the contrary, our markets tend to enhance cash market liquidity as well as provide an important means by which inherent economic risks can be shifted to those who are more willing to assume it. The net result is a strengthening of the economic fabric of this nation.

# The Coveted Scapegoat

*The ultimate bane of futures markets is their arcane existence. It is the source of a multitude of pejorative beliefs about our marketplace that have plagued us since time immemorial. It has made our markets the ideal scapegoat.*

*This is not to say that our markets are without fault—utopia has not yet arrived on the floors of futures markets. Rule violations, greed, and avarice are ubiquitous human characteristics and occur in every endeavor. Futures markets are no exception. However, futures markets and their traders are often the brunt of grossly unfair prejudices and accusations that simply have no basis in fact.*

*The process of repudiating the unwarranted and repugnant slander directed at futures markets throughout history is, to say the least, difficult. One must begin by openly calling attention to the demagoguery and debunking false beliefs.*

Keynote Address before the American Enterprise Institute, Washington, D.C., October 31, 1985. Published in the *Futures Industry Association Newsletter*, December 1985

"It's ludicrous to think that foreign exchange can be entrusted to a bunch of pork belly crapshooters," proclaimed a prominent New York banker back in 1972 on the eve of the Merc's launch of the International Monetary Market.

"The New Currency Market: Strictly for Crapshooters," echoed *Business Week* (4-22-72) and wrote that "if you fancy yourself an international money speculator but lack the resources . . . your day has come!"

Derogatory comments, defamatory innuendos, inflammatory jokes, false accusations, misleading opinions, half-truths, out-and-out lies: these represent the fate and burden of futures markets. Thus it has been throughout time, thus it will

131

no doubt continue because predicting the future has always been a hazardous occupation. Good news was universally welcomed, but its failure to materialize—or its counterpart—was shabbily treated. "Behead the messenger of bad tidings" was not an uncommon reward.

Futures and options markets—that little understood corner of business activity, that complex arena of esoteric economics, that noisy place shrouded in mystery, that distant cousin of the financial world—have served as an ideal scapegoat since time immemorial. And why not? Visit the tumultuous, colorful, rowdy trading floor. Observe the rough, boisterous, undignified members and brokers. Clearly, there is something sinister going on there! Obviously, no legitimate business is being conducted. And, even worse, speculation is going on there. Certainly, dens of speculation cannot be a place for serious investment. Read the headlines—their members are always out to make a killing. Those markets have nothing to do with capital formation. Those markets create volatility. Futures markets, the ideal scapegoat.

Has anything changed? In 1973, a group of Chicago housewives marched on the Chicago Mercantile Exchange to protest *high* food prices. A few years later, during the 1977–1978 farm crisis, U.S. farmers drove their tractors to the Chicago Board of Trade on LaSalle Street to protest *low* prices on their agricultural products.

Has anything changed? After the War of 1812 played havoc with the U.S. farm economy, antispeculative sentiment was rampant. Buying forward was acceptable, but any market that also allowed the opposite—forward sales—was unacceptable. The New York legislature, applying its ultimate wisdom, enacted legislation banning all forward selling.

Has anything changed? In January 1985, 70 years later, leaders of the American Agriculture Movement demanded that short sales in futures be banned because "selling depresses prices." Later in the year, mounting frustrations over the nation's failed agriculture policy, its low farm prices, its record crop surpluses, and sagging land values inspired farm spokesmen in search of a scapegoat to denounce the Chicago exchanges as the *Bermuda Triangle of agriculture*. A U.S. senator piously agreed, pointed his finger in our direction, and proclaimed that "never have so few done so little to make so much from so many."

Has anything changed? In 1976 when the U.S. Treasury bill and Treasury bond futures markets were introduced, countless articles were published that warned of the negative impacts of these new inventions, of their unfavorable effect on the underlying cash markets by causing price distortions, of their disruptive market influences because of fraudulent acts by traders, and of their adverse consequences to the U.S. Treasury's debt management activities. If our eventual 200-billion-plus dollar deficit had been known then, these futures markets surely would have been an excellent candidate for its cause.

The respected *Economist*, in its January 17, 1976, issue, in reporting on the new interest rate markets wrote, "Like Linda Lovelace, the girl with the 'deep throat,' the International Monetary Market (IMM) of the Chicago Mercantile Exchange tries to make money by being more outrageous than its rivals. Now that its currency futures market is well established—it was opened in 1972 by women in fancy dress—the IMM has this month opened a trading pit in United States Treasury bill futures. Bidding for the government paper takes place on the same floor as for pork bellies, live cattle and three month eggs."

Surely, futures and options markets are not immune from criticism. Surely, they are not utopian—what enterprise is? Surely, there are rule violators, greed, and avarice. Surely, they are not without sin. We agree. But neither are they the work of the devil! And as an industry, they are a great deal better than most.

The next time you hear a story, see a headline, or hear a rumor maligning futures and options, ask yourself the following questions: Would the world's financial system have survived the economic stresses and strains of the 1970s and early 1980s as well as it did without these markets? Would the shrinking base of private sector capital have been equal to the increased public sector demands without throwing the free world into financial turmoil, were it not that futures markets provided a new and more efficient means of capital utilization? Would the speculative fevers unleashed by volatile price movements due to unprecedented inflation and record interest rates, followed by unprecedented disinflation and falling interest rates, not have materially disrupted the world's financial fabric were it not that futures and options acted as a buffer and a pressure valve? Would our shrinking world—where a bank in South East Asia is as near as your downtown counterpart, where an event in Abu Dhabi is as close as your nearest telephone—not demand a means, such as our markets provide, to instantly partake and protect yourself from the financial effect of a significant world event?

If there had not been futures and options markets, wouldn't they have been invented by now? And if there were no economic justification for financial futures, how could these markets have achieved such phenomenal growth in just 13 years? How could they have attracted so many financial institutions, so many banks, money managers, foreign exchange traders, and pension fund managers worldwide? How could exchange membership scrolls have swelled so quickly with the names of so many of the world's most prestigious institutions? How could the transaction volume of these markets have experienced such unparalleled increases unless there were a fundamental need for them as a modern tool of business, finance, and risk management? How could these markets be as evil as their detractors claim and yet be as coveted and copied as they are by every major world financial center?

And how could these markets have completely fooled four U.S. federal agencies—the Federal Reserve Board (Fed), the Commodity Futures Trading Commission (CFTC), the Securities and Exchange Commission (SEC), and the U.S. Treasury—in their recent study to determine the effects on the U.S. economy as a result of trading in futures and options? This study, mandated by the U.S. Congress and conducted under the helmsmanship of the Fed, was so all-inclusive that it covered virtually every issue ever raised about these markets. The resulting document, together with the Fed's separate report on securities and futures margin, represented the most comprehensive report on the subject ever produced.

Ask yourself how these reputedly wicked markets could be the recipient of the following Federal Reserve Board findings: That financial futures and options serve a useful economic purpose by providing a more efficient way to manage risk; that the liquidity of related cash markets such as those for U.S.

Treasury securities and common stocks has been improved by the presence of futures and options; that the Fed's ability to conduct open market operations in an orderly manner across a range of maturities in government securities has been enhanced by futures and options contracts; that the Treasury's ability to conduct debt management operations has been similarly enhanced; that the improved liquidity in the Treasury securities market means interest rates paid by the taxpayer on debt incurred by the federal government is lower than it would be without financial futures markets; that the ability to hedge corporate bond underwritings results in a lower all-in cost of funds for the private sector; and that there appear to be no significant regulatory problems concerning either manipulation or customer protection.

If you asked yourself these questions and reflected on the answers, you would, in all candor, become skeptical about the derogatory comments, defamatory innuendos, inflammatory jokes, false assertions, misleading opinions, half-truths, and out-and-out lies you read and hear about futures and options.

Can we therefore now expect things to change? Can we expect a fairer review now that the mandate of Congress has been satisfied, now that we have some credible answers to those age-old concerns that historically have plagued and inhibited these markets? Can we now expect futures and options to become a universally accepted and integral tool of risk management?

Forget it. Listen to the cover story of *Business Week*, September 16, 1985, "Playing with Fire: As Speculation Replaces Investment Our Economic Future Is at Stake." The article states: "Ah, progress. Spurred by deregulation, the financial inventors have been working overtime. They've churned out a vast array of new instruments and created whole new markets. It's now possible for even the average citizen or company to take a financial position almost instantaneously in just about anything, anywhere. What only 15 years ago was an oppressively restrictive financial system has been recast in a pluralistic, almost anything goes mold. . . . by stoking a pervasive desire to beat the game, innovation and deregulation have tilted the axis of the financial system away from investment toward speculation. The U.S. has evolved into what Lord Keynes might have called a 'casino society'—a nation obsessively devoted to high-stakes financial maneuvering as a shortcut to wealth."

Imagine that, *Business Week* paying homage to Lord Keynes. Will wonders never cease!

Or listen to *Barron's,* "Pin-Striped Pork Bellies: Why Stock Index Futures Are Red Hot": "Like their lightening-paced video game counterparts, stock index futures offer instant gratification or instant annihilation depending on the accuracy of your impulses and the quickness of your reflexes."

Some things never change. Thus, it is imperative that we inform and instruct, divulge and debunk, proclaim and protest, again and again.

# Fixed Exchange Rate Foolishness

The Merits of Flexible Exchange Rates: An Anthology, *published by George Mason University Press in 1987—for which I acted as editor—contained a chapter I wrote on the creation of the International Monetary Market. The chapter began with the following thought: "Few things are more symbolic of flexible exchange rates than the International Monetary Market (IMM) in Chicago. Indeed, the birth of this futures exchange on May 16, 1972 is inextricably intertwined with the death of Bretton Woods, occurring as it did but a few months after President Nixon officially closed the gold window and ended the system of fixed exchange rates."*

*Consequently, whenever the repudiated specter of fixed exchange rates resurfaces—which happens periodically—it is incumbent upon IMM idealogues, as well as all those who understand this issue, to speak out. Indeed, the Anthology was an outgrowth of an ad-hoc coalition of leaders from academia, business, and commerce who shared the idea that world economic stability and viability is best achieved through adherence to free market principles. That coalition—the American Coalition for Flexible Exchange Rates (ACFX)—was organized in 1986 at our instigation when once again there was a growing clamor for a return to a more fixed international monetary system.*

*The ACFX was founded on the following propositions:*

- *That free markets are the best arbiter of supply and demand, providing the most efficient determinant of price.*

- *That the free market exchange system reflects, does not cause, fundamental economic factors at work in various nations.*

- *That the value of a nation's currency depends on a complicated analysis by the free market of the differences between that nation and others in price levels and inflation rates, interest rates, national money supplies, national incomes, trade and investment flows, government and private debt, and political risk.*

- *That these complex factors are best assessed and balanced through the flexible free market exchange system.*

- *That a stable international monetary system is fostered by market-driven exchange rates.*

*The ACFX successfully repulsed the anti-free market forces of that day. The following* Wall Street Journal *op-ed article served as the opening volley of our counterattack. It is highly instructive as well as frightening to see how often this same issue returns to the fore. Here in late 1992, recent international FX upheavals have made the views reflected in this article as pertinent as they were when it was written.*

---

**Published in *The Wall Street Journal*, April 24, 1986**

---

In 1985, we witnessed a pivotal round in an unusual struggle between the forces of nature and human wiles. It was a year during which the power of the free market proved as seldom before its unequaled strength in determining fair value. Alas, it was also the year that humans, their eyes tightly shut to the clear evidence about them, schemed once again in a futile quest to overcome the honest evaluations of supply and demand.

On one hand OPEC (Oil Producers' Economic Cartel)—the all-powerful international price-fixing cartel—found it increasingly difficult to maintain its long-standing system of artificial price edicts in the face of unrelenting market forces. Similarly, the London Metals Exchange desperately fought to survive the massive default caused by the artificially supported tin prices of the International Tin Council (ITC). On the other hand, the U.S. Treasury, in unison with several other ministers of finance—the Group of Five (G-5)—picked up the torch on behalf of artificial price rule by committee.

This time they tell us it will be different; that the universal laws of supply and demand are different for foreign exchange than for oil or tin. Indeed, they point with pride to the recent instant success of their magic bullet and attempt to assuage our doubts by insisting that the motivation is pure. Meanwhile, some of our most principled free market advocates shamefully look the other way, mumbling something about the occasional virtues of pragmatism over idealism.

False! The fundamental truths that govern the value of money are no different than those for all commodities. The market forces that overpowered a man-made method to artificially ordain the value of oil will similarly undo the manipulations of the G-5 or any artificial system that attempts to dictate the relative value of the dollar. In today's world, a fixed rate or targeted range for currency in international capital markets can last for only so long as market forces agree with it.

The G-5's September 22, 1985, quick fix was successful simply because the market agreed with the result. The dollar had already established its top after enduring the blow-off stage of its four-year long bull market. By early September, it had already fallen 23 percent against the Deutsche mark, 33 percent against the British pound and 10 percent against the Japanese yen. The dollar was in the final stages of consolidation after this initial down-leg when the G-5 struck. Their timing was excellent. With prospects for lower U.S. interest rates in sight, the dollar responded to the added pressure of the moment. Had the ministers not acted, free market forces would have achieved a similar result.

The danger of believing otherwise is the same as in the case of any false messiah. We will be forced to appeal to our new intervention god again and again with increasingly negative results. Greater uncertainty, higher volatility, and accentuated price dislocations will be among the predictable achievements. Eventually, the stark truth will reveal itself when the participating ministers no longer see eye-to-eye, or when the market totally refuses to obey our dictates. This inevitably will happen—witness OPEC and the ITC. Indeed, in the history of mankind, there are few examples where policy makers have been able to outsmart—for any extended period of time—the collective judgment of buyers and sellers in the marketplace. It will then be of small value to claim that we adopted the new religion only to prevent a worse fate; that the prevailing U.S. political climate for protectionism threatened the sanctity of world commerce and that therefore a little intervention was far better than a little trade war. Alas, just as in the case of pregnancy, there is no such thing as only a little fixed. Intervention, as with every intoxicating elixir, has a certain mass appeal.

Once again, it became fashionable to call for a return to the Bretton Woods system of fixed exchange rates that was adopted by the Western world directly after World War II. Instantly, a parade of U.S. and world experts extolled the virtues of that old order. While each approached the issue from a different philosophical viewpoint, all proclaimed the high dollar value was evidence of a failure of flexible exchange rates. Consequently, they called for a new international Bretton Woods conference to reestablish rigidity in foreign exchange.

The world of 1985 does not in any way, shape, or form resemble the world of 1944. The war had then completely ravaged every aspect of international commerce and trade. The U.S. financial system and its dollar were the sole survivors of the free world's economic fabric. The agreements achieved at Bretton Woods—at a time when the United States could virtually dictate any economic resolve—could no longer be duplicated today.

The U.S. "fixed exchange rate" advocates have the best of intentions in calling for a return to a more fixed monetary order. All of them are highly dedicated to global prosperity, modification of a tax code that penalizes savings and investment, reduction of the budget and trade deficits, and the removal of global trade barriers. Unfortunately, they are in error believing that those worthy goals can be advanced by revisiting the Bretton Woods system of fixed exchange rates. They should carefully examine what brought down that world arrangement. Though free market economists such as Milton Friedman advocated flexible exchange rates as early as 1950, a consensus in the banking world against fixed rates did not evolve until 20 years later. By then the Bretton Woods system could no longer cope with the intrinsic value changes responding to daily supply/demand statistics.

Since the abandonment of fixed exchange rates, free market forces have correctly reflected economic realities. Our dollar's value declined sharply during the 1973 to 1980 period when the United States experienced high inflation and weakened economic conditions. The dollar rose in value beginning in 1981 when our policies dramatically changed under the leadership of the Federal Reserve Board. Certainly this record does not bespeak of a failure on the part of flexible exchange rates.

The issue fueling a desire for fixed rates stems from our current massive trade deficit. It is argued that the main culprit of the trade imbalance is the high price of the dollar which makes it cheaper to import than to export. While that is obviously true, it is not the complete picture. The price of the dollar is not a cause but, rather, a symptom of the problem. Price is but a reflection of a fundamental value in the market. To argue that the high dollar impacts adversely on our economy does not explain how or why the price got there, nor does it prove that the flexible exchange rate system has failed. Rather, the opposite is true.

Our extraordinary federal budget deficit could only be funded in one of three ways: restricting investment, increasing savings, or exporting our debt. We rejected the first alternative, were insufficient in the second, and relied heavily on the third. Accordingly, rather than being the cause of our trade deficit, the strong dollar resulted because it was the main equilibrating factor that enabled trade exports and imports to make the adjustment necessary to satisfy our extra large debt appetite.

It is imperative to understand and correctly evaluate the actual role of floating exchange rates in the present situation. Given the need for foreign capital and the inevitable trade deficit it entails, permitting the price mechanism of floating exchange rates to determine how that trade deficit is to be achieved is the most equitable, and certainly the most efficient, means of getting a very difficult job done. Surely, such an appraisal of the facts is not meant to deny that there are substantial economic costs resulting from the high dollar. Such consequences should not be allowed to panic us into unsound or unwarranted actions. Floating exchange rates, while far from perfect, are the best system we can offer to sort out the complexities that makeup the relative value of currency.

As economist Gottfried Haberler proclaimed, "The politicalization of exchange rates is a dangerous game. It has caused much turbulence in the foreign exchange markets. Free markets do a better job of setting exchange rates than governments do." Or as E. Gerald Corrigan, President of the New York Federal Reserve Bank, said recently in a speech before the Japan Society ". . . the widespread sense of frustration with the current system of floating exchange rates is understandable and we certainly should be sensitive to opportunities to strengthen the system, but to think that a return to fixed exchange rates or to something like a gold or commodity standard is going to provide magical and painless solutions to our problems is sheer folly."

In 1985, we dramatically learned the futility and folly of interfering with free market values. How odd that, in the same instant, we are urged to repeat our mistakes. Is this not Santayana's warning? Or was it his curse?

# The Debate over Index Participation Contracts

*The conflict between futures exchanges and securities exchanges erupts periodically. It is often the result of one specific issue: which industry has the right to trade a given instrument or product line. Much rests on the answer. Not only does the answer determine which federal regulatory agency—the Securities and Exchanges Commission (SEC) or the Commodity Futures Trading Commission (CFTC)—will regulate the product in question, but more important, the direction of business flows.*

*Since the distinction between a futures instrument and a securities instrument can be complex—often blurred and getting increasingly more difficult to ascertain with every passing year—a clear definition is difficult to write into law. Periodically, Congress wrestles with the problem, but more often than not the issue goes to court.*

*Index Participation (IP) contracts were created by some of the securities exchanges as a competitive instrument to the highly successful index futures contracts at the Chicago Mercantile Exchange and other futures exchanges. While few of us in futures believed IPs to be a competitive threat, nevertheless we believed the securities exchanges should compete on a level playing field with the futures exchanges. In our opinion, IPs were nothing more than copycat futures instruments. Accordingly, they should be traded pursuant to futures market rules under the auspices of the CFTC. We were determined to protect our business sphere.*

Published in *The New York Times*, August 25, 1989

Sometimes you just can't win!
In 1982, when futures markets conceived the idea of stock index contracts, we were told by the securities industry that it was a silly idea that wouldn't work. Later, when

the contracts were successful, they told us it was the work of the devil and ought to be banned. Later, when respected federal officials and academicians lauded these contracts as innovative and cost-efficient risk management tools indispensable to money managers in today's financial environment, the securities exchanges decided that maybe it was a good idea after all. You would think that was the end of the story, yes? Wrong!

The American Stock Exchange (AMEX) and Philadelphia Stock Exchange (PHLX) went about creating their version of stock index futures, the so-called Index Participation (IP) contracts. So far so good. But then they brashly stated that these were not copycat futures contracts, but their own new securities innovation. How silly can you get? Every honest appraisal concluded these were futures contracts. As Gertrude Stein might have said, "A future, is a future, is a future."

But okay, so what's the big deal? Why be so technical? For years, the Russians claimed they invented the model T Ford when everyone knows they really invented the Salk vaccine. We didn't let a little technicality like that stand in the way of *Glasnost*, did we?

Ah, but the plot thickens. There is a reason behind the labeling squabble. If IPs are futures, than they must be listed under the authority of the Commodity Futures Trading Commission (CFTC). On the other hand, if IPs are securities, then the Securities and Exchange Commission (SEC) has jurisdiction. Moreover, both the AMEX and PHLX have futures divisions at their respective exchanges and could have listed IPs there *without* any legal objections. But a legal hassle is precisely what these securities exchanges wanted. And that's what I call *chutzpah!* Even the Russians didn't have the nerve to press their fictitious claim before the World Court.

The securities exchanges got just what they deserved. On August 18, 1989, a federal appeals court concluded that IPs have all the attributes of futures contracts, such as daily settlement, expiration, and payment in cash, etc. Conversely, they do not possess any of the usual indicia of an equity product; that is, unlike with shares of stock, the purchaser gets no interest in the governance of any company, nor does the purchaser even own the underlying shares. Thus the court ruled that IPs are subject to CFTC regulation.

The AMEX, PHLX, and SEC screamed bloody murder. *"We wuz robbed! The decision is stifling innovation! Congress must intervene!"*

Not only is the Appeals Court's opinion correct as a matter of logic and law but the complaints of the AMEX, PHLX, and the SEC are a smoke screen on broad policy grounds. It is yet another attempt to capture the benefits of futures industry innovations without competing on a level playing field. If IPs are worth their salt, why did the AMEX and PHLX not simply list them as futures contracts on the futures divisions? In such a case, the futures industry would have no legitimate complaint.

Point in fact, even as the AMEX and PHLX were trying their Russian gambit, the New York Stock Exchange (NYSE) proposed the development of a *genuine* securities basket product whereby a purchaser would actually own the stocks in the basket. The futures exchanges had no objections. The NYSE product is precisely what was recommended by those who analyzed the 1987 stock market crash.

So, having lost the legal argument, the AMEX, PHLX, and SEC are now resorting to specious cries that the court's ruling *stifles competition* and that this must be cured by Congress, presumably, either by changing the Shad/Johnson Agreement to further favor the SEC (which in our opinion already favors the SEC over the CFTC by a country mile) or by creating a single regulator (in other words doing away with the CFTC).

The idea for a single regulator has been advanced for a variety of purposes—usually to the advantage of the securities industry. Dr. R. Fischel, Director, Law and Economics Program, University of Chicago, who analyzed the Brady Report with respect to this issue, dismisses the one-agency concept by declaring that there is no evidence to imply that competition among regulators is harmful or that regulatory cooperation, when desirable, cannot occur without a single agency.*

Similarly, SEC Commissioner Edward Fleischman points out that the fundamental differences between securities and futures are sufficient reason *not* to give the SEC regulatory jurisdiction over financial derivative products. He too concludes

---

*Daniel R. Fischel, "Should One Agency Regulate Financial Markets?" *Black Monday and the Future of Financial Markets*.

that regulatory competition is "an extraordinary healthy development . . . [which is] . . . beneficial to both regulators."*

You need only take a brief historical glance to grasp why the two-agency concept has been beneficial to the American financial community. For instance, who recognized that modern techniques of financial risk management will require an array of new products? Who recognized in 1972 that the collapse of fixed exchange rates required a market for currency futures? Who understood the need of a hedging mechanism for interest rate risk exposure? Who conceived the concept of stock index contracts? In every case, it was the futures markets. Would that have happened under the SEC? Would the SEC have encouraged such innovation? Problematical at best. Exchange traded options, the only successful new securities product during this period, was devised by a futures exchange.

So c'mon guys, give us a break. Take the court decision (loss) like a good trader and invent something of your own.

---

*Edward Fleischman, Address before the Commodities Law Institute, Chicago, Illinois, October 21, 1988.

# PART IV

# THE 1987 CRASH

*In my judgment, the Chicago Mercantile Exchange experienced three calamities of a nature which most observers would describe as serious crises. In two of the instances, the emergency was more or less a local matter. In the other situation, it was an industry-wide problem, affecting every futures and options exchange in the United States.*

*The first episode was purely local. It took years to evolve to a critical point and climaxed during the late 1950s and early 1960s while I was still a novice on the trading floor. The predominant product line of the CME—storage and frozen eggs—was in its death throes. The egg production cycle was disappearing and with it the need for a futures market in eggs. Trading slowed to a crawl. The Exchange was losing money every year. Membership prices sank to $3,000, at which point the exchange instituted a support program. On the trading floor, the atmosphere of death hung in the air. The days of the CME seemed numbered.*

*Although I experienced this crisis from a distance, having had nothing to do with the history that brought it about, it served as a powerful lesson: To be viable, an exchange cannot rely on only one product line—it must diversify. In subsequent years, this lesson became the cardinal theme of my long-range strategy for the CME. It was the underlying rationale for continuously seeking new and diverse instruments for futures trade.*

*The most recent crisis unfolded in January 1989. It resulted from the federal investigation of trading activities on the floors of the Chicago exchanges. Unfortunately, I am constrained at this time from fully commenting on this episode since there are still some legal matters pending against several of our members. However, I am not constrained to state that the media can be faulted for the grossly over-blown manner in which the proceedings were reported. To our dismay, many in the media erroneously assumed that the investigation rivaled the insider trading scandal of the securities markets in both size and intent. And while any trading infraction cannot be countenanced, the subsequent trials of futures traders showed that the amounts involved were relatively small and many of the violations technical in nature.*

*During these proceedings, the exchanges and their officials found themselves in a very difficult position. It was incumbent upon them to be totally cooperative with the federal investigation and they were. The exchanges are committed to keeping the transaction process free from members' transgressions. Anything less than such a policy would violate the exchanges' responsibilities to the public trust, could have resulted in a diminished credibility with Congress and a corresponding diminished right to self-regulate. Consequently, some of the actions undertaken by officials of the Chicago exchanges may have seemed unsympathetic or even indifferent to the difficulties experienced by their memberships as a result of this investigation. This unfortunate impression was untrue. The exchanges and their officials never doubted that the vast majority of their membership was totally innocent of any wrongdoing. Indeed it was, and remains our strong opinion that the ethics, conduct, and trading practices of Chicago futures and options traders can withstand the scrutiny of any test and compare favorably with any markets in the world.*

*One distinct constructive result of the investigation was that, in spurring the exchanges to an even stricter enforcement policy, it expedited their embrace of advanced technology in the execution process. The exchanges' adoption of technological innovations has immeasurably benefited their members, making these markets much more efficient and cost effective. This is destined to promote continued business flows to Chicago as we enter the twenty-first century—a century bound to be highly competitive and technologically driven.*

*The final crisis was of a global nature. It was the stock market crash of 1987. In my view, this emergency was by far the most dangerous and critical of any of the problems we encountered during the two decades of my leadership of the CME. Consequently, I have devoted this section of the book to an analysis of the crash and the problem it represented. Although this emergency was caused by world events, although the markets of futures and options were not at fault, although our markets performed flawlessly during the crisis, although the facts substantiated our claims, our markets came dangerously close to being labeled the culprit and legislated out of existence.*

*The 1987 crash is equally significant for what it did for the markets of futures and options. The national publicity generated by this unprecedented event and the consequential scrutiny our markets received resulted in recognition of our markets as a serious and important component of the world's financial structure. More significant, the testimony to Congress by Federal Reserve Board Chairman Alan Greenspan that stock index futures have inherent value and are an important tool in the management of equity risk, combined with the statement of U.S. Treasury Secretary Nicholas F. Brady that the stock market, the futures market, and the options market are parts of one market, served to raise the stature of futures markets beyond our most ambitious expectations.*

# A Call to Arms

*With every passing week that showed an increase in the transaction volume of S&P 500 futures, there was a commensurate increase in the attack against them. This negativism was part of an expanded attack on index investing, a relatively new investment methodology. The trend toward index enhancement investing was growing and perceived as a threat to orthodox equity investment strategies. It was the beginning of a difficult conflict between these two forces.*

*Index enhancement strategies utilize index futures and options. Consequently, our markets became the target. Since index futures were new, arcane, and had no establishment constituency, they took the brunt of the attack. No one spoke up on our behalf, no one came to our defense, and no one explained our function or necessity.*

*We developed a long-range strategy. However, we needed assistance from the financial establishment to initiate our short-range plans, which involved an immediate counterattack. We looked to our equity-based members who were index futures users and arbitrageurs. They understood the index market and the role of futures; they used our market to the benefit of their customers and their firms; and they understood that index futures were an outgrowth of modern investment strategies and had become an integral part of the equity market. These member firms had credibility with the media and we had to energize their voices. We implored that they assist us in a counterattack.*

---

**Presented at the Index Trading Coordination Committee meeting, New York, New York, September 30, 1986**

---

Anyone who is not aware that index investing and, consequently, index futures markets are under attack, is either dead, asleep, or living in Alice-in-Wonderland. In the past two weeks, I have heard and read more negative diatribe about index strategies, program trading, triple witching, and stock market volatility than I have in the past two

151

years. Everyone, it seems, who has the power of the pen, and is even remotely connected with the financial arena, has felt compelled to expound on the evils unleashed by index investment strategies and the use of index futures. And, let's face it, the new strategies are often connected to futures and options—*instruments suspected as the work of the devil.* The exchanges for trading these mysterious instruments are predominantly located in Chicago, not a locale that is associated with virtuous finance or a place that inspires confidence. So why not attack the credibility of these markets? Why not question their necessity? Why not cast doubt on their value?

I need not explain the problem to anyone in this room. I need not explain that index investment methodologies are perceived to threaten orthodox investment strategies. I need not illustrate that this conflict boils down to income flows between two different profit centers. I need not illuminate that futures markets have taken the brunt of this attack. That our markets are blamed whenever the stock market goes down but receive no credit when the stock market goes up. Even former SEC chairman John Shad admitted recently that all the undesirable effects of program trading—the volatility and price swings on expiration dates—get all the publicity, while the desirable effects of their nature go unnoticed.

Imagine that! After a four-year long bull market, with a budget deficit larger than we have ever before witnessed and no relief in sight, with a record trade deficit, with economic forecasts and data that are rather weak, with interest rates ticking up, with inflation showing some sign of life, and with a tax reform package that penalizes you 18.5 percent for holding on to your investment, it is still necessary to find a culprit for a market correction. And if a culprit is needed, why not blame index futures.

Represented in this room are members of our community who understand and are concerned about the problem, and who, we believe, can help us do something about it. We called you together because we feel you represent the predominant users of index futures and options, because you know the value of these instruments in index investment strategies, and because you can act as a source for our credibility with the media and the public. You are the professionals and experts the media respect. We asked you to join with us today so that we could underscore the severity of the problem; provide you with substantive facts and statistics with which to combat the problem; and implore you to help us educate the media and aggressively come to the defense of the markets that you utilize.

The truth is that index enhancement strategies represent relatively new, cost-effective methodologies for equity investment. Our markets allow you to effectuate these innovative strategies in a rapid manner. Simply stated, our markets represent an alliance of modern market strategies, modern portfolio management, and present-day technology. The orthodox investment establishment does not like what we represent. They view us as a threat to status quo. To satisfy their preference, or the preference of those who simply fear change, we would have to discard modern investment theory, destroy the computer chip, throw the cathode-ray tube out the window, abort the telecommunication revolution, and return to the day when the rotary telephone was our main link with the world.

Index investing, as with block trading, mutual funds, futures, stock options, Treasury bill futures, and many other innovative and revolutionary ideas of the past 20 years, is indicative of the changing times. These innovations are a result of the here and now. It is incumbent on those of us who witnessed and participated in these changes and who understand the changes and the reasons for their necessity to stand up and be counted.

We are here to ask you to help us explain the virtues of our markets. We need assistance in educating the media about the function of futures in modern investment techniques. We need you to say why our markets are important to the marketplace. We need you to help us get the word out. Otherwise, all we will have in public view is the irresponsible, misguided, misinformed, and sometimes intentionally malicious impressions from those who do speak to the writers of financial columns (who themselves know so little). Unfortunately, it does not end with the media. Remember, there are people who read this nonsense. The readers are the voters, voters affect the legislators, and legislators affect the regulations. And whether you like it or not, most people believe what they read. And if I'm paranoid, as the saying goes, it does not necessarily mean I'm wrong.

Remember, there are enemies of markets who are against change, against innovation, against the free market system in general, and against index investment strategies in particular. A misinformed press is powerful ammunition for their weapons. And if anyone here thinks I exaggerate, that I overestimate the danger, allow me to dislodge you from this notion. I am no newcomer to this scene. You are hearing it from someone who has been on the firing line for the past 20 years. I have encountered the enemy before. They use real bullets and they mean business.

We have a comprehensive defense strategy that includes both long-range and short-range plans. Our long-range plans include a mass education program that will focus primarily on academic institutions. We need colleges and universities to include modern investment strategy and the use of our markets in their academic programs. We will also authorize and encourage studies about futures and their impact on volatility, investment, capital formation, and the equity market. But such programs take time.

Short range, we propose an immediate media counterattack. To this end, we want you, your associates, and anyone else you can influence to assist us. We suggest you stop dodging the questions from reporters. Stop hiding. Become visible. We even want you to seek out the members of the financial press and give them your opinion. Educate them and get your viewpoint into print.

Explain to them the difference between triple witching (which occurs four days a year) and the use of futures in index investment strategies (the other 361 days). Explain our markets. Explain that arbitrage is as old as humankind, that it serves an important purpose in leveling differences between different markets, that while by definition, it is riskless, there are risks, and that it requires know-how as well as capital. Help us educate the media about the benefits our markets provide to investors—both large and small. Explain to them how professional money managers use index markets to increase the return on investors' portfolios.

You can show them that small investors who invest in mutual funds benefit by these strategies. You can tell them that the world has changed and that we represent that change. You can tell them that you cannot go back in time. You can explain how our markets provide buyers when the sellers want to sell and vice versa. You can discuss fundamentals that affect market movement and explain that our markets—the same as cash markets—respond to supply and demand. And you can help us explain that these markets represent efficient, cost-effective, and modern-day techniques that work in harmony with the stock market. Explain to them that we are all one market and cannot exist without each other.

If you all roll up your sleeves, become visible, and make your voices heard, you will provide the immediate return of fire needed now. This will coincide with some of our other short-range plans that are aimed at educating the financial press. More important, your immediate actions will give us time to put in place our long-range strategy, which is designed to permanently preserve our markets and your right to use them.

# Embracing Reality

*The 1987 stock market crash was a shocking event. It unleashed an un-
paralleled torrent of unfavorable accusations, sentiment, and publicity
aimed at futures markets. For a time, it became so bad that it was unclear
whether our markets could survive the negativism that was being hurled
at us. The assault took form both in legislative proposals that would crip-
ple our existence as well as in a highly adverse national image. It required
all our courage, skill, intellect, and careful strategy to repel the onslaught
and keep our markets viable.*

*Our strategy was fourfold: Meet the attack head on, bring out the truth
(the facts were highly favorable to our markets), explain the underlying
fundamentals that caused the crash, and point to the solution of the problem. Thus, we wrote and published a host of material, testified before
many congressional committees, and gave innumerable speeches. Particularly important was the understanding and assistance of our own membership. As in many prior instances, I used the CME Annual Report as
an avenue to educate our members and establish the "party" line. Afterward, the theme was amplified and carried forward to the outside world.*

*The conflict was anything but easy and lasted almost two years. In the end,
our strategy not only proved successful, it resulted in catapulting futures
markets to the forefront of the financial arena. The Chicago Mercantile Exchange, in many ways, became equated with the New York Stock Exchange—
a measure of stature and respectability unimaginable a few years ago.*

*The unwelcome episode unwittingly served as the constructive begin-
ning of a new growth era for futures markets and initiated our epoch of
globalization.*

---

**Published in the Chicago Mercantile Exchange 1987 Annual Report**

---

W hen the United States Congress began an investigatory process to determine the cause of the October 19 stock market crash, I suspected what would happen. I
was not disappointed.

The congressional hearings, the regulatory inquiries, the media pressures, and the multitude of studies (official and private) focused the attention of Congress and our nation on *how* the stock market crashed and diverted its consideration from *why* it crashed. Clearly, why the market crashed is the more fundamental issue, albeit harder to resolve. The concerns stemming from underlying economic conditions and factors that ultimately determine values of investments ought not be relegated to second place. And an investigation to determine these conditions and factors was not necessary. There was a plethora of legitimate candidates.

At one end of the spectrum were the momentous and complex twin problems of the record budget and trade deficits, the mounting pressure from their dire consequences overshadowing all else. At the other end of the continuum was the simple explanation that after a five-year uninterrupted bull market, a correction was long overdue. There were an overabundance of bulls, and price–earnings ratios were at historically high levels.

Then, of course, there were the concerns over the tightening of monetary policy by the Fed; some loss of confidence in American leadership; federal legislation that would, among other things, disallow interest deductions for any significant takeover borrowing, thereby directly affecting a market activity that had acted as the major fueling force for the U.S. stock market; the dangerous specter of protectionist trade legislation; and the increasing unfavorable disparity between the return on stocks versus the return on fixed income investments.

Beyond this backdrop of fundamentals, there were some psychological concerns: an unsettling Persian Gulf situation with stepped-up Iranian hostilities; some dire predictions about inflation as well as a recession; a falling dollar; an open policy disagreement between the U.S. Treasury and the German Bundesbank spelling an end to the Louvre Agreement (targeting exchange rates) and thus exploding the myth that foreign exchange values can be ordained by government edict; falling prices on foreign stock markets; and finally, a raft of articles comparing October 1987 to October 1929. Surely the combination of these factors was more than ample cause, both real and psychological, for a market collapse.

Perhaps Alan Greenspan, Chairman of the Federal Reserve Board, summed it up best in his report to the U.S. Senate Banking Committee on February 2, 1988:

> Stock prices finally reached levels which stretched to incredulity expectations of rising real earnings and falling discount factors. Something had to snap. If it didn't happen in October, it would have happened soon thereafter. The immediate cause of the break was incidental. The market plunge was an accident waiting to happen.

Thus, in our haste to look responsible and explain the crash, in our need to find a villain, in our ambition to prevent a recurrence, we have not only diverted our attention from the obvious, we have also focused our concerns in the wrong direction. Indeed the answer to why the market fell so quickly is no mystery. Overvalued markets can become very painful; when everyone wants to sell, there are never enough buyers. In other words, perhaps there is nothing we can do about this reality.

However, we can learn something from the October crash. The event provided us with a fundamental insight that we dare not ignore. We learned to what extent our technological competence had outdistanced our market mechanics. To put it bluntly, most of our traditional markets were operating on a technological standard equivalent to the steamboat, while those who make market decisions were using the jet plane.

As Walter Wriston, the former chairman of Citicorp, the largest U.S. bank, recently wrote (*Forbes*, December 14, 1987):

> Today there are more than 200,000 computer screens in hundreds of trading rooms, in dozens of countries, which light up to display an unending flow of news. It takes about two minutes between the time the President or prime minister reads a statement and the time traders buy or sell currency, stocks or bonds based on their evaluation of the effect of that policy on the market.

While Mr. Wriston's assessment of the number of computer terminals is far too low and his estimate for the reaction time too high, his point is precisely on target. The technological revolution has given us what he calls the information standard, which he states is far more draconian than the gold standard or the Bretton Woods standard. With the information standard, it does not matter what market legislation we attempt. The screens will continue to light up with information, and the market participants will continue to act on the information as they deem fit. As Wriston puts it, "the new global electronic infrastructure has doomed the effectiveness of a cosmetic political fix." I agree and would go further: The new global reality has placed demands on our markets that cannot be met by current transaction mechanisms.

The solutions to October 19 do not lie in new federal regulations, new federal authority, nor a ban on program trading or other market strategies. Such cosmetic or political fixes may serve perceptional needs, but will delay us from applying the real solutions. Indeed, they are fraught with danger and point in the wrong direction. Nor will the answers be found in better coordination between the markets or the federal agencies, although that is clearly welcome and necessary. Rather, the solutions that are possible lie in structuring the world marketplaces, both internally and externally, so that their procedures and transaction mechanisms are more efficient and more reflective of the realities of specialization, globalization, and the technological revolution.

It is with a measure of pride that the CME can boast of having recognized the realities of the information standard and accepted the technological challenges it represented long before the events of last October. Indeed, we had been struggling with these issues for a long time. And, in the same revolutionary spirit with which we introduced the IMM and spawned the financial futures revolution, in the same innovative mode with which we created the CME/SIMEX Mutual Offset System, we prepared to embrace the technology of the present era and respond to the demands of globalization.

The CME chose to meet this challenge head on. As our members well know, in September of last year, in a bold and far-reaching joint undertaking, the Chicago Mercantile Exchange and Reuters Holdings PLC entered into a long-range agreement to create an after-hours global electronic automated transaction system for the trading of futures and futures-options. CME members overwhelmingly approved the proposal on October 6, 1987.

The concept embodied in P-M-T (Post Market Trade—its working designation)* is clearly a historic milestone in the development of futures trading. It embraces the realities brought about by technological advancements of recent years and takes a giant step toward unification of the world's separate financial centers.

This is our response to the demands brought about by the technological revolution as well as to the challenges of globalization. We believe it will translate into opportunity and cost-efficiency whether you are a banker in Tokyo, a risk manager in London, or an investor in the United States. It is a solution in sync with the markets of the future. Thus, the CME has led the way once again. While P-M-T was not devised as a consequence of the October stock market collapse, it represents the correct direction for the solutions to that episode.

Markets subject to the flows of institutional capital demand a transaction system responsive to the needs, uses, and strategies of professional managers. Markets subject to the flows of global information demand a market mechanism responsive to the 24-hour trading day. Markets subject to the consequences and strains of modern technology demand systems and procedures of equivalent competence. Nothing less will suffice. Simply stated, the solutions to October 19 will be found in embracing reality.

---

*Ultimately its name became GLOBEX.

# Who Killed Cock Robin?

*The witch hunt for the culprit of the 1987 stock market crash was in high gear. The consensus was that the culprit was futures markets. After all, so many of this nation's financial wizards—all inhabitants of New York City—were standing on the roof of the New York Stock Exchange and piously pointing westward to Chicago. How could the verdict be otherwise?*

*Was there a glimmer of hope? A last chance to change someone's mind? A slim possibility that someone somewhere would look at the facts, listen to reason, and respond to logic? Perhaps not, but despair wins no war. We would continue the fight until the bitter end.*

*In an act of final desperation, I entered the holy inner sanctum of the movers and shakers of the American Bar Association. It was an act of courage above and beyond the call of duty.*

Presented at the American Bar Association Committee on Futures Regulation, Acapulco, Mexico, January 23, 1988

Whoever chose "Who Killed Cock Robin?" as the topic for my remarks must have been a mind reader. The title is perfect for what I wish to say. It is perfect because it attests to the mania that existed in the world prior to October 19, 1987. Because no one killed Cock Robin, at least not on the 19th. Cock Robin—the stock market bull-mania that enveloped the American public, Congress, the media, the financial community, and virtually everyone else—had been dying by inches for years. Indeed, by October 19th, the real Cock Robin was already long dead. Like others of his breed, he was simply running about with his head missing!

The disease that did him in was the slow creeping kind. It took years to do its work. It was voodoo—the voodoo economics that gave us the largest budget deficit in Western memory; that transformed this prosperous nation from a creditor to a debtor for the first time in its history; that turned our financial fabric upside down, created a monumental trade gap with all our trading partners, a record low value for the dollar, higher interest rate prospects, and higher inflationary expectations. These results did not occur on October 19th. What happened on that day was a sudden realization by the financial wizards of the world that Cock Robin might be missing his head.

Suddenly the mania was over. Suddenly reality dawned. Suddenly the stock market was at a ridiculously high level. Suddenly panic set in. Suddenly everyone was running about—like Cock Robin—without their heads. Instantly the search for the villain was on; that same awful fellow who told the emperor that he had no clothes. There he is, I see the culprit! He is the portfolio insurer! No, he is the specialist on the NYSE! No, he is the futures market! No, he is the program trader! No, he is the computer!

Of course, we would not dare do anything to the real culprits because there are too many of them. We all know who they are. They are all those silly people who believed that the "tulip mania" of the 1980s would never end; that the stock market would continue to rise forever; that economics had nothing to do with it; that the Dow Jones Industrial Average was going to 3600; and that everyone would get out at the top, or at least before it crashed! To paraphrase Pogo, "We have found the villain, and he is us."

Think about it. Suppose you run this little law firm with six or seven lawyers working for you, you are successful, your net earnings are $1 million per annum, and your future is bright and secure. Along comes this yokel with a barrelful of money and offers 22 times your annual earnings for your practice—$22 million—without so much as a noncompete. Would you sell? You bet you would, you say now. But this is post-October 19th. Before the 19th, you know what you said? Hell no, no way! If this joker thinks I'm worth 22 mil, I must be worth at least a million or two more. I'll wait.

And after the stock market mania comes crashing down around our ears, do we blame our own stupidity and greed? Don't be silly. We run about looking for the real culprit. We demand an investigation. Who killed Cock Robin? Let's lynch the son-of-a-gun. Let's have some hearings—let's have some studies.

We'll hire old Katzenbach.* He's a wise old lawyer, he'll find the real villain. And sure enough he did. By golly, it's the futures markets, he said. It's those Chicago pits. They are evil, they are dens of speculation, purposeless and immoral. They should immediately be done away with—and should be moved to New York. Or else we'll get good old Brady.† He knows all about the stock market. He'll find the answer. And he did. It was an astounding revelation. All the markets are interrelated, he discovered. What a unique thought. It's one big market, after all. Amazing! Or we'll get good old Ruder‡ to study up on it. That's the ticket. The SEC's the thing. It can be depended on. After all, it discovered that there was insider trading going on at the New York Stock Exchange when all these years we thought the market was sinless divinity.

And do you know what Ruder and the SEC will discover? I'll give you my prediction. It'll be another revelation. That the financial world has changed during the past decade. How about that! Institutions and their traders are now a powerful lot and dominate the marketplace. Astounding, isn't it? Well, that's right. Messrs. Brady and Ruder are quite correct. The world *has* changed, institutions *are* dominant, and it is *one* market. And what's more, futures are very much part of this new world.

In fact, futures sensed the coming change long before the other financial markets. We recognized that values of financial instruments were going to fluctuate dramatically because the world was getting smaller and the economics more uncertain. We knew that uncertainty breeds risk and that risk seeks insurance. So we created tools with which to better manage the risk. We created markets that became essential for money managers in a world plagued by uncertainty. And these markets are more efficient than their securities counterparts. But

---

*Nicholas deB. Katzenbach, former United States Attorney General, who authored—at the behest of the New York Stock Exchange—*An Overview of Program Trading and Its Impact on Current Market Practices,* December 21, 1987.

†Nicholas F. Brady, Chairman, Dillon Read, and subsequently U.S. Secretary of Treasury.

‡David S. Ruder, Chairman, Securities and Exchange Commission.

they are not more speculative. That's right, not any more speculative than the New York Stock Exchange.

In case you had a different notion, allow me to explain that the role of the NYSE in capital formation is not achieved when a stock is listed there for trading. The primary capital formation process is over by the time John Q. Public offers its capital. The NYSE role in the capital formation process is to provide a market that will assure the underwriter or original investor that his investment can be spread to the masses. In simple terms, the NYSE is the security blanket. Its role cannot be underestimated. However, it is precisely the same role financial futures play.

And Katzenbach was right also. Sure, there is a lot of speculation in futures markets. But what he neglected to mention was that there is a lot of speculation in the stock market as well. It's the fuel that keeps both markets going. But speculation does not change the fact that both markets are an integral part of the capital formation process. Don't take my word for it, check out the studies of the Federal Reserve Board.

And no matter how we regulate them—no matter who does it—the need for futures markets will not go away. They could not have succeeded as well as they have unless they were an important commercial tool for risk management in today's world. To name just a few: Investment banks use interest rate futures to hedge new bond underwritings; broker-dealers use interest rate futures to hedge inventories acquired as market makers; primary securities dealers use interest rate futures to hedge their Treasury auction purchases and exposures; block traders use stock index futures to reduce the systematic risk in their positions; banks and savings and loan institutions use futures to quickly and cheaply adjust their interest rate exposure; financial institutions hedge their short-term liabilities in futures and can swap transactions as a result; pension funds and insurance funds use financial futures to manage bond portfolios and adjust their exposure; corporations use financial futures to manage their working capital, hedge their cash portfolios, and smooth returns on their cash flows; multinational corporations and banks use currency futures to reduce foreign exchange exposure in an efficient manner; interbank participants use currency futures to reduce their credit line exposure; fund managers of every sort use stock index futures to assume or reduce investment exposure quickly; and, investment bankers use stock index futures for hedging against major market changes when underwriting new security issues. And on and on.

If we do something stupid to these markets, their necessity will not go away. The futures industry will simply be taken from U.S. markets like some other American industries. Foreign competitors are out there now and there isn't a foreign financial center that is not envious of what we have created in futures and planning to copy or wrest from us what we have. In today's technological world, these markets can exist anywhere. And our foreign competitors will not be any more bashful about it than they were in steel or autos or so many other sectors of the American economy.

But what about Cock Robin, you ask? Surely his demise could have been less painful. Can't we somehow protect ourselves from a future October 19th? Well, I don't know. Tulip manias come along every so often and there isn't very much humankind can do about it. The next time it may not be in the stock market or it could be the stock market again.

But we did learn of some weaknesses in our system. We can make the markets better. The futures markets will propose a package of changes in the way our markets operate as well as in financial protections to make our markets safer and better. To protect against another freefall, we at the Chicago Mercantile Exchange were first voluntarily to impose a daily price limit. Those are Brady's circuit breakers. We intend to refine them and make them permanent. Similarly, the NYSE is experimenting with some ideas that will act as circuit breakers. They also will improve their DOT system so that it can handle larger volumes.

These are the positive results of Cock Robin's demise, but they are not enough. Nicholas Brady's underlying theme was that it is one market. We embrace this philosophy. But as Brady stated, this does not mean there need be only one regulator. Indeed, that might prove counterproductive. The markets all have different functions and work differently. Each requires a regulator steeped in the different expertise. Brady's goal is to achieve better coordination between the markets. We emphatically agree. However, there is more than one way to achieve this result. Ours would be through the private sector. There are already in existence the organizational structures to achieve this result. Creating a new federal regulator is unnecessary.

We also believe the necessary expertise to achieve a coordinated approach to protective market measures lies with the markets themselves. We believe that such an approach is far better than additional federal regulation. Just as the CME and the NYSE solved the triple witching problem without regulatory involvement, so can we now find the correct solution to coordinated interaction between our markets. We stand ready to work toward this goal.

Allow me to leave you with this thought. We live in a reactive society that demands something be done. It is a society that must find the villain in every drama; a society that believes that there are always those who are the good guys and those who are the bad guys. Well, let me argue that this time we temper our demands with good judgment. If we end up strangling our markets in search for Cock Robin's killer, we will have strangled ourselves.

# Chicken Little Revisited

*This parody, written in the aftermath of the 1987 stock market crash, was inspired by one of our many trips to the East Coast to meet with executives of the major securities firms of the New York Stock Exchange.*

*Sometimes, sitting on the airplane on the way back to Chicago, I was struck by the obstinate, pious, and blind refusal by otherwise highly intelligent and successful members of the U.S. financial world to accept that index arbitrage was simply a market mechanism and not an inherently evil strategy whose only purpose was to lower stock prices.*

> Presented before a group of New York-based members of the Chicago Mercantile Exchange's Index and Options Market (IOM), New York, New York, February 1988

When I first began working as a runner for Merrill Lynch on the old floor of the Chicago Mercantile Exchange, I was about as green as you can get. I knew nothing about futures, and was equally ignorant about all aspects of the marketplace. But that did not disqualify me for my new job. As a runner, I wasn't required to know anything. Besides, I would learn. My school, so to speak, would be all around me—what I would see and hear.

The process worked. My teachers were my contemporaries, those clerks and runners on the floor of the Exchange who had been there at least a day longer than me. I idolized every one of them and hung on their every word.

The dean of our little band was a clerk named Peter who was much older and had been there longer than any of us. In fact, I recall wondering why he was still a runner but dismissed the thought on the basis that I really didn't understand how the system worked. Besides, it didn't matter since, to my good fortune, Peter became my friend. He was a very serious fellow who spoke with a keen sense of authority and knew everything. In short, Peter's word was gospel.

One day, Peter swore me to secrecy and divulged why he was still a runner. "It is the best place to learn," he said in a whisper and explained that as soon as he learned everything he would become a trader and make a million dollars.

Since it was clear that I was trustworthy, Peter imparted to me still another secret, a discovery that, in his words, "was bound to make me a ton of money."

"I call it," he confided with a measure of pride, "the pink law of market dynamics."

"Wow," I exclaimed, duly impressed, "what does it mean?"

"It means," he whispered, looking about to see if anyone was listening, "it means that colors control the direction of the market."

"The direction of the market? You're putting me on."

"No I'm not," he said emphatically, "colors control."

"You mean a color can make a market go up or down?"

"That's right," he nodded solemnly, "it's a discovery I've made about market dynamics. I know for a fact the color pink makes the market go lower."

There was an embarrassing moment of silence while I pondered the revelation and then shamefully admitted I was a dunce and didn't quite get it.

Peter smiled and with a fatherly pat on my back told me not to worry. "In time you will understand."

In fact, years later I did understand.

It seems that Peter was working for a major brokerage firm that had hired a new floor manager. The new manager was innovative and adopted a unique procedure to help brokers quickly execute the firm's business. The new policy required that all "buy" orders be written on blue order forms and all "sell" orders be written on pink order forms.

In Peter's mind, the procedure took on a deeper meaning. After all, no sooner would he deliver a pink order to a broker, then the market would tend to go lower. (Sell orders do have this curious effect on a market.) Over time, to Peter, the color became the controlling element. Pink was no longer the messenger, the vehicle. Instead pink assumed the substantive role. Pink became the reason for the market's decline.

Years have passed. Believe it or not, Peter's unique sense of logic did not hamper his success in the world of markets. Today, Peter is chief clerk for a fund manager managing billions of dollars. By accident, I ran into him the other day and, after reminiscing about the good old days, I jokingly asked him if he remembered his old pink law of market dynamics.

A knowing look crept into his eyes. "Damn good law," he said lowering his voice, "except that its applicability is much broader than I realized at the time. It goes far beyond the color pink."

"Like what?" I asked, ready to go along with the gag.

"Like index arbitrage," Peter responded with conviction.

"Wait, let me guess. You mean index arbitrage makes the market go down just like the color pink?"

"You bet."

I hesitated. "Peter, you can't be serious?"

"You bet I am."

"But Peter, that's stuff and nonsense. Arbitrage is simply a transference between two or more markets. Net, net it does not add any new pressure to the process. It is a reactive procedure with a zero sum gain."

"Believe what you like," Peter responded with anger.

"Peter," I tried again, "I hate to break this to you, but arbitrage is no more the cause of a market decline than is the color pink. It is a practice as old as the market itself. In fact, index arbitrage is beneficial to the marketplace by adding liquidity and balancing out price differentials."

I was about to say more, but one look at Peter's face told me that this was not a subject to pursue. Things could get violent.

You see, Peter never forgot the lessons he learned as young man in the business. In the recesses of Peter's mind, his pink law of market dynamics lives on. He has simply replaced the color with index arbitrage. The principle is the same, its simplicity undeniable. After all, no sooner is there index arbitrage (as a consequence of "sell-programs") then the stock market goes lower. (Actually the reverse is equally true as a consequence of "buy-programs," but Peter's logic doesn't bother with rising prices since they are always welcome and need no specific cause factor.)

In Peter's mind, index arbitrage has become the controlling element. To him, index arbitrage is no longer the messenger, the vehicle. Instead, it has assumed the substantive role. Index arbitrage, like the color pink, became the reason for the market's decline.

If you are still having difficulty comprehending Peter's logic or his pink law of market dynamics, allow me to make a modest suggestion. You will need to study the finer points of the marketplace. I suggest you begin with the story of "Chicken Little." Read it carefully and in no time you too will understand why the sky is falling.

# Excerpts from Testimony Relating to the 1987 Stock Market Crash

*Congressional testimony is one of the most serious burdens of exchange leadership. It demands a carefully worded and meticulously balanced statement, one that embodies the exchange's fears, hopes, and strategies concerning a particular issue that is presented before Congress at a particular juncture in history. It is usually prepared in consultation with exchange senior staff and legal counsel.*

*The full written testimony is seldom read at the hearing before the Congressional Committee; rather an oral opening statement is made before questioning ensues. However, the written testimony—which is always made part of the official record—is often read and scrutinized by Committee members and staff, the media, and opponents of the views represented. Thus, Congressional testimony is a highly important element in the life of an institution and can be pivotal to its continued credibility and viability.*

*The 1987 stock market crash was as momentous an event in U.S. financial history as memory allows. For futures markets—which many immediately blamed as the cause of the crash—it could have spelled the end to their potential and growth. As expected, there was a rash of Congressional investigatory proceedings and an interminable number of Congressional hearings. These became the focal points of media attention and the cause of follow-up debates and countless news reports. The official testimony we offered in these proceedings was a crucial component in our strategy to repulse the false accusations and reverse the negative image occasioned by our markets as a consequence of the crash. It was as critical an endeavor as anything we have undertaken in the history of financial futures. The following are excerpts of two examples of oral statements made in conjunction with testimony relating to the crash before two Congressional Committees.*

## 1. ORAL STATEMENT: U.S. SENATE COMMITTEE ON BANKING, HOUSING AND URBAN AFFAIRS, FEBRUARY 4, 1988

M r. Chairman, this is the second time we have appeared before this Committee with respect to the events of October 19. When we appeared before you the first time, just 10 days after the crash, we testified that our preliminary findings demonstrated that the CME (Chicago Mercantile Exchange) had carried out its responsibilities in a flawless fashion. Nothing that has happened since that testimony, no evidence or report has contradicted this fact. Indeed, our finding that the CME provided a pressure valve for a large number of investors to hedge their stock risks has been borne out by all the evidence. We have now seen many reports, each from a different viewpoint and motivation. It seems to us that of these reports, only three can be viewed as truly independent—the one authorized by the President (the so-called Brady Report), the one by the GAO (General Accounting Office), and the report from the Federal Reserve Board. All these reports have many common points, and none of them lay any blame on the futures market.

In our opinion, the report most likely to gain your attention is the one from the Brady Commission. The Chicago Mercantile Exchange is pleased to embrace its central theme, namely, that the stock market, the stock options market, and the stock index futures market are, in fact, components of "one market." We also emphatically agree that there needs to be better coordination among all these markets.

As our written testimony explains, there is more than one way to achieve that result. It is our opinion that the expertise to achieve better coordination among the markets lies within the markets themselves. Thus our suggested approach is through the private sector rather than through additional regulatory authority. The CME stands ready to work with every exchange toward this goal.

The Brady Report recommended that the Federal Reserve Board act as the supercoordinator for the principal intermarket areas of concern. In this respect, the Chicago Mercantile Exchange is in accord with the testimony of the

Federal Reserve Board as well as the CFTC. Our recommendation is for the creation of an Inter-Market Coordination Committee (IMCC) comprising all the securities and futures exchanges as well as representatives from the CFTC, SEC, and Federal Reserve Board. This can be achieved by expansion of the existing Inter-Market Surveillance Group (ISG), an entity created and operated under the auspices of the SEC.

The proposed IMCC could then act as the coordinating forum for the sharing of cash flow and trading data among the commodities and securities exchanges. This will include the ability to provide lenders comprehensive information on a clearing firm's position, thereby facilitating bank financing and reducing liquidity pressures of the type that were experienced by some firms during the crash. This centralized information sharing will greatly enhance the financial integrity of all the exchanges and will facilitate detection of inter-market violations such as front-running.

In addition, the CME has submitted a comprehensive package of internal trading, procedural, and financial rules to the CFTC. These proposals are in accord with the Brady recommendations described in the following sections.

### Circuit Breakers

The CME has proposed a set of permanent "daily" price limits as well as a new concept of "opening" price limits. It should be noted that the CME was the first exchange voluntarily to impose such emergency circuit breakers, long before the Brady Report concluded such a procedure was central to ensuring that October 19 does not recur.

### Rationalization of Futures Margins and Securities Margins in Line with Professional Margin on Securities

While we strongly disagree with this proposal, since the function of futures margin is substantially different than that in securities, we nonetheless have proposed the following improvements:

- The CME proposes to adopt a new and highly accurate system for measuring option risk.
- The CME has petitioned the CFTC to add a risk-based capital requirement that will impose higher charges on firms that represent above-average risk.
- The CME proposes to substantially increase the level of liquid assets guaranteeing performance by its clearing house.
- The CME will maintain its initial speculative stock index margin at a level of approximately 15 percent of the value of the contract. This percentage will bring our futures margin into substantial alignment with professionals' margin on securities.

### Enhancement of the Clearing System and Settlement Process

The CME will act promptly to resolve the specific problems that interfered with expeditious fund transfers during the crash. In particular, we will modify our intraday pay/collect procedures and coordinate with the other futures exchanges and the Options Clearing Corporation (OCC).

Mr. Chairman, allow me now to turn to another aspect of this discussion, the underlying nature of our financial markets, their differences from traditional markets, and their global significance. The Chicago Mercantile Exchange, the Chicago Board of Trade, and the other futures markets in our country understood that the world had entered an era of great financial uncertainty—that uncertainty breeds risk—that risk seeks insurance. Thus we created markets and procedures that responded to the needs of sophisticated users. Were this not the case, we could not have possibly grown or succeeded in the phenomenal fashion we have. Unfortunately, because these markets represent sophisticated applications to instruments of finance, because they cater better to present technology, because they function differently from older traditional markets, the nature and importance of futures markets is sometimes misunderstood.

It is perhaps important to note one of the unique differences of futures that has a profound impact on their regulation and use: All futures market positions are marked-to-market on a daily basis; that is, any price changes in futures positions representing losses must be paid for in cash at least before the next market day. This financial system is substantially safer than traditional systems that are credit-based and allow losses to accumulate for many days.

Nevertheless, futures often become easy targets in our uncertain and complex world. Some have derided them, calling them dens of speculation, casinos, and worse. While this is not funny, there is an amusing irony about such beliefs. Most non-capitalistic societies have held similar views about all our financial institutions—the NYSE (New York Stock Exchange), in particular.

Mr. Chairman, in truth, the U.S. futures markets are the envy of every financial center in the free world. There is not a capital market in existence, be it London or Tokyo, Paris or Singapore, Sydney or Zurich, that does not seek to copy the formula of our American success, or wrest from us the business we have garnered. In the telecommunications era of this day and age, that is no idle threat. Futures markets can be re-created in any financial center. Even as we debate the cause of the recent stock market crash and the right of futures to exist as efficient markets, the Japanese government proudly announced its decision to proceed with the formation of a Tokyo Futures Exchange.

Indeed, our markets have been hailed by the academics as the most important financial innovation of the past 20 years. They provide a most efficient risk transfer mechanism and an effective price discovery system, offer large transaction cost savings, and are an integral component in capital formation.

Our markets are utilized by investment bankers and broker-dealers, by primary security dealers and block traders, by banks and savings and loan institutions, by corporations and financial institutions of every sort and by pension funds, insurance funds, and mutual funds. Over one third of our business flows are from foreign shores, providing a meaningful and positive factor to our balance of payments.

Mr. Chairman, we urge that Congress avoid policies that impose unnecessary restrictions on these markets and drive this industry to a foreign competitor as has been our unfortunate experience with so many other American industries.

We urge that simply because our markets are different, we not be forced to become the same. That because we have advanced into the technological present, we not be forced to retreat to a less technological past. That because we are efficient, we not be forced to become mediocre. That because we have succeeded in an arena that some mistakenly view as the exclusive domain of New York, we not be forced to relinquish our market share.

## 2. ORAL STATEMENT: U.S. SENATE COMMITTEE ON BANKING, HOUSING AND URBAN AFFAIRS, SUBCOMMITTEE ON SECURITIES, MAY 18, 1989

Mr. Chairman and Members, good morning. We welcome this opportunity to appear before this Committee to address the October 19, 1987, world stock market collapse and the aftereffects of that phenomenon. At the outset, allow me to compliment this Committee for the foresight and prudence you exhibited in the weeks following the frightening events of that October. It should serve as a model lesson to all congressional committees and members of the Congress. Amid the near-panic conditions that then pervaded the media, amid the calls for market reforms by many, amid outlandish statements and irresponsible accusations by some who pointed in one or another direction for the perceived cause or culprit of the crash, this Committee retained its composure, refrained from any emotionally dictated reaction, and was not panicked into any unwarranted legislative action. Today, historical hindsight allows us now to assess the wisdom of this Committee's deliberate inaction. Any legislative response would have been misplaced and counterproductive, and would have interfered with the marketplace to its ultimate detriment.

Nearly one year ago, this Committee heard testimony from the White House Working Group,* which analyzed the events of the October 1987 crash and clarified the Brady Report recommendations on clearing and settlement procedures, information flows, margin requirements, financial safeguards, and cross-market circuit breakers. These intricate and complicated

---

*Alan Greenspan, Chairman of the Federal Reserve Board of Governors; George D. Gould, Undersecretary of the Treasury for Finance; David S. Ruder, Chairman of the Securities and Exchange Commission; and Wendy L. Gramm, Chairman of the Commodity Futures Trading Commission.

areas prompted Chairman Greenspan to advise this Committee that "The most important result of the crash is that market participants learn and act. They have done so and are doing so."

Indeed, all actions taken to date have indicated that the present regulatory environment is capable of addressing issues raised by the crash and of instituting changes that can address rampant market volatility in the future. We see no signs of any "gaps" in regulatory oversight, no unnecessary duplication of oversight, nor any need to consider a consolidation of government regulation of the futures and securities industries.

The most important trend affecting securities markets and capital formation is the acceleration toward international markets. Capital moves across national boundaries with increasing ease, reflecting both enhanced opportunities and sophistication on the part of investors to exploit the opportunities. The Chicago Mercantile Exchange early on recognized the importance of this phenomenon with the development of foreign currency and Eurodollar futures and options. Most recently, the development of our global electronic transaction system, GLOBEX, is a demonstration that not only do the trading instruments need to reflect an international orientation, but that the mechanism of trading must fit in the international community as well.

Steps to keep our economy in a position to benefit from this trend must be made today, or the United States may lose its place of preeminence in the world capital markets. Private U.S. firms have demonstrated an ability to move quickly and effectively in this environment, but regulatory burdens and institutional inertia on the part of some major institutions should be addressed promptly.

Regulation of securities and futures markets internationally has shown little consistency across national boundaries. While regulation should be adequate, great care must be taken that our regulations do not place unnecessary constraints on the U.S. securities and futures industries. Many instruments are traded at several different locations around the world, and regulatory inequities could chase U.S. business to foreign markets.

Institutional change is also needed to keep up with these rapid developments. Traditionally our banking system has been oriented to domestic business, but to remain competitive, it is necessary to change. Allowing U.S. banks to hold foreign currency deposits beginning in 1990 is a major positive step, but many more will be necessary. Our central bank now operates during our business day, leaving the important tasks of clearing, settlement, and oversight of international monetary flows to other national banks. It is likely that some national bank will expand its activities to cover more of the 24-hour span. If the U.S. Federal Reserve Board moves in that direction first, it would ensure that our facilities and policies, which are currently the focus of the entire world, would maintain their dominant role. If another central bank seeks this role, our influence internationally could be diminished.

The past few years have demonstrated the degree to which the markets for securities and futures have become increasingly linked internationally. This is not a trend that is likely to be reversed. Private U.S. companies are very dynamic and capable of adjusting to these challenges. The goal of Congress should be to provide the regulatory and institutional framework that will allow effective competition and maintain the U.S. economy in the forefront of the international arena.

We agree that the regulators of financial institutions and markets, both foreign and domestic, should coordinate regulatory activities and exchange information with each other. However, we believe that legislation is not necessary in this area. Both the CFTC and the SEC have entered into or are negotiating memoranda of understanding with their counterparts in the major financial centers of the world.

The CME has had extensive experience in coordinating with overseas exchanges. In 1984, the CME and the Singapore International Monetary Exchange (SIMEX) entered into a mutual offset arrangement in which a trade executed on one exchange could be offset by a transaction on the other. More recently, in connection with CME applications to trade futures contracts based on Japanese, British, and world stock indexes, the CME entered into agreements to share surveillance information with the Tokyo Stock Exchange and The Securities Association in London.

In September 1988, the CFTC, the CME, and other U.S. futures exchanges agreed with three United Kingdom regulators to exchange financial information respecting companies with branches in the other jurisdiction.

The CME recognizes that the financial markets are becoming increasingly international in scope. Trading can be done in

London or Tokyo as easily as in Chicago or New York. In the past five years, new futures exchanges have opened or been announced in London, Paris, Hong Kong, Sydney, Toronto, Singapore, New Zealand, Brazil, Osaka, Zurich, Tokyo, Dublin, Frankfurt. Every financial center knows the value of integrating actual or possible movement of London's FTSE 100 and Tokyo's NIKKEI indices as harbingers of the day's S&P 500 movement.

Indeed, in response to the demands of the globalization of markets, two years ago the CME entered into a long-range agreement with Reuters Holdings, PLC to create GLOBEX, an automated, "after-hours," transaction system for futures and options. The GLOBEX system will provide access to the CME's markets by overseas investors during their regular business hours while the CME's trading floor is closed.

However, GLOBEX is much more than an after-hours transaction system for CME markets. The CME also is cooperating with other futures exchanges, both domestic and foreign, in connection with the establishment of GLOBEX as a shared international communications network and order matching system. In that manner, GLOBEX can be used by members of every participating exchange to trade its futures and options contracts during the hours that the exchange's trading floor is closed. GLOBEX will allow transactions in futures, options, and selected foreign financial instruments to be executed from anywhere in the world, instantly, and with financial integrity.

For GLOBEX to work effectively, GLOBEX order entry terminals must be placed in the major financial centers of the world, such as London, Paris, Geneva, Tokyo, and Hong Kong. The CME is examining the laws of those jurisdictions to determine whether any legal or regulatory problems exist that might prevent the introduction of GLOBEX terminals into their territory. One potential concern is that the government of one or more of those countries may block the installation of GLOBEX terminals in its territory, not for legitimate regulatory reasons, but to protect the local exchanges in such country from competition. If we determine that GLOBEX is being kept out of a country for protectionist reasons, we will promptly notify the U.S. Trade Representative of the situation and seek assistance in overcoming any obstacles that may prevent us from offering GLOBEX services internationally.

# Quintessential Lessons

*One of the most amazing results of the 1987 stock market crash was its boomerang effect on the stature of futures markets.*

*The initial perception of many in the financial world was that futures markets were the culprit responsible for the crash. But the facts and the ensuing process did not bear out this mistaken belief. Of the 77 studies undertaken in the aftermath of the crash, virtually none found blame with futures markets.*

*On the contrary, futures markets ultimately received the highest praise possible from academicians everywhere. Indeed, most highly qualified experts characterized futures as a critical mechanism for risk management in today's modern global markets.*

---

**Presented before the National Association of Futures Trading Advisors, Chicago, Illinois, July 22, 1988**

---

The 1987 stock market crash was an awesome event. It provided many lessons and proved many things. Allow me to name at least five.

First, of course, it was brutal market punishment for the sin of a global mania that had swept good sense to the side and taken world stock prices to levels far beyond rational levels. Alan Greenspan, Chairman of the U.S. Federal Reserve Board, summed it up best in his report to the U.S. Senate Banking Committee on February 2, 1988:

> Stock prices finally reached levels which stretched to incredulity expectations of rising real earnings and falling discount factors. Something had to snap. If it didn't happen in October, it would have happened soon thereafter. The immediate cause of the break was incidental. The market plunge was an accident waiting to happen.

Second, it was an expensive lesson, proving to what extent our technological competence had outdistanced our market mechanics. To put it bluntly, most of our traditional markets were operating on a technological standard equivalent to the steamboat while those who make market decisions were using the jet plane. In other words, the disparity between markets and their participants is growing. It is primarily the result of the changed nature of the decision-making power in matters of finance. Scientific and technological advancement have forced the world to become highly specialized and professional, a trend that will not abate and is nowhere more obvious than in finance.

In the United States, investment managers now represent over 33 million mutual fund shareholders and over 60 million pension plan participants and their beneficiaries. These funds equal nearly $2 trillion in assets compared with only $400 billion a mere decade ago. The reason is obvious. Large pools of capital offer access to professional management, enabling even small investors to equal the profit capabilities of institutional participants. As a result, a myriad of specialists, techniques, and strategies have evolved. Moreover, technological sophistication has enabled these professionals to apply their strategies with lightening speed. Unfortunately, traditional market mechanisms, particularly in stocks, are simply not structured to accommodate the massive and sudden money flows these managers command. On October 19, 1987, we learned the foregoing truth in a very real and painful fashion. Financial managers with colossal market positions under their control attempted to institute similar market decisions at the same moment. The stock markets could not possibly handle the sudden surge of money flows these orders represented when combined with the extraordinary flood of general selling that was at hand.

Third, the 1987 stock market crash provided clear and convincing evidence that market globalization was upon us. Early on the morning of October 19, hours before the sun began its ascent over the East River and even longer before the New York Stock Exchange opening bell rang, grim news from Tokyo, London, and elsewhere was flickering on computer screens throughout the United States. Some portfolio managers, anticipating the worst, were moving to beat a selling avalanche in New York by unloading shares in London. Rarely was the impact of globalization on the markets more amply demonstrated.

Fourth, to our chagrin, we learned how shallow is the understanding by a large segment of the financial universe about markets in general and about futures markets in particular. From the outset, a belief arose that the October 1987 stock market crash must have been the fault of a specific cause. After all, financial advisers who had been telling their clients to hold on to their investment or buy more could not possibly be so wrong. There had to be an explanation: some special factor must have intervened; some villainous sabotage that stopped the bull market in its tracks. Never mind that the October collapse was a global event. Never mind that all speculative bubbles must finally burst. Never mind the plethora of accumulating fundamental economic and psychological factors that could cause the collapse. Never mind all of that, and let us instead search for a specific culprit. And search we did. A large number of studies, official and ad hoc, were launched to seek the answer to the question: Who or what caused the crash? When a demon is hunted, a demon will be found.

It did not take long. Quite soon the fingers were pointing to technology. The words were catchy. Mindless computers on automatic pilot were the culprits. Technology has outdistanced its effectiveness. Efficiency needs a brake pedal! Then the search got specific: *program trading.* Then even more specific: *index arbitrage.* All the while, the fingers were pointing westward in the direction of futures and options.

Throughout the witch hunt, the media was the medium, used and abused. Because the October crash was extraordinary and frightening, because the issues were deeply complex, because so many within the financial world seemed to agree that there was a specific villain to be found, the media generally accepted the premise at face value. And Congress played its part: Was there really a problem to be fixed? Or simply an issue to be had. Either way, an investigation was in order, an opportunity for a public forum.

And there were those who had a special motivation to find a culprit. With volume and brokers' commissions down, someone or something had to get the blame for loss of investor confidence. *Volatility* became the watch word of the day. Volatility caused the lack of investor confidence. Volatility, rather than the simple logic that after a major market decline, only the imprudent would blindly rush back to the market. Volatility, rather than have someone conclude that there was a bear market about, that business and volume might suffer, that jobs might be in jeopardy.

Indeed, the movement gained momentum and an impressive following. Demagoguery and misinformation are powerful combinations. On May 10, 1988, the most prestigious U.S. investment banking firms bowed to this nonsensical pressure and announced their withdrawal from proprietary index arbitrage. It was a particularly sad day in American financial history. The movement might have grown further except that it reached a level of near-hysteria with a call for a ban on index futures. For most of the financial community, this went too far. For most, it served as a sudden, chilling tonic bringing them back to reality. A call to ban was indeed too much.

*When I was but a child on the floor of the old Chicago Mercantile Exchange, long before financial futures, long before futures became a respected and even indispensable risk management tool, Elmer Falkner, an old line CME member who had made and lost many a fortune, took me by the hand. "Don't let our futures market get too successful," he ominously warned, waving his big cigar in the air (Elmer was a little guy, something under 5 feet tall and his cigar was almost as big as he was).*

*"Why not?" I innocently inquired.*

*"Because," he replied, "futures markets tell the truth and nobody wants to know the truth. If the truth is too bad and too loud, they'll close us down."*

*I learned all to clearly how sage Elmer's advice was on October 19, 1987, when the futures index markets were the first to tell the truth. The truth was indeed too bad and too loud.*

*Who was Elmer Falkner? Why is he important? Allow me to digress a bit and tell you something about the little guy. I have often been asked who invented index futures. I don't know the answer. Clearly, it wasn't I. The idea had been around long before I showed up on the scene as a runner for Merrill Lynch. But it was Elmer Falkner who first told me about it.*

*"The ultimate futures contract," he confided to me, "is stock market futures."*

*When I didn't immediately understand his meaning, he whis-*
*pered, "you know, like Dow Jones futures. But," he quickly*
*added waving his cigar again, "it will never happen. You can't make*
*delivery."*

I never forgot Elmer or the things he taught this young and
innocent disciple. Three decades or so later, we advanced the
concept of cash settlement to make Elmer's ultimate contract a
reality.

Today, as before the crash, the CME's Standard & Poor's
500 futures contract is the most successful stock index futures
contract in the world. Its success stems primarily from the fact
that it represents an equity risk management tool for the
present day and offers the most liquid and cost-efficient environment yet devised.

Finally, the fifth lesson of the 1987 October crash proved
that it was no exception to the rule that every cloud has its
silver lining. For in the final analysis, the truth will out. After all the studies were in, after all the evidence was presented, after all the analysis was done, after all the
misinformation was laid to rest, futures markets were not
only exonerated from blame, they were vindicated by receiving high praise from the most knowledgeable experts. Indeed, these experts could not be deemed fellow travelers of
the Chicago exchanges. Rather they were classic products of
the Wall Street community.

Allow me to quote some pertinent testimony of the Chairman of the Federal Reserve Board:

> There is no avoiding the fact that, as our economy and financial
> system change, our financial markets are going to behave dif-
> ferently than they have in the past. We cannot realistically hope
> to turn back the clock and replicate behavior of the past. Rather,
> we need to understand better how the system is evolving and
> the consequences of such change. Our efforts need to focus on
> making sure that the financial system is more resilient to
> shocks rather than embarking on futile endeavors to artificially
> curb volatility.
>
> What many critics of equity derivatives fail to recognize is that
> the markets for these instruments have become so large not be-
> cause of slick sales campaigns but because they are providing
> economic value to their users. By enabling pension funds and
> other institutional users to hedge and adjust positions quickly

and inexpensively, these instruments have come to play an important role in portfolio management.*

And allow me also to quote some equally strong support for the futures market from the U.S. Treasury in the person of George D. Gould, the Under Secretary for Finance:

> There are numerous factors that have made markets react more quickly today to changes in the fundamental determinants of stock prices. First, the nature of stock ownership has changed substantially over the past twenty years, led by private and public pension funds. There have evolved very large individual aggregations of capital of a size unknown in an earlier period. . . . Thus, stock index futures markets have evolved as the lowest cost, most efficient response to these changed needs. "Trading the market" and hedging are not in and of themselves either good or bad—they are economic facts that are not going to go away.

> Much public criticism of index arbitrage is a classic case of wanting "to shoot the messenger" that brings the bad news of selling on the CME to the floor of the NYSE. If selling is going to take place to a degree that pushes prices down sharply, then cash markets will not be made immune by eliminating index arbitrage.[†]

And to those who would criticize futures markets as dens of speculation, the Chicago Federal Reserve Bank had the following to say:

> At the heart of the economic role of a futures market is risk transfer. Futures contracts provide a way of transferring risk from hedgers who seek to reduce risk to speculators who would bear risk in the hope of profiting by it. Attempts to curb speculative activity on these contracts by raising futures margins overlook the fact that such curbs would also reduce an investor's ability to sell off unwanted risk by hedging.[‡]

---

[*]Alan Greenspan, Chairman, Federal Reserve Board of Governors, *Testimony before the U.S. House Subcommittee on Telecommunications and Finance of the Committee on Energy and Commerce,* May 19, 1988.

[†]George D. Gould, Treasury Under Secretary for Finance, *Testimony before the U.S. House Subcommittee on Telecommunications and Finance of the Committee on Energy and Commerce,* May 19, 1988.

[‡]Herbert L. Baer, Maureen V. O'Neil, *Chicago Fed Letter,* The Federal Reserve Bank of Chicago, May 1988, p. 1.

Impressive support, powerful testimony, compelling arguments, you will agree. Thus, the silver lining. These quintessential lessons of the October crash have served to strengthen, rather than weaken, futures markets worldwide. The evidence is all about us.

Take the recent agreed to initiatives between the Chicago Mercantile Exchange and the New York Stock Exchange, the two markets where most of the equity business critical to the issues at hand takes place: to institute a system of coordinated "circuit breakers"; to develop a system of "shock absorbers" that would be triggered by smaller predesignated price moves; to transform the present "collar" rule (which limits use of the NYSE's DOT system after a move of 50 Dow points) into a coordinated system that temporarily diverts program trading from the DOT system at approximately 100 points on the Dow; and to create a common definition of "front-running."

These agreements could not have been achieved unless or until our futures markets were able to take their deserved and honored seat at the financial table. Indeed, these initiative are a direct result of the process that focused national attention on the fact that the financial markets—both stocks and futures— are strongly linked and of equal importance in today's competitive global environment.

The achievement is the direct result of the joint efforts by the Chicago Mercantile Exchange and the Chicago Board of Trade in proving that futures markets represent the *avant-garde* of today's market demands and are indispensable as modern risk management tools. The agreements represent compelling evidence that American financial markets can work together to achieve the necessary solutions and that federal legislation is both unnecessary and would be counterproductive to the complex and sophisticated markets of today.

The evidence that the lessons of last October served to strengthen futures markets is even more evident from a global perspective. Even as the United States deliberated the role of futures in the October 19 market collapse, the London International Stock Exchange published its conclusion that the solution was in more—not less—index arbitrage. At the same time, the Japanese Ministry of Finance announced its decision to establish two futures markets in Japan. And the headlines on business pages the world over confirm this judgment:

"Luxembourg Ponders Futures and Options Exchange," "Japanese Markets to Cover Domestic and U.S. Interest Rates as Well as Stock Index Contracts," "LIFFE Canvasses Support for German Bund Contract," "Finnish Futures Exchange to Start Soon," "ICC Sets Sights on New York," "Stockholm Foreign Exchange Market Welcomed," "China Plans Futures Markets," "French Proceed with Stock Index Plans," "German Stock Index to Be Established."

Today every major center of finance must either possess or be connected to a futures and options market just as it must possess or be connected to a stock market or a major bank. As Secretary Nicholas Brady concluded in his report to the President, "there is but one market." Futures are an integral and indispensable part of it.

# The Jaws of Victory

*The fallout from the 1987 stock market crash lasted nearly two years. The debate became ugly before it got better. Index arbitrage—and consequently futures—were blamed for nearly all the ills of the stock market and beyond. Futures markets were innocent of blame. The underlying problem was not with index arbitrage or program trading, but with modern equity investment techniques and their impact on traditional investment strategies.*

*The latest trend in portfolio management utilized index enhancement strategies—techniques that required constant adjustments to portfolios and utilized stock index futures markets. Unfortunately, these portfolio adjustments caused price movements (volatility) in individual stocks that had no relationship to fundamental values. As a result, futures were perceived to be the cause of volatility in the market. The issue became quite serious and threatened the life of the stock index futures contract.*

Presented at the Fifth Annual CME London Finance
Symposium, Le Meridien Piccadilly Hotel, London, England,
November 13, 1989

The subject of program trading, particularly the aspect of it known as index arbitrage, unfortunately has become a somewhat heated topic in U.S. financial circles. While this American debate may sound peculiar and insignificant to the outside world of finance, it is even more profound than a surface examination will divulge. The issues unfortunately include some serious anti-free-market implications. I cannot therefore help but muse that we Americans have chosen a rather strange moment in history to question our successful market philosophies. For we stand at the historical juncture when the triumph of capitalism and free market economics is undeniable and nearly worldwide. Perhaps the debate is only indicative of a U.S. penchant to snatch defeat from the jaws of victory.

There are four kinds of program trades.* The first three do not require stock index futures and use futures only when they meet the objectives in a cost-effective way.

The first and most general form of program trading is defined by the New York Stock Exchange (NYSE) as "the simultaneous placement of buy or sell orders for a portfolio of at least 15 different stocks valued at more than $1 million." A broker executes these transactions using DOT, the NYSE automated stock order-routing system. DOT, which requires computer utilization, has greatly increased the efficiency of stock executions.

Portfolio insurance, the second type of program trading, is also known as dynamic hedging. This technique sometimes utilizes the futures market and is effectuated whenever the cash market index falls to a predetermined level. Though this strategy was found somewhat inadequate during the 1987 stock market crash, it is beginning to make a comeback. Its alleged inadequacy during the crash was likened to a homeowner's attempt to buy fire insurance *after* his house is on fire—it can be rather expensive.

Tactical asset allocation, the third program trading strategy, examines the relative value of stocks, bonds, and cash equivalents. A predetermined formula makes trading decisions in an attempt to achieve the highest yield for an investment portfolio by exchanging one asset for another. This strategy has been gaining popularity steadily with many money managers worldwide. Programmed computers, including the NYSE's DOT system as well as futures and options markets, can be and often are utilized to effectuate this strategy.

Index arbitrage, the last category of program trading, is the strategy that is usually called into question and is the topic of the current debate. Traditional arbitrage activity—not to be confused with that of risk arbitrage—is as old as markets themselves. Not only is there nothing sinister about the activity, but it greatly benefits the markets with which it interacts by adding liquidity and equalizing price differentials. Simply

---

*The author wishes to acknowledge the assistance provided by Todd Petzel, CME Senior Vice President and Chief Economist.

explained, arbitrage works this way: If the widget market in New York is higher priced than the widget market in Chicago, an arbitrageur will—after accounting for transportation costs—sell New York widgets and buy Chicago widgets, and vice versa.

In index arbitrage, an arbitrageur monitors both the equity cash market at the NYSE and a stock index futures such as the S&P 500 contract at the Chicago Mercantile Exchange. On the date the futures contract expires, its price will converge with the underlying stock cash price. However, during the life of the futures contract, its price will often differ from the cash market. Whenever the futures and cash index price differ by any appreciable amount, an arbitrageur can lock in a profit by buying the lower-priced market and selling the higher-priced market. It is an age-old and totally legitimate practice that offers an arbitrage profit from price differences that develop between two or more markets. In the case of equities and futures, the price differential results because futures markets react quicker to market information. The reason is that futures markets are more cost-efficient than their counterparts in the cash market.

Quite often, when money managers want to adjust their portfolio quickly, they will choose to initiate the indicated transaction in futures. This will cause the futures market to achieve a different price level than the cash market. The transitory price difference offers the index arbitrageur an opportunity for profit. His resulting arbitrage activity works to even out the price differential between the two markets. The practical problem occurs whenever such activities result in a lower price for the stock market, a consequence of an arbitrage-related sell program. To someone in the cash market, the arbitrage activity appears to be depressing the stock market. There is then a hue and cry against program trading. Conversely, there are few complaints when the result of such arbitrage activities is a higher price for the stock market. As former Treasury Undersecretary, George D. Gould, explained, "Futures markets act as the messenger." When the message is good, everything is lovely; but you know what happens to the messenger of bad tidings.

In 1987, the attack against program trading as one of the primary causes of the crash, took on the proportions of a witch hunt and proved without merit. Not one of the 77 postmarket studies on the crash found evidence to substantiate this belief. Today, the attack has a somewhat different focus: Program trading causes volatility, and volatility is driving the individual investor away from the market. Whether there is more volatility today or not, whether volatility per se is good or bad, whether it is driving individual investors from the market, and whether or not it can be stopped are all important questions of yet another dimension. Indeed, there is much evidence to suggest that, when measured over long periods, there is no greater volatility today than years ago. Nevertheless, the issue before us is whether program trading—specifically index arbitrage—is the primary cause of volatility in the market.

There can be no dispute that volatility and liquidity are related. The more liquid the market, the less the volatility. It could then be assumed that since volume at the NYSE and other markets has grown substantially over the years, liquidity has benefited as well. However, in a letter to clients, Stanley B. Shopkorn, Vice Chairman of Salomon Brothers, explained why this is not the case. Mr. Shopkorn focused on a factor of volatility that is little discussed and may be structural to the marketplace. Stock market liquidity, Shopkorn states, comes from two traditional sources: specialists and block trading firms.

As a consequence of the removal of fixed commission schedules in the mid-1970s, both specialists and block traders suffered a dramatic decline in their commissions and floor brokerage. Transactions that would have brought a broker $.40 a share in the 1960s might bring less than $.04 a share today. This has had devastating consequences on liquidity. According to Shopkorn, the higher commissions of two decades ago provided a kind of insurance. Block traders, for instance, "were willing to make bids and offers that would stabilize the market because at former commission levels they could afford to provide liquidity during periods of stress, even if it meant losing money on a specific trade." This is no longer true. Current commission schedules "offer insufficient incentive to cover the risks of significant block positions."

Similarly, the drop in commissions for specialists has forced them to rely heavily on trading. In the early 1970s, Shopkorn explains, "about two-thirds of the typical specialist's income came from floor brokerage commissions and the balance came from trading." Today, the relationship is reversed. Moreover, the growing reliance by specialists on trading comes in an environment of increased competition from other markets and has led to a narrowing of the bid/ask spreads. A narrower spread reduces the specialist's profit per transaction.

The combined effect of these dramatic changes in business has increased the risks and reduced the incentive to provide liquidity in the traditional manner. Thus Mr. Shopkorn points out, "Low commission levels for block traders and specialists do not allow them to accumulate a cushion sufficient to provide the liquidity that becomes so essential for smoothly functioning equity markets during periods of stress." If this is so, Mr. Shopkorn has pointed to a structural reason for inadequate liquidity that, in turn, has a fundamental effect on market volatility.

But this is by far not the only possible cause of modern-day volatility. Today, large institutional investors control huge sums of money. The decision-making power for these funds is held not by vast numbers of investors, but by a relatively small number of portfolio managers. Their investment decisions—often instantaneous and quite often similar—create a sudden and much greater impact on the market than would the separate decisions of thousands of disparate investors. And whether we like it or not, whether good or bad, is not the issue. Scientific and technological advancements have forced the world to become highly specialized, technologically oriented, and professional—a trend that will not abate and is nowhere more obvious than in finance. In the United States, investment managers now represent over 33 million mutual fund shareholders and over 60 million pension plan participants and their beneficiaries. These funds equal $2 trillion in assets compared with only $400 billion a mere decade ago.

Furthermore, new technologies have spawned a myriad of new techniques and the ability to apply them instantaneously. As Mr. Shopkorn states and most experts know, the majority of today's trading activities are no longer conducted relative to fundamental evaluations. Current portfolio managers often apply index enhancement strategies that require adjustments to portfolios resulting in price movements for individual stocks that bear no relationship to fundamental values. The nation's 200 largest pension funds now have 30 percent of their assets committed to some form of indexation.

Tangential to globalization as a factor of volatility is the impact of foreign investors on our markets. Their force—both on a long-term and intraday basis—is an immense and relatively new influence. Japanese investors alone represented nearly 30 percent of the $180 billion in U.S. stock purchases made by foreigners in 1988. In 1983, Japanese investors accounted for less than 3 percent of $70 billion in foreign purchases. Indeed, the U.S. equity market is no longer the dominant force it was years ago. In 1975, the U.S. accounted for 75 percent of world equity markets; today it accounts for only 25 percent.

Nor can we underestimate the volatility consequences of today's interest rate and currency fluctuations or those flowing from LBOs, high-risk junk bonds, or the current massive global debt structure. Indeed, impacts on price stability in today's global village are quite different from several decades ago when American markets were fully insulated from competing financial centers.

Today, the financial landscape of the United States—as well as that of the world—is considerably different. The postulation that the current U.S. stock market is more volatile can be attributed to plenty of substantive causes. To conclude that program trading is the single or even most prominent cause is at best simplistic and at worst self-deluding. Alas, the issue has taken on ominous proportions. Indeed, there is currently a dangerous environment in the United States, one that if unchecked will blame index arbitrage—and consequently futures markets—for all the ills of the stock market and beyond. Witch hunts have a certain undeniable appeal and can serve as a ready answer to affix blame for a variety of serious problems.

Already there is a strong view that program trading is weakening public confidence in the market and that it disrupts capital formation. Already it is an accepted truth that sell programs—executed in conjunction with futures markets—are depressing stock prices. Already there is a view that this activity is manipulative and that it profits a few institutional players by taking advantage of individual investors. Already there is a movement to stop doing business with firms and individuals that do index arbitrage. Already there is testimony and proposed legislation in favor of curbing or even banning this market procedure. In such a climate, it is easy to see how index arbitrage could become the central villain should the stock market turn bearish, an eventuality not to be dismissed lightly. How far a step is it then to a presidential action of the following magnitude:

> It has come to my attention that certain persons are selling short in the commodity market. . . . These transactions have been continuous over the past months. I do not refer to the ordinary hedging transactions, which are a sound part of our market system. I do not refer to the legitimate . . . trade. I refer to a limited number of speculators. I am not expressing my view upon the economics of short selling in normal times, but in these times this activity has a public interest. It has one purpose and that is to depress prices. It tends to destroy the return of public confidence. The intentions to take a profit from the loss of other people . . . the effect may be directly depriving (others) of their rightful income. If these gentlemen have the sense of patriotism which outruns immediate profit, and desire to see the country recover, they will close up these transactions and desist from their manipulations.

That address was delivered by President Herbert Hoover on July 10, 1931. Scary stuff, isn't it?

However, the United States often reaches the brink of disaster before wisdom prevails. Indeed, the recent editorial in the *Wall Street Journal* is testimony that wiser heads are entering the discussion. The editorial cautioned that in such complex issues, we should not jump in favor of conclusions based on popular misconceptions. Blaming computers will have its price. Exchanges, the *WSJ* editors correctly state, have a difficult task in these matters and have the obligation to strike a balance between maintaining an orderly market and allowing the market to freely perform its function. Let us hope—as does the editorial—that if we err, it will be on the side of free markets.

# PART V

# GLOBALIZATION AND THE NEW WORLD ORDER

*There was at least one striking consequence of the new world order that was unexpected. Globalization ushered in a new era of common goals between two arch competitors—the Chicago Board of Trade and the Chicago Mercantile Exchange, the world's two largest futures exchanges.*

*Of course it was predictable. Throughout time, these two giant Chicago markets have put on a united front whenever there was a common danger; generally this involved legislative or regulatory authority in its incessant attempt to encroach or burden the free market process. Over the years, the CME and the CBOT have had an excellent record of fending off unnecessary and burdensome legislation by uniting forces and working together.*

*Suddenly, there was a new common danger: globalization. The competitor was no longer the other exchange in Chicago, it was the new exchange in a foreign land. The contracts invented and developed by the Chicago futures exchanges could not be copyrighted or patented. Globalization meant that foreign exchanges could use the contract specifications of these financial instruments and list them for trade during their own business hours. This meant that Chicago's futures and options markets were no longer safe from international competition. The market share of our products had become the target of foreign competitors. Indeed, as a consequence of international competition, by the year 1990, the U.S. market share of total world futures transaction volume had been reduced by 35 percent.*

*At first the CME and CBOT acted separately in a similar quest to protect their primary financial instruments. The CME forged a tie* *with the Singapore International Monetary Exchange (SIMEX), a market in another time zone; several years later, the CBOT launched an after-hours market in U.S. Treasury bond futures. But by 1987 the CME's Strategic Planning Committee\* had come to the revolutionary conclusion that the ultimate answer to the competitive realities of globalization was to embrace a technological solution that could provide an after-hours, around-the-clock trading capability. Subsequently, the CBOT reached the same conclusion.*

*This history proved to be the magical formula for cooperation. Out of the fray of fierce competition between the Chicago exchanges came the realization that the greater danger was external, not internal. The present contracts of trade at the CBOT and CME do not compete directly with one another, and the exchanges had no problem allowing the marketplace to make its determination about future competitive products. On the other hand, both exchanges saw the clear and present competitive danger posed by other world exchanges trading the traditional CBOT and CME products in their own time zones. The same anxiety was voiced by every exchange around the globe. Globalization meant that any futures or options instrument, no matter what locale was its natural home or where it had been developed, could be transplanted by another financial center.*

*It was this ubiquitous concern that later prompted the CME to materially change its original electronic after-hours concept. The exchange agreed to internationalize GLOBEX by expanding its scope and inviting other exchanges from around the world to list their unique products on the system. This internationalization of purpose brought to GLOBEX its first partner exchange—the Paris-based* Marché à Térme International de France *(MATIF). It is to the everlasting credit of Gérard Pfauwadel, chairman of MATIF, who not only understood the enormous value of joining an electronic trading system that would allow MATIF products to be traded internationally on a 24-hour basis, but had the courage and foresight to lead his exchange toward this unprecedented agreement.*

*The foregoing global reality was sufficient cause for the CME and CBOT to act in unison, but there were other compelling reasons.*

---

\*For historical purposes it is important to record the names of the members of the CME Strategic Planning Committee that forged the GLOBEX concept and that I had the privilege to chair: Brian P. Monieson, vice chairman, John T. Geldermann, Philip L. Glass, M. Scott Gordon, Richard J. Kapsch, Larry B. Leonard, Barry J. Lind, Laurence M. Rosenberg, Louis G. Schwartz, Steven E. Wollack, Robert E. Zellner and John F. Sandner, CME Chairman.

*The development of a global electronic system is quite costly. To develop two such systems, when one can suffice, is an outrageous waste of capital. Moreover, two after-hour electronic systems, each with different listed contracts, would necessitate the U.S. futures industry to maintain both systems in order to service its global clientele—a highly inefficient and gross waste of capital. As expected, the Futures Industry Association (FIA), in the persona of their president John Damgard, their past chairman David J. Vogel, as well as their current chairman Hal T. Hansen, were a driving force on behalf of unification of the CME and CBOT electronic systems. The final agreement reached followed the prescription the CME had forged with Reuters Holdings PLC—the giant international communications vendor would develop the system for both exchanges. This arrangement was extremely advantageous for the exchanges since they did not have to expend the capital necessary for research and development; it was equally advantageous for Reuters with respect to the long range profit potential it represents.*

*However, no rationale is necessarily of sufficient compelling persuasion given the history of rivalry between these two fiercely competitive exchanges, their separate heritage and pride of memberships, and their common and long standing distrust of each other. This unification of systems might never have occurred were it not for the good sense of the leadership at both institutions. It took the wisdom, courage, and great foresight of the CBOT's then chairman, Karsten Mahlmann together with its president Thomas R. Donovan to respond favorably to the CME's initial offer extended by myself as chairman of the CME Executive Committee and John F. Sandner as senior policy advisor—with the blessing of then chairman of the board, John T. Geldermann, and president, William J. Brodsky—to begin negotiations toward unification of our respective GLOBEX and Aurora systems. But CBOT total commitment toward this difficult undertaking did not take shape until the entrance and accord of their present chairman William F. O'Connor. His embrace of system unification served to cement the current common goals environment between the two exchanges. He also became the CBOT's strongest advocate for technological innovation.*

*The ultimate agreement achieved—to become equal partners of the GLOBEX system—did not come easy. Negotiations which began in the summer of 1989 were arduous and heated, took some 18 months, often came dangerously close to breakup, and resulted in a substantial overhaul of the original specifications and agreement with*

*Reuters. It is imperative to credit the members of the negotiating team who, in addition to the leaders of both exchanges, had the persever-ance to stay with the process: At the CBOT: David P. Brennan, David J. Fisher, Mark Shlaes and Jay S. Sorkin, Directors, and Bur-ton J. Gutterman and Neal E. Kottke, members of the Technology Subcommittee; at the CME: John T. Geldermann, M. Scott Gordon, Barry J. Lind, Gordon J. McClendon and William R. Shepard. It is also imperative to credit Andre Villeneuve and John Hull of Reuters, for their indefatigable efforts toward the result. However, this unique and formidable achievement could not have been accomplished suc-cessfully without the brilliant and devoted work product of senior staff at these institutions.\**

*On June 25, 1992 GLOBEX became a reality. No one at the CME or CBOT expects instant success. GLOBEX represents as revolution-ary a change for the futures industry as did the introduction of finan-cial futures two decades before; that revolution took the better part of ten years to succeed. Irrespective of the time required to become ac-cepted, GLOBEX inaugurates a new era in futures and options mar-kets. In the near term, if GLOBEX serves to protect our financial futures contracts from global competition, it will have achieved its primary purpose. Long term, GLOBEX exemplifies the world of the 21st century.*

---

\*At GLOBEX: Gary Ginter; at the CBOT: George Sladoje, Glen W. Belden, Carol A. Burke, and Scott E. Early; and at the CME: Jerrold E. Salzman, T. Eric Kilcollin, Kenneth R. Cone, Donald D. Serpico, John P. Davidson, III, Carl A. Royal, and James R. Krause.

# Responding to Globalization: A CME Perspective

*The CME's official announcement of P-M-T, the after-hours electronic trading system—whose permanent name was later to become GLOBEX— sent shock waves through the futures industry. It represented a violent break with tradition, something to be feared and abhorred.*

*To those of us who had envisioned this revolutionary concept, it represented quite the opposite. To us, use of technology represented the recognition of reality. It embodied the use of mechanisms that could protect our market share from foreign competition as well as from competitive and hostile domestic pressures all about us. To us, the march of technology was a force no one could deny or ignore.*

*But how were we to convince the rank and file of an industry—one so committed to open outcry that the very thought of automation sent shivers down its collective spine—to accept technology? The task was not easy. The odds were long, and the bets were against us.*

*The following represents the rationale for our action. It became the CME GLOBEX manifesto. It was imperative that it be understood and accepted by our members. It was imperative that it be heard around the world. It was imperative that the mechanism we proposed become the only international system for futures and options. Today, this GLOBEX rationale represents the orthodox view of the futures industry worldwide.*

**Published by *Global Investment Management*, 1987**

In a bold and far-reaching joint undertaking, the Chicago Mercantile Exchange (CME) and Reuters Holdings PLC (Reuters) entered into a long-range agreement to create a global electronic automated transaction system for the trading of futures and futures options. The system, called P-M-T (Post Market Trade—its working designation) will operate worldwide before and after regular U.S. business hours. P-M-T will allow transactions to be matched directly against CME open positions and will be cleared by the CME clearing system. The undertaking was overwhelmingly approved by referendum of the CME membership on October 6, 1987. The concept embodied in P-M-T is clearly a historic milestone in the development of the futures trading. It embraces the realities brought about by the technological revolution of recent years and represents a giant step toward unification of the separate world's financial centers. It puts the CME light-years ahead of its competition.

Since the fundamental principle of the CME/Reuters agreement involves a significant departure from "established" futures industry philosophy, it is imperative to begin this discussion by addressing its impact on the quintessential element of present-day American futures: open outcry.

It is fair to say that most observers and users of futures markets hailed the CME announcement with admiration and approval. Yet, it should be of little surprise to anyone that this view was not unanimous. There are many within our industry who are vocal critics of any movement toward automation, or (in some extreme cases) even the adoption of technological advancements. These critics argue that such reforms advance the black box and hasten the end of open outcry. Obviously, the CME feels differently. Although we too hold open outcry sacred, we do not agree that such a philosophy requires a blind adherence to status quo.

Futures and futures options are dynamic and continuously evolving. As our markets became the standard tools for risk management the world over—as their applicability extended to new products, new techniques, and new users—we grew from a 1976 volume of approximately 37 million contracts to a 1986 volume of 216 million contracts. Today, the futures industry is not in any way, shape, or form the same industry that spawned the financial futures revolution in 1972. Nor does this industry bear much resemblance to the one that fought to prove its merit during its formative years. We are today but a distant cousin to that which gave us life, and while we must respect our heritage, we must not be held back by its limitations.

Throughout our dramatic metamorphosis and expansion, the open outcry system for execution of futures has been the only proven system for achieving the degree of liquidity necessary to produce and maintain a viable market. This is still the case, and it would be futile for anyone to argue otherwise. However, to assume blindly that it will always be so is to be lulled into a false sense of security and to forgo any opportunities for enhancing or advancing our way of doing business. Such a policy is both foolish and dangerous.

Open outcry, for a multitude of reasons, is under attack. Whether it is because of the system's inherent limitations, new and more efficient technologies, new users and uses, competing securities exchanges, foreign pressures, or competitive off-exchange applications, the fact is that open outcry is being scrutinized and its efficiency and necessity are increasingly being questioned. Those who close their eyes to this truth do the open outcry system a severe disservice.

Indeed, to preserve open outcry, it is imperative to examine the state of our industry in light of current demands on our markets and in the context of those very competitive and technological pressures that attack the present system's viability. We must not only examine these issues, we must be willing to respond to them in a manner that is consistent with the findings. At a minimum, this means we must be ready to accept those aspects of technology as well as those transaction modifications that can be integrated with and applied to open outcry without materially detracting from its inherent values. While this may not by itself guarantee the continued life of open outcry, it will certainly enhance its chances and serve to protect future business flows to our exchange floors.

The recommendation to create P-M-T stemmed from a comprehensive, year-long study undertaken by the CME's Strategic Planning Committee, which is charged with reviewing fundamental industry issues and problems. Not surprisingly, the Committee determined that three critical issues face the futures industry: globalization, automation, and off-exchange expansion. Its recommended solution was a single response embodied in an automated after-hours transaction system.

The marriage of the computer chip to the telephone changed the world from a confederation of autonomous financial markets into one continuous marketplace. No longer is there a distinct division of the three major time zones. No longer are there three separate markets operating independently of external pressures by maintaining their own unique market centers. Today, users of every market come from around the globe because news is distributed instantaneously across all time zones. When such informational flows demand market action, financial managers no longer wait for local markets to open before responding. Rather, they have the capacity to initiate immediate market positions—a capacity that has come to be known as globalization. With globalization, each financial center has become a direct competitor to all others, offering everyone new opportunities and challenges.

During the past several years, exchanges have attempted to meet the globalization challenge by searching for alternative solutions to preserve local business flows and attract business generated on foreign shores. With varying degrees of success, these actions involved either electronic linkages with foreign exchanges or, more recently, extended trading hours. While it is still too early to evaluate fully the long-term effectiveness of these alternatives, neither appear to represent an adequate response to the opportunities and perils of the 24-hour trading day.

Electronic linkage, via a system of Mutual Offset (MOS), was pioneered in 1984 by the CME and the Singapore International Monetary Exchange (SIMEX). It proved that markets in separate time zones can be linked to allow safe access to each other's open interest, thereby giving both markets the advantage of the other's nonregular trading hour business flows. Although successful, the CME/SIMEX experiment and other similar linkages that followed identified certain limitations to their overall effectiveness: that linkage is not useful or successful for every type of financial instrument; that regulatory and legal complications make it uncertain whether electronic linkage can be achieved on a worldwide basis; that competitive considerations between different market centers complicate the implementation of a worldwide linkage system; and that no single link-up can cover the entire 24-hour trading period.

The concept of extended trading is not new. From time to time, all exchanges have restructured and extended their regular trading hours (RTH) to accommodate new business flows. Such past trading extensions have more or less proved successful. However, extensions of RTH beyond the parameters of normal business hours, as was recently instituted by the SIMEX, the Chicago Board of Trade, and the Philadelphia Stock Exchange (with other exchanges planning to follow suit), are far different in scope from RTH extensions in the past. The problems of these new RTH extensions are considerably more severe.

There are the human issues: the ability to attract a sufficient number of capable nighttime market makers, the strains on personnel, the disruption of traditional life patterns. There are the liquidity concerns: Will domestic nighttime business flows be sufficient to maintain a liquid market until the anticipated foreign business is developed? There are the monetary considerations: the cost to member firms in maintaining nighttime trading and back-office facilities until the operations become profitable. On the surface, nevertheless, the night session seems successful; transaction volume has been good and, some say, better than expected. Moreover, these sessions have and will benefit from sporadic surges in volume whenever events occurring after RTH warrant market action.

However, some fundamental concerns about these night sessions remain unanswered:

- Extended night trading, as a response to globalization, addresses only a small portion of the hours of the foreign business day.
- It is highly unlikely that the session can be successfully extended the full 16 hours necessary to cover the other two principal financial time zones.
- The extended night session, at best, can only be applied to selective instruments of trade and will become increasingly more difficult as additional products are attempted.
- It is highly doubtful extended night sessions in the U.S. time zone will dissuade a foreign financial community from instituting its own exchange, in its own time zone, during its own RTH.
- Once a foreign RTH exchange has been successfully established, it will very likely become the dominant center for business from its own locale; it will then act as a

strong magnet for all business flows during its own RTH, thus impeding the growth and purpose of a night market on a distant shore.

Consequently, while it is far too early to be definitive, unless unforeseen events intervene, the extended trading solution of a night market in the United States seems to have limited potential. While, undoubtedly, it will be a window of opportunity for the next several years, ultimately it can only hope to attain a secondary market niche by way of arbitrage and minor business flows.

P-M-T is the Chicago Mercantile Exchange response to the demands of globalization. It will be an after-hours automated transaction system that will utilize the Reuter Dealer Trading System (RDTS). The P-M-T concept combines elements of electronic linkage with those of extended trading and integrates them with the open-outcry system. In effect, it draws the best from the present and marries it to the technology of the future. The ingredients of the new trading system will include all the critical elements of a viable trading environment: the liquidity and open interest of the CME financial markets, representing the comprehensive spectrum of instruments that constitute the CME financial markets as well as selected foreign financial instruments; a communications organization with the largest international network of communications hardware as well as the technological capability to create and conduct an automated transaction system; and the capability, creditworthiness, and established financial integrity of the CME clearing system.

The international implications of P-M-T are self-evident and will be felt throughout the world financial community. It translates into opportunity and cost-efficiency whether you are a banker in Tokyo, a risk manager in London, an investor in any part of the world. P-M-T means that the financial markets of the Chicago Mercantile Exchange—with their operational capabilities, liquidity, and safeguards—are open not just during the regular trading hours of the CME trading floor, but around the clock. Unlike electronic linkage, P-M-T can be applied to every market equally. Its worldwide implementation will be simple when compared with the practical and legal complications of the electronic link-up alternative.

Clearly, P-M-T has universal application and appeal. Since our announcement, we have been approached by members from virtually every center of finance for information about how to participate in the global system we envision. It is well these questions are asked. For it is fully the intention of the Chicago Mercantile Exchange to extend its P-M-T concept to every center of trade and finance.

We intend and will devise methodologies that will accommodate direct access and participation for all communities the world over. It is not our intention to keep P-M-T so closely to ourselves that we exclude participants who can meaningfully contribute to the success of the concept. To the contrary, we have advised all that have come forward that the built-in flexibility of the P-M-T structure will allow for the participation of their community and individual members. We invite all other representatives from world centers of finance to join in this revolutionary concept and help us create a truly universal transaction system.

P-M-T is a bold and comprehensive response to the opportunities resulting from globalization as well as the dangers posed by automation and off-exchange expansion. It represents a global transaction capability whose time has come. When combined with CME's regular trading hours, it can provide the world with its first literal 24-hour trading system.

# The Third Milestone

*It was axiomatic that a trading system that utilized automated electronic capabilities epitomized the ultimate threat for members of the futures industry. It erroneously represented the proverbial Darth Vader who would destroy their coveted open outcry world and eliminate the trading pit in favor of the "black box"—a computer-driven marketplace. But it was equally axiomatic that automation, electronic competence, and technological advancements were inexorable forces that would overwhelm anything that stood in their way. Those who ignored the march of technology were soon banished to the historical scrap heap of failures. In other words, use it or lose it.*

*The foregoing ideological conflict seemed to represent a dilemma of Hobson's choice proportions for many within our industry. It caused many simply to shun the issue, for to contemplate technological automation in the transaction process was suicidal. Still, for some of us, the challenge was inevitable. To bow to the demands of status quo simply because of fear of change was unacceptable. To me, innovation was no idle concept to be admired from afar. Indeed, market innovation was as essential to me as the very oxygen we need to stay alive—it was the critical trait that made us different and empowered us to bring the Chicago Mercantile Exchange to the forefront of financial markets worldwide.*

*Thus, the concept of GLOBEX was born. Because we could not ignore the reality of competitive demands engendered by modern technology, because we realized that without automated electronic competence, our futures contracts would be limited to the regular business hours of the American time-zone, because our market share was threatened by foreign competitors, we chose to meet the challenge with a computer-based electronic after-hours trading system. The trick was to convince our members to embrace this reality.*

*In a referendum held on October 6, 1987, the members of the Chicago Mercantile Exchange voted overwhelmingly in favor of the GLOBEX concept by a vote of 3,939 to 526. The following was the rationale behind our victory.*

---

**Published in the Chicago Mercantile Exchange 1988 Annual Report**

---

Financial futures have occasioned two milestones in their short history. These milestones, both of a revolutionary nature, occurred on the floor of the Chicago Mercantile Exchange. The first milestone was their creation itself. The departure by traditional futures from their century-old agricultural base and entrance into the world of finance dramatically changed their direction and history. By definition, no financial futures history could have ensued without its conceptual inception. It is clear today that the revolutionary concept sponsored by the CME 17 years ago, was destined to change the world of finance and become an indispensable risk management tool the world over. Indeed, the invention of financial futures has been hailed by Merton H. Miller, PhD., Professor of Banking and Finance, University of Chicago, as "the most significant financial innovation of the last 20 years."

Alas, hardly anyone recognized that event as significant back in 1972. Indeed, hardly anyone believed it to be of any consequence at all, and few gave it any chance of success. Pundits and critics mocked the idea, regarding it as no more than a joke or, at best, a quixotic impossible dream. Some simply thought it ludicrous that a "bunch of pork belly crapshooters" would dare to contemplate treading on the hallowed ground of foreign exchange. But succeed we did. The reason? Quite simple! Victor Hugo explained it when he told us that no general is smart enough and no army strong enough to suppress an idea whose time has come.

The second milestone—cash settlement—came nine years later. In 1981, the Merc's Eurodollar contract became the first to settle by way of payment in cash rather than by delivery of the instrument itself. Once financial futures shed the requirement of physical delivery, the curtain was opened to instruments and concepts previously unthinkable. Cash settlement represented the gateway to index products and seemingly limitless potential.

Today, financial futures are poised at the threshold of their third milestone. Not surprisingly, the CME is again leading the way. As was the case in the with the first two instances, the third has generated a good deal of discussion and even controversy. For all the landmarks have a single common denominator; each represents a dramatic departure from status quo. GLOBEX, the third milestone—the automated global transaction system being developed by the CME and Reuters Holdings PLC—represents a move toward automation in the transaction process. It touches the very nerve center of status quo in our industry and has incurred the criticism of those who would oppose any movement toward change in automation or adoption of technological advancements. To them, such reforms advance the black box and hasten the end of open outcry.

The unequivocal truth is that the world of futures is dynamic and continuously evolving. Complacency is the enemy; innovation and change are at the heart of our success. As our markets' applicability extended to new products, new techniques and new users, as our markets became the standard tools for risk management, the changes we engendered were dramatic and revolutionary.

In 1977, I wrote an article on the mechanics of a commodity futures exchange for the *Hofstra University Law Review*. The article concluded that an automated transaction process cannot supplant the trading floor nor the open outcry system. While that assertion was made with respect to a world quite different from today, GLOBEX does not run contrary to this view. GLOBEX is not designed to replace but rather to enhance the present transaction process. Nor did my conclusions of a decade ago intimate that our industry should ever be precluded from experimenting with change. Indeed, we must continually evaluate the state of our industry in light of current demands and competitive pressures on our markets, and in recognition of the effects of scientific and technological changes in the world around us.

There is no doubt that throughout our dramatic metamorphosis and expansion, one thing has remained constant. In the United States, open outcry has been the liquidity engine for our success. This remains the case. The CME, similar to other American exchanges, has a continuing commitment to the preservation of this transaction process. However, the CME also believes that to assume blindly that open outcry is the perfect system for all time is to be lulled into a false sense of security and forgo any opportunities to strengthen or advance our way of doing business. Such a policy would be both foolish and dangerous and could lead to disaster. While we must always respect our heritage, we must never let ourselves be held

back by its limitations. We must recognize the greater truth—
that those who ignore or fear to embrace reality will quickly
become history. Therein, of course, lies the rub.

Historian Barbara Tuchman succinctly told us that "men
will not believe what does not fit in with their plans or suit
their prearrangements." Walter Wriston, the former Chairman
of Citicorp, is more explicit: "When major tides of change
wash over the world," he tells us, "power structures almost inevitably reject the notion that the world really is changing,
and they cling to their old beliefs."

The change that has washed over our end of the world is
the telecommunications revolution: Sophisticated satellites,
microchips and fiber optics changed the world from a confederation of autonomous financial markets into one continuous
marketplace. There is no longer a distinct division of the three
major time zones—Europe, North America, and the Far East.
No longer are there three separate markets operating independently of external pressures, maintaining their own unique
market centers, product lines, trading hours, and clientele. Today, news is distributed instantaneously across all time zones
and when such informational flows dictate market action, financial managers no longer wait for local markets to open before responding. The old order offered our financial markets a
geographical security blanket that kept them relatively free
from the dangers of international competition. That order is
history. Globalization, caused by the telecommunications revolution, has ushered in the information standard. Every financial market is now a potential competitor of the other.
GLOBEX recognizes and embodies that change. GLOBEX
symbolizes the technological revolution that has engulfed
every walk of life—and none more than ours. A global electronic "after-hours" trading system embraces reality and
shakes the very foundations of complacency about us.

Two additional observations. First, successful open outcry
is a predominantly *American* phenomenon. With few exceptions, other world centers have not long had this tradition nor
much success with its application. As a consequence, many
non-U.S. centers have, from the outset, opted for either a partially or totally automated execution system. Second, while the
futures market pits remain the single most important source
of present-day liquidity, they are no longer the only source.

Today, there exists an army of upstairs traders whose trading methodology is not dependent on eye-to-eye pit contact, but rather on two technological instruments: the computer screen and the telephone. Using these instruments, upstairs traders buy and sell in rapid fashion throughout the day—similar to pit traders—and provide a continuous flow of orders to the market. These traders represent a liquidity source virtually nonexistent a decade ago. While they will not, in the near future, replace the liquidity source of pit traders, there is no denying they represent a growing universe with no visible limitation on its expansion. GLOBEX should present no problem for the upstairs trader.

The CME perceived the globalization reality when it instituted the mutual offset link with the Singapore International Monetary Exchange (SIMEX) in 1984. It was the first successful attempt to link the trading capability of two different markets in two different time zones. It served as a model for others to follow and took the world one step closer to a global market. This experiment provided the CME with invaluable expertise and living proof that world markets can be safely and efficiently linked. It also led us to the next logical evolutionary step.

GLOBEX combines elements of electronic linkage and integrates them with the open outcry system. In effect, it draws the best from the present and marries it to the technology of the future. It is critical to understand this point. We did not set out to re-create open outcry. We sought a way to secure it—a way to marry it to the technology of the future, a way to extend its market day—but not to re-create it. While we recognized the value of open outcry and the liquidity it generates, we sought to do better. We recognized the inadequacies of open outcry—its inherent unfairness. We knew that an automated system provided us an opportunity to do away with those inadequacies, an opportunity to make the system more fair.

At the same time, GLOBEX represents a giant step toward unification of the separate world financial centers. GLOBEX will offer the world a transaction capability that is as advanced as the imagination will allow and as far-reaching as the future itself; a transaction capability that will allow the products of all the world's great exchanges on the same system—on the same screen—to be utilized by everyone around the clock. The very words are breathtaking.

We envisioned a global, interactive, shared system for futures and options: a system whereby no partner exchange will relinquish its autonomy; whereby every partner exchange will continue to clear and guarantee its own products; and whereby the rules of the respective governments will continue in force, as before. Yes, we envisioned a transaction structure for the ultimate unification of the world's separate marketplaces. That is the essence of GLOBEX.

GLOBEX is a major departure from status quo. Consequently, it has drawn heavy criticism from those who fear change, as well as those who recognize the competitive edge the new system will offer our institution. Those are some of the very reasons the CME conceived GLOBEX. Of course, there are no guarantees. There are many hurdles to overcome, some are of a technological nature, some are in the government domain. Unfortunately, our government officials often fail to appreciate the prophet in their own backyard. All too often, American innovations are ignored or repressed by virtue of shallow reasoning or bureaucratic red tape. Such examples are too numerous to mention. We trust, however, that will not be the case with GLOBEX. We trust U.S. federal officials will recognize that GLOBEX is the trailblazer, the model for all to follow, and that it is a product of American ingenuity to be assisted and encouraged.

Again Wriston says it well. "If today's leaders in government and business fail to recognize that the world has changed" because what they see, in Tuchman's words, 'does not fit in with their plans or suit their prearrangements' they will follow into oblivion a long list of leaders who have made similar mistakes. Those who can understand and master change will be tomorrow's winners.

The first two milestones the CME engendered offer unequivocal proof that our institution does understand change; that we are both willing and capable of embracing the realities it represents. The third milestone carries forward this tradition in a grand fashion.

# GLOBEX and World Markets

*In 1981, the Chicago Mercantile Exchange was the first U.S. futures exchange to recognize the potential of European business flows by opening a full-time office in London and instituting an annual financial futures seminar for the European community. In 1987, the CME adopted a similar approach with respect to Japan.*

*Our first Tokyo financial symposium in 1989 was an enormous success and the event has become an important annual component in our effort to establish a strong futures presence in Japan. But the subsequent advent of the common goals era between the CME and the CBOT changed the competitive policy between our two institutions as it related to international presence and programs. In 1991, the CME and the CBOT merged their respective London and Tokyo offices and combined their separate programs for those two centers of finance. Today, by virtue of this change, the London and Tokyo symposiums are a combined undertaking of the CME and CBOT and a critical signal of our combined strength.*

*The theme of this first CME event and my address is as topical today as it was at that time. The issues pertaining to globalization, protectionism, the trade deficit, the role of futures, and GLOBEX are still the agenda of the day.*

---

Presented at the Chicago Mercantile Exchange First Annual Tokyo Financial Symposium, Tokyo, Japan, May 30, 1989

---

Today's occasion is noteworthy, not merely because it symbolizes Japan's emergence as an international financial center, nor simply because it underscores that the CME is a world institution. This symposium in Tokyo, as well as the similar seminars the CME conducts annually in London are stark testimony to two inescapable truths: First, financial futures and options represent indispensable risk management tools in today's business environment; and second, the world is increasingly becoming smaller.

Financial futures and options represent unique and indispensable risk management tools in today's business environment. The proof can be found in a few simple statistics. Since their introduction in 1972 at the CME's International Monetary Market (IMM), financial futures experienced a transaction explosion that rivals any new product on the business scene. Futures and options volume in the United States reached a total of 225 million contracts last year, compared with only 3.9 million in 1978. This represents a growth factor of nearly 6000% for the past 10 years alone. The dollar volume that these transactions represent is in the trillions of dollars.

Not only has the success of these markets been evidenced in transaction growth but the markets themselves have multiplied with offspring all over the world, look-alike structures that attempt to replicate the capabilities once found only in Chicago and New York. In the past 5 years, new financial futures exchanges have opened or been announced in London, Paris, Hong Kong, Sydney, Toronto, Singapore, New Zealand, Brazil, Osaka, Zurich, Dublin, Frankfurt, and, next month, here in Tokyo. Little wonder that Merton H. Miller, PhD, Professor of Banking and Finance, University of Chicago, named financial futures as "the most significant financial innovation of the last 20 years."

The implication of the second truth—that the world is increasingly becoming smaller—is equally simple to prove. What were once dozens of scattered, national economies are inexorably becoming linked into one interrelated, interdependent world economy. The world's financial markets are quickly following pace. In many instances, they are in fact setting the pace, demonstrating the ease with which capital can follow the sun, seeking out investment opportunities regardless of national boundaries or time zones. Indeed, recent failed attempts by central bankers to dictate the price of the dollar is clear evidence of the overwhelming power of today's marketplace in determining values on the basis of free market forces alone.

The evidence of the emerging economic global village is all around us. What were once merely domestic economic problems are now issues we all must face: The U.S. budget and trade deficits are not just American problems, they impact every nation that deals with the United States; the Third World debt crisis is not just a burden to be borne by the underdeveloped nations of the world but a cross we must all help carry; the coming of Europe 1992 is not just a national or even a pan-European issue but is an event that will affect us all; the new economic might of Japan and the fast-track economies of its Pacific neighbors are not just national or even regional matters, but rather events of international significance.

In times of crisis, there are no longer national markets, there is only one world market responding to world events. For example, when a U.S. unemployment or trade deficit report is released, do European or Japanese traders patiently wait until their markets open the next day to react? When the Bundesbank or Bank of Japan acts to change rates, do U.S. traders merely yawn and go back to sleep, content to wait until morning to act? Of course not. In a world where minutes of hesitation can translate into millions in losses, traders simply cannot afford to wait. Anyone who doubts that fact need only look at two market-shattering events of the past decade for proof.

Recall what happened in 1984 when rumors began circulating of troubles at a major American bank. Japanese institutions did not wait for American banking hours before they decided to withdraw billions of dollars from Continental Illinois National Bank. Nor did European account holders. By the time Continental opened its Chicago headquarters that fateful spring day, it was already in the eye of a storm that had begun thousands of miles away.

And who can forget October 1987? What occurred then was not merely an American stock market crash—it was a global pullback of massive proportions. Portfolio managers, who had become increasingly international in outlook, found there were no safe havens when economic events conspired to unnerve the investing public.

What issues will preoccupy the world of tomorrow? What events will create the risk and opportunity for financial managers of the coming decade? That is difficult to predict. We can be certain only that there will be surprises. Some things, however, are quite evident. I touched on them earlier.

Without doubt, the central economic problem that will haunt us in coming years is the massive amounts of debt pummeling nearly every sector of the world's economy. Neither Japan nor the rest of the world's major powers can afford to ignore this international dilemma.

In the United States, the twin deficits—trade and budget—continue to vex policy makers and cast ominous world shadows. The current budget compromise represents but a fancy accounting ballet that simply sidesteps the difficult issues involved. *Time* magazine, alluding to an old country-western tune, calls the agreement "a Sixteen Tons budget that, will just leave the government 'another year older and deeper in debt.'"

The official estimate for the 1990 deficit under the compromise is $108 billion. But seasoned Washington hands expect the actual figure to approach $130 billion. Already Congress has discussed a $50 billion thrift bailout plan that would not include that sum in the deficit calculations. Such unrealistic approaches to the federal budget process will do nothing to calm world markets not to speak of solving the predicament. Consequently, worries have already surfaced regarding the fiscal 1991 picture. Gramm-Rudman deficit targets will not be met that year without tax increases, many argue. But tax increases of any appreciable size could spell an abrupt end to the long economic expansion of the United States. And if even a recession should be underway by 1991, tax increases could deepen and broaden its reach.

And let us not forget the other U.S. deficit, the trade deficit. The greatest danger the trade deficit presents is not only its ultimate impact on interest rates or the dollar but the impetus it gives to the advocates of protectionism. Seemingly rational people in the United States, Japan, and Europe insist on advocating measures that look painfully similar to trade barriers of a previous era. The consequences of trade wars of the 1930s are a sufficient reminder of the financial havoc such a trend can provoke. While tariffs are no longer the prime tool of the protectionist, the import quotas, market restrictions and regulations disguised as standards but really aimed at restricting foreign competition are now the weapons of the modern-day protectionist arsenal.

*Fortune,* in a February 27, 1989, article, noted that nontariff trade barriers have been multiplying since the 1970s. In a February 6, 1989, article, *Forbes* warned that the world faces the unpleasant possibility of becoming divided into three protectionist spheres—Europe, the Pacific Rim, and the Americas. It notes that during the past eight years, the level of total U.S. imports subject to quotas or official restraint has risen from 12 percent to 23 percent. Recent U.S. actions under the so-called "Super 301" against Japan, India, and Brazil serve as ominous signals of this dangerous trend.

The coming unification of Europe in 1992 may also echo protectionist tones. The Common Market's own projections note that trade inside Europe will grow 10 percent over the next 6 to 10 years while imports from nonmembers will rise a mere 2 to 3 percent.

There is, unfortunately, no scarcity of potential upheavals on the financial scene. How will world markets respond to these pervasive problems or the surprises that are bound to occur? No one knows. Still, wherever and whenever economic uncertainty exists, there is opportunity and risk. And, the need to hedge against that uncertainty is ever present.

To its credit, the futures industry, in general, and the CME, in particular, were farsighted in anticipating the linkage of national economies. The CME was the first U.S. exchange to anticipate the end of fixed exchange rates when it launched currency futures in 1972. With its Eurodollar contract, the CME was the first exchange to introduce cash-settled futures to expand the concept of risk management beyond the world of physical commodities. We were also the first to create a linkage with a distant market, Singapore, in a different time zone. The CME then became the most successful exchange in creating stock index contracts to track the flow of national stock markets.

Then, on September 2, 1987, the CME was the first exchange to conceptualize an after-hours electronic transaction system. GLOBEX, the CME's electronic 24-hour transaction system developed in conjunction with Reuters Holdings PLC, symbolizes the technological revolution that has engulfed every walk of life—none more than ours.

When GLOBEX begins operation, it will both reflect and facilitate the new globalization of capital and markets. Although it may take time before GLOBEX is accepted, with it, financial managers will be in a position to react instantly to events that buffet the world economy no matter what time of day it happens to be in that corner of the world. By providing financial managers the ability to initiate market decisions instantly—rather than wait the hours or sometimes days it may take for their local markets to open—GLOBEX will provide the ideal hedging tool for the opportunities and risks of the changing economic times ahead. While GLOBEX embodies current realities, it did not cause them or hasten their occurrence.

In 1972, the IMM did not precipitate the financial upheaval of the coming decade. It did, however, benefit from being in place at the right time. Its success was explained by Victor Hugo when he told us that no general is smart enough and no army strong enough to suppress an idea whose time has come.

Similarly in 1989, GLOBEX will not cause globalization, but its launch acknowledges that world financial markets are already linked. Globalization of markets is a trend that is as inexorable as it is unmistakable. GLOBEX simply recognizes that reality and embraces state-of-the-art technological capabilities to provide the international business community with the means to respond effectively and quickly to the financial changes that are bound to occur.

Of equal importance, GLOBEX envisioned the ability to link a number of world markets electronically. This single unified system recognizes that the days of isolated markets that respond only to local economic events have passed. To survive in the 1990s and beyond, risk managers will need to react quickly, efficiently, and intelligently to developments around the globe.

GLOBEX will meet that need. It will offer the world a transaction capability that is as advanced as the imagination will allow and as far-reaching as the future itself. This transaction capability will allow the products of all the world's great exchanges on the same system, on the same screen. GLOBEX will provide a 24-hour system. It will present regional markets to an international arena; it will allow market applications, strategies, and experimentation with a product mix never before possible; it will represent the ultimate unification of the world's separate marketplaces.

And today I can affirm the historic announcement made on the eve of our departure from Chicago. On May 26, 1989, the Chicago Mercantile Exchange and the Chicago Board of Trade (CBOT) agreed to begin discussions aimed at unifying our respective electronic systems. The successful culmination of these discussions will result in a single, unified, after-hours trading system that combines the unique features of CME's GLOBEX with those of the CBOT's Aurora. This momentous step is the result of the undeniable logic dictating that a joint electronic system between our two exchanges will immeasurably benefit all our members, all our member firms, and the futures industry worldwide.

# The Impossible Dream:
# Free Markets in Moscow

*The most significant part of this address is where it was delivered. Had anyone suggested a year earlier that I would be standing in an open forum in the Soviet Union delivering a speech about market-driven economic order, I would have counseled that the person seek medical assistance.*

*The idea that representatives from the Chicago Mercantile Exchange and the Chicago Board of Trade—the embodiment of free markets—would be invited in 1990 as honored guests of the city of Moscow and the Federation of Russia, was so unbelievable as to be nothing short of science fiction.*

*The words I used were substantially the same as those I had used countless times before to countless audiences—but always in the free world. For the first time in modern history, or perhaps even the first time in history, someone was flagrantly preaching to a very large audience in Moscow—in the shadows of the Kremlin—that the only Messiah for the Soviet people was capitalism.*

**Presented at the Seminar on Futures & Options, USSR
Council of Ministers on Food and Procurement, Moscow,
USSR, November 1, 1990**

Two months ago, on August 22, 1990, the Chicago Mercantile Exchange (CME) announced that it would consider an eventual futures contract on the Russian ruble. This represents a new and dramatic chapter in the revolutionary history that began some 18 years before. Indeed, the birth of the CME's International Monetary Market (IMM) on June 16, 1972, is symbolic of the power of an idea whose time had come—an idea that has caused fundamental changes in the financial landscape of the world, and one that is intertwined with events in the Soviet Union and every corner of the globe. An idea that recognized that the structural changes in financial markets as a consequence of the telecommunications revolution would make traditional market concepts obsolete; that they would disintegrate market barriers resulting from geographical borders; and that they would demand bold and new financial risk management tools.

That financial futures have become an integral component of the world's financial markets is self evident. Futures markets are symbolic of the economic order that demonstrated its supremacy over an economic system whose structure and function were dependent on central economic controls. Indeed, there are few better examples of price discovery as a consequence of the free forces of supply and demand than the markets of futures and options. Their indispensability to the structure of a market-driven economy was quickly recognized by none other than President Mikhail Gorbachev as he called for the immediate creation of securities and commodity exchanges in the Soviet Union. We applaud this sentiment as well as the recently announced revolutionary steps of your government in the difficult journey toward economic reform.

Not only do futures markets exemplify the infrastructure of a market-driven economy, but the very same technological advancements that gave rise to their birth are the same that made *perestroika* inevitable. Indeed, the telecommunications revolution of the past several decades—or what former Citicorp Chairman Walter Wriston called the information revolution—made it impossible to continue the charade and hide the uncompromising truth that an economy dependent on government edict was doomed to failure. Modern communications techniques, coupled with massive media penetration in disregard of national boundaries, offered a stark, unyielding comparison of economic systems. As journalist Mike O'Neil predicted years before the 1989 historic events in Eastern Europe: The consequences of the new telecommunications technology "is hurrying the collapse of old order, accelerating the velocity of social and political change, creating informed and politically active publics, and inciting conflict by publicizing the differences between people and nations."

As it has throughout the history of humankind, technology again has dictated fundamental change in the world's social structure and reshaped both the political and economic landscape of our planet. Its immediate impact on the populations of Russia and Eastern Europe is now a historical reality. And Messrs. Gorbachev and Yeltsin both understand the same fact as Federal Reserve Board Chairman Alan Greenspan, namely: The acceptance and growth of financial futures is the consequence of a need in our volatile world for a cost-efficient market mechanism with which to discover price and hedge financial risk.

However, if anyone in the Soviet Union believes that financial futures can instantly reform your current economic status into a vibrant, successful market-driven economy; if anyone in the Soviet Union or reemerging nations of Eastern Europe believes that creating securities or futures exchanges within your respective borders will instantly transform stagnant economic conditions into prosperous standards of living for all— allow me to quickly persuade you that this is not the case. Indeed, nothing can be further from the truth. Nothing can serve to impede your journey to economic success more than the mistaken belief that there is an instant solution: For one does not exist. The road to economic success is painful, long, extremely difficult, and laden with pitfalls that can delay the process, divert you in a wrong direction, or lead you toward a dead end. To be perfectly blunt, conditions here will get much worse before they get better: But there is no other choice.

While they have their differences, Messrs. Gorbachev and Yeltsin both recognize the efficiency of a market economy and that the prerequisites to the effective functioning of the market include the right of private property, the shift from government to private ownership of assets, the restructuring of the banking system to create a central bank independent of the government, the need for commercial banks to be independent of the central bank, and the need to create a single convertible national currency. These are the fundamentals upon which the road to a free market economy can successfully be built. And while none of these can be accomplished overnight, there will be stages. For instance, the recent announcement that four exchange rates will soon be established for the ruble are encouraging, if they will in fact take place.

However you achieve it, through slow stages or through a more painful rapid mechanism, ultimately there must be a single, fully convertible rate for the ruble—one that can meet the fair market test on the international arena—for only then can the ruble be convertible.

Your current plan recognizes the critical Soviet need for foreign investment capital. To rely solely on foreign government loans to bolster your economy would be a serious mistake; indeed because the United States today finds its own economic house in disorder, our flow of government funds to the Soviet Union will be limited. Consequently, it is imperative that foreign private sector capital be sought. To accomplish this result, it is mandatory that current restrictions on exporting profits be dropped and that foreign investors know how to calculate their rate of return. Therefore, the announced ruble plans are essential elements in the journey to a market economy, and while such moves are fraught with the danger of enormous inflation and pain for the average citizen, they are steps that cannot be avoided. In this respect, the Chicago Mercantile Exchange will carefully monitor the results as we attempt to determine at which point we can assist the process by instituting a viable futures market in the ruble.

I am heartened by conversations with Sergei Stankevitch, Gennady Poleshuk, and Vladimir Paplauski and have a great deal of faith in their intellect. I respect their basic understanding of futures markets. The statements of your Mayor, the Honorable Gavriil Popov, are refreshing and encouraging for he is not only an advocate of a market economy, but is providing the infrastructure to encourage its implementation. The Moscow Commodity Exchange is but one significant example of his efforts. And while the Moscow Commodity Exchange may not, at its inception, look or trade in the same manner as do the Chicago markets—indeed its wares of physical commodities are very different from our financial indexes and intangibles—nevertheless, this exchange represents the all-important beginning. I salute you for this first milestone.

While the world is cognizant of the 500 Day Plan approved on September 11, 1990, by the Parliament of the Russian Republic, we are also aware of the philosophical differences that exist regarding the rapidity by which the intended reforms can occur—issues such as decollectivizing farming and the restructuring of farm land from state to private ownership, and issues such as tax collection and central authority. These issues represent difficult internal Soviet political and economic questions. My opinion—as an external observer—is that the sooner you begin the reform process the better because no matter how swiftly you intend the necessary reforms to be implemented, they will take longer. There is little doubt you will encounter major economic disruptions as well as serious unexpected difficulties. These may produce serious civil pressures and cause segments of the Soviet public to call for a return of the old order. But, such reactions would be foolhardy; the old order was without hope and brought about today's conditions. More than one third of your population earns less than 100 rubles per month and the average monthly wage is only 250 rubles—the price of 10 packs of American cigarettes on the black market.

Clearly, the old order is no answer. Your only hope is that from the strife of the coming years will emerge a new Soviet world based on the precepts of individual freedom and a market-driven economy. And although your task will be arduous and will take many years, you have the resources to be successful. Your first and foremost resource is the people of Russia. For a nation that gave birth to Tolstoy, Dostoyevsky, Pushkin, Gorky, Borodin, and Tchaikovsky is a nation of an immensely rich and resourceful culture, one that has the depth of talent to lead toward economic victory. Indeed, the Soviet Union has endured much misery in its history, but it has persevered. And it can persevere through this as well.

Certain of Russia's most admirable characteristics will need to be redirected in the process of moving toward a market economy. Your spiritual soul will need to develop a somewhat materialistic counterpart. As author Hedrick Smith recently wrote: "*Perestroika* has to happen in the mind for it to work. People's outlooks have to change and that happens as society changes. It is a push-pull, gradual process. It cannot be decreed."

At this juncture, however, it is critical for your leaders to concede their differences, compromise divergent points of view, build on their basic agreements, and assist your nation in achieving common objectives. Indeed, the greatest disservice to the Soviet Union at this time is for divisiveness among the leadership to detract you from the goal you seek. Therefore, urge your leadership to embrace common goals and join hands to lead your nation on the road to a market economy.

Along the way, you will need to build futures and options markets, for these markets are without substitute in providing a mechanism for price discovery. They are an open forum where market participants—buyers or sellers, producers or consumers, investors or speculators—have the ability to direct their price opinion on the value of the product to the auction process. Through this process, a fair price for the product is discovered. And for that moment in time, until the next set of variables changes the price, value is established. No other mechanism can boast a more certain avenue at determining value than the markets of futures and options.

Today's established futures and options markets offer the widest array of agricultural and financial instruments in virtually every center of finance—from beans to bonds, from cattle to crude, from stocks to silver, from gilt to gold, from euros to yen, from coffee to the CPI. These markets offer a measure of liquidity not available elsewhere; a cost-efficiency of incomparable narrow bid/ask spreads; an ability to swiftly institute a variety of strategies, programs, or fine-tuning techniques; the ability to cost-effectively adjust portfolio exposure; a flexibility to choose the most fairly priced alternative instrument at any time; a facility to preserve credit lines within a system offering the highest degree of creditworthiness; a fluency to access all markets on a global basis; a speed and certainty of execution difficult to duplicate; and soon, market coverage on a 24-hour basis. These aspects of futures and options—their price discovery apparatus, their hedging ability, and their profit potential—have made these instruments integral to the infrastructure of global finance and indispensable to a market-driven economy.

Finally, GLOBEX, the newest addition to the revolution sponsored in Chicago in 1972, will again revolutionize the markets of the world. GLOBEX is an electronic trading system currently being developed between the Chicago Mercantile Exchange, the Chicago Board of Trade, and Reuters Holdings PLC—the world's largest international market telecommunications entity. When GLOBEX becomes functional, it will allow all our American futures and options products to be traded worldwide on a 24-hour basis. It will also allow all the major futures markets to participate with their unique product lines. Indeed, the MATIF, the Paris-based futures exchange that is today number one in Europe, is already a partner to this system. Ultimately, GLOBEX will be the central trading system for all the world's futures and options markets. And in the future when the Soviet Union is well along in its free market journey, the Moscow Commodity Exchange may also become a proud member of the GLOBEX family of world futures exchanges.

Until that day, allow me to congratulate you on the momentous step you have taken in opening the doors to the Moscow Commodity Exchange. On behalf of all the members of the Chicago Mercantile Exchange, best wishes. We stand ready to assist you in every way possible.

# Free Market Victory

*At the end of October 1990, a group of senior officials from the CME and CBOT visited Moscow at the behest of the Soviet government in order to sign a commodity market cooperation agreement. While there, we had a firsthand opportunity to witness and assess the depth of the devastation that 70 years of Communist central planning had perpetrated on this nation and its people.*

*From Moscow, I traveled to London to attend the CME's annual International Finance Symposium and was provided a most appropriate opportunity to give a comprehensive report. As is indicative from my rhetoric, I was struck by the extent of the havoc Communist rule had perpetrated on the Soviet economy and the bleak prospects for its reconstruction.*

*At the time, my grave assessment was rather unusual since there was little common knowledge of the true abysmal economic condition of the Soviet Union. My report carried two central themes: the collapse of Communist rule was a clear victory for a market-driven economic order; and the problems faced by the Soviet Union were such that it might take a full generation to cure.*

**Presented at the Sixth Annual International Finance Symposium, London, England, November 8, 1990**

Wrote Victor Hugo, "*An invasion of armies can be resisted, but not an idea whose time has come.*" Certainly history has provided us with many examples to prove this wisdom, but none better than what we have witnessed in recent days.

Clearly, the inexorable idea of freedom for people as well as for markets was an idea more powerful than all the armies behind the Iron Curtain or all the generals the Kremlin possessed. It has obliterated the once dreaded Berlin Wall and allowed the people of the Soviet Union, indeed the people of all of Eastern Europe, to rise and throw off the shackles of tyranny and the chains of a centrally dictated economy. When at last the glorious idea that freedom must dictate the basic structure of human endeavor could no longer be suppressed, when at last the dam burst open, it happened with such ferocity and with such stunning speed, that no general nor army would have dared to stand in its way. And so, for the Soviet Union and Eastern Europe, it is a brave new world: a world from which more statues of Lenin vanish each day (including from City Hall in Moscow); a world in which the truth about empty stores, long lines, rotting wheat and potatoes, frustrated and desperate people, and collapsing roads and buildings can no longer be hidden nor tolerated.

Said U.S. Federal Reserve Board Chairman Alan Greenspan: "It is almost as if a great economic experiment had been undertaken some 70 years ago. The world was divided into two parts. In one part, there would be a market-driven economic order, and on the other, a centrally planned economic system. Today we can compare the results."

And now, President Gorbachev, as a means of breathing life into his moribund economy has abandoned the bankrupt Communist order and explicitly embraced the idea of a market-driven economy inclusive of futures markets. "We must get down to creating a full-blooded domestic market," he told the Soviet Congress of the Peoples Deputies last spring. ". . . Price, supply and marketing reforms, changes in the way state orders are placed, and steps to create first commodity and then stock exchanges will become necessary in this respect."

What Mr. Gorbachev knows is that markets—particularly those of futures—are in their essence voting booths. The participants therein, in continually buying and selling contracts are in fact expressing their informed opinions as to the future price of some underlying commodity, be it a pork belly or an index of stocks. This invaluable price discovery mechanism in turn aids producers, processors, investors, and a host of other economic players in determining where and how to allocate resources; that is, what to plant, how much to produce, and where to invest. As a consequence of futures markets, hedging and price projection have aided national economies in leveling the extreme peaks of overproduction and extreme valleys of undersupply—precisely the mechanisms that are so lacking and desperately needed in the Soviet Union. And Mr. Gorbachev also knows that the same attributes that served agriculture were later transformed to serve finance when the Chicago Mercantile Exchange launched the IMM in 1972 and began trading futures contracts on foreign currency.

From this revolutionary concept stemmed a host of financial futures instruments that included government securities, bonds, Eurodollars, and finally stock index futures. The success of these markets propelled the futures and options industry to unparalleled greatness. In the 1980s alone, U.S. volume in futures and options skyrocketed from 76 million transactions in 1979 to a record 323 million in 1989. And our success became a model for the world, resulting in non-U.S. futures and options volume growth from virtually zero in 1985 to 180 million contracts in 1989. Some 30 exchanges are now situated in virtually every world financial center and now trade financial futures and options. The London International Financial Futures Exchange (LIFFE) established in 1982 was the first. Next came the MATIF (*Marché à Térme International de France*), founded in 1986.

However, while futures markets are an essential component of a market-driven economic order, they are not magic. The leaders of the Soviet Union have the mistaken impression that a magic wand can wipe out the sins of Stalin and all those who followed for so many decades and instantly grant them prosperity; that they need only establish some securities and futures exchanges and declare themselves in favor of a market-driven order and it will happen. The problems and troubles are much deeper than most of us in the West realize.

Several days ago, we (officials of the Chicago Mercantile Exchange and the Chicago Board of Trade) returned from Moscow where we signed a cooperation agreement with the City of Moscow, the Moscow Commodities Exchange, and the Federation of Russia to assist them in the process of creating a commodity exchange. While there, I had a firsthand opportunity to witness and assess the depth of the devastation perpetrated by 70 years of Communist rule. To say the country is bankrupt is to misconstrue the actual desperation of the situation. Indeed, their economy has achieved a new meaning for the word *bleak*, and the problem may be generational. The Russian public has been inculcated to totally disbelieve everything the government tells them, to distrust all public officials and institutions, to expect corruption and live by its rule, to hoard, to steal in order to survive, to disrespect laws, to expect pain, suffering, hunger, depressed living conditions, and even inhumanity. As a consequence, the Russian people have lost what in the West is known as the work ethic. In the Soviet Union there is a saying that explains it well: "They pretend to pay us, and we pretend to work." Malaise is now a national trait. "If we in America are dominated by the workaholic," says Hedrick Smith, the bureau chief of the *New York Times* and well-known authority on the Soviet Union, "then the Soviet Union is mired in hard-to-motivate Type Bs."

In the Soviet Union, it all depends on who you are. There is nothing for the masses and everything for the privileged. Indeed, the country has been bled dry in favor of armaments and space programs with nothing remaining for the people. My guide confided that "Moscow is just like New York. In New York you can get anything for dollars. In Moscow, too."

Cynicism underlies the entire Russian infrastructure. Cheating and fakery are an accepted way of life. Little else is understood. You do as little as possible, one observer explained to me. Many workers, he said, come to work in order to sleep. The same attitude pervades at the highest levels. Managers and local party officials constantly deceive higher-ups. In addition, decades of central planning and dependence on the state have obliterated most incentives in the average Russian. He is averse to risk and very conservative. If the average worker had a choice between the free market and a guaranteed salary, he is apt to choose the guarantee. Moreover, most citizens are envious of success, no matter how it is attained. There is something wrong with "making it," with being better off, and with achieving a better standard of living than the next fellow.

Decades of Leninist indoctrination do not easily dissipate. For the great masses of Soviet people, capitalism is still a dirty word. Millions of people distrust the market and fear being outsmarted by sharpies. They still feel a profit motive is immoral. Explains Mr. Smith, "In debates at the Supreme Soviet, the most passionate arguments involve accusations that the free market will enable speculators to get rich by exploiting the working class."

"*Perestroika,*" says television commentator, Vladimir Pozner, "has to happen in the mind for it to work. People's outlooks have to change, and that happens as society changes." That will not come easy. A former *New York Times* correspondent summed it up succinctly, "In America, it is a sin to be a loser, but if there is one sin in the Soviet Union, it is being a winner." Indeed, there is a psychological intolerance toward those who make more money, no matter how honestly they earn it.

It is bound to be a painfully slow process. It cannot be decreed and no institutional market—not even one blessed by the Russian Pope as was the Moscow Commodities Exchange—will be the magic answer. And conditions will get much worse before they get better. By government estimates, roughly 3 million people were thrown out of work from 1985 to 1989, and approximately 15 million more jobs will be eliminated during the balance of this decade. More than 40 million citizens work in jobs at substandard income levels, even by Russian standards. Shops are empty, there is even a lack of bread. Prices at private farmers' markets—the only places where food in quantity exists—have already increased 25 percent in the first nine months of this year. Spiraling inflation is inevitable, with the government itself hiking the price it pays for meat and other agricultural products by about 50 percent since October 1. And retail prices, it is estimated by Grigori Yavlisky, the Yeltsin advisor, could shoot up by 400 percent overnight.

There may be hunger and even famine in some parts of Russia. And there will be civil unrest. Indeed, many of the Republics wish to secede and that may certainly occur. No one can with certainty predict the outcome of the current revolution now taking place behind what Churchill once called the Iron Curtain. According to the report by the Organization for Economic Cooperation and Development, not only have the credit ratings of all East European countries been downgraded by the world private markets during the past year as the risks inherent in the transition from centrally planned economic systems to market economies becomes evident, but the Soviet Union can probably no longer be viewed as an entity for investment opportunity, rather the investor must look to the separate republics.

My purpose in recounting the difficulties that lie ahead for the people of the Soviet Union is to prepare for the possibility that suddenly one day you may hear some in the Soviet Union say they want to return to the good old days of Communist rule; that it was better than this. It may indeed have been. But that is foolish and foolhardy since it was the old order that brought about this desperate result. The old order was without hope and could only get worse. Thus, while the journey to a market economy will be painful and long, at least they have taken that first step and at least there is certainty of a successful result at the ultimate goal.

If this then represents the worst of times for the Soviet Union, by any comparison the rest of the world is living in nearly the best of times. New ideas—ones that no one can stop—continue to motivate those of us who live in the other part of the world where the experiment of Adam Smith, Milton Friedman, and Alan Greenspan has proved so successful.

Technology, as it has throughout the history of mankind, is again dictating fundamental change in our social structure, reshaping both the political and economic landscape. Satellites capable of beaming news instantaneously, powerful computers that slide into briefcases with room to spare, and fiber optic cables that span both the Atlantic and Pacific oceans have changed the world for all time. Not to mention the Paris–London tunnel!

Imagine the difference in our two worlds. There I was in the Kremlin, with Russia's second most important official, trying to place a telephone call to the CME for the opening of the market. This was not possible—not from the hotel, not from the street, not from a briefcase, not even from the Kremlin itself!

Yes, there are two worlds. And the task from our part of the world is to adapt the futures trading idea to this new technologically sophisticated and globalized world. Thus we developed GLOBEX, an automated, electronic trading system capable of operating around the clock. Although, the implementation of this system is still in the future, surely one of its most significant achievements has already occurred. Recently the Chicago Mercantile Exchange (CME) and the Chicago Board of Trade (CBOT) agreed to unify the CME's GLOBEX with the CBOT's Aurora electronic systems. While most industry observers bet against this possibility and said it would never happen, they underestimated the power of an idea whose time had come. The successful discussions with the CBOT culminated in an overwhelming referendum vote by the CBOT membership in favor of GLOBEX. The resulting single, unified, after-hours trading system is bound to become the standard for the world. This momentous occurrence is the result of the undeniable logic that a joint electronic system between our two exchanges will immeasurably benefit all our members, member firms, and the futures industry worldwide. Indeed, when GLOBEX becomes operational, with the combined volume of the CME, the CBOT, and MATIF, it will automatically include over 50% of the world's financial futures and options business.

Most importantly, however, we invite all the major exchanges to join us in this endeavor. It is of particular importance for this community that LIFFE become part of GLOBEX, since London is and will always remain a central hub of world finance. Ultimately, we envision linkage with all the other world markets—be they in Japan, Germany, Australia, Singapore, or elsewhere. At the final seminar in Moscow, we were confronted by a delegation from a nearby province that demanded we include them in GLOBEX because, they boasted, they already have a computer.

Of course, there really are not two worlds. We live on one planet in a technically driven world, where physical travel is swift and informational flows are at lightening speed, so that no nation is truly independent of the other. Indeed, we are all intertwined and interconnected—even with the fate of the Russian and East European people. What happens there will certainly impact all of us. Such is the state of the world at the advent of global trading. It is a world in which risks are radically more complicated and where capital flows at the blink of an eyelash and the stroke of a key. Traders today must weigh difficult variables and then adjust positions in reaction to events—with so much uncertainty, so much strife, so much at stake: change, volatile financial markets, *perestroika*, Kuwaiti invasions, budget deficits, inflation worries, record world debt burdens, the cost of German unification, third world problems, banking illiquidities, a united Europe in the making, a single European monetary unit, and on and on.

And that world—the world of interdependence, the world of formidable risks and conversely immense rewards—is the one to which futures and options markets are ideally suited. It can be argued that futures and options came into their own at almost the precise moment when it became clear that this international economic interdependence could no longer be ignored.

# Financial Markets in the Coming Decade

*The cataclysmic upheavals in the Soviet Union spelled the end of the Cold War and the beginning of a new world order. While none of us are sage enough to know precisely the ultimate outcome of those events or the repercussions they yet portend, it is incumbent on us to attempt to put those remarkable happenings in perspective, particularly as they relate to world markets.*

*Clearly, the market-driven economic order epitomized by the United States was the most important victor in the struggle between East and West. But at what cost to our own financial structure? What role did futures and options markets play in this drama and what will be their function in the new world order? Will the world now enter an era of economic equilibrium or are there new disorders to be faced? Will the debt accumulated during the 1980s result in trouble for the 1990s? What will the markets be like in the coming decade?*

*While predicting the future is dangerous at best, it is often imperative that we make the attempt.*

Published in *Futures* Magazine, November 1990

It seemed like just another traditional May Day celebration in Moscow Red Square. As usual the government top brass were all present, as usual there were banners and marches and song, as usual there was all the expected pomp and circumstance. But something was drastically different. It was the banner! The colors were right—yellow letters on a red background—but the words were all wrong. "Communists: have no illusions—you are bankrupt," it blatantly proclaimed! Right there, in the middle of Moscow Red Square, on May Day 1990!

The occurrence of this incredible event, that it occurred without fear of retribution, is first and foremost vivid and commanding testimony of the failure of Communism. Or to state it in the affirmative, it represented a magnificent triumph of capitalism, of democracy, of market-driven economic order, of Adam Smith, Ayn Rand, and Milton Friedman. "It is almost as if a great economic experiment had been undertaken some 70 years ago. The world was divided into two parts. In one part, there would be a market-driven economic order, and on the other, a centrally planned economic system. Today we can compare the results."

The results are stunning. President Gorbachev himself admits the Soviet Union is suffering from "economic deadlock and stagnation." Or as reported by Irwin M. Stelzer, political columnist for the London *Sunday Times*, who succinctly sums up the situation in the USSR by quoting Nikolai Shmelev and Vladimir Popov, two prominent Soviet economic experts, "There is not enough of anything, anywhere, at any time." The inexorable result: An impending plan to dismantle central economic controls and move to free markets.

Tangentially, of course, the experiment was equally a triumph for the markets of futures and options. These markets are integral and indispensable to the economic order that demonstrated its supremacy over an inferior economic system whose structure and function are dependent on the edicts of government. Indeed, what markets better epitomize price determination by virtue of the free forces of supply and demand than do the markets of futures and options?

But the Red Square banner is testimony to still another truth one that has even greater implications to the world of tomorrow. Let's face it, the failure of Communism is not news, it failed long before the autumn of 1989. What is news is that the populations that were hostage to this economic and political order suddenly had the temerity and courage to publicly denounce the system that had enslaved them. What is news is that the truth—officially kept secret within a world isolated by the Iron Curtain—was out.

Unquestionably, Andrei Sakharov, Mikhail Gorbachev, Lech Walesa, and, no doubt, many others whose names historians will ultimately determine, deserve a substantial measure of the credit. These giants of human history forged a political environment that made the events of autumn 1989 possible. However, with all due respect, their monumental achievement was not conceivable without the parallel consequence of yet another human endeavor: the inexorable march of technology. More than any other single factor, the telecommunications revolution—or what Walter Wriston dubbed the information revolution—made it impossible to continue the charade and hide the unmitigated bankruptcy of the Communist order. Modern communications techniques between people, coupled with massive media penetration in disregard of national boundaries, offered everyone a stark, uncompromising comparison of economic systems.

As journalist Mike O'Neil, years before the historic events of 1989, predicted: The consequences of the new telecommunications technology "is hurrying the collapse of old order, accelerating the velocity of social and political change, creating informed and politically active publics, and inciting conflict by publicizing the differences between people and nations." To put it another way, the technological revolution of the last decade made *perestroika* inevitable.

Thus, as it has throughout the history of mankind, technology again is dictating fundamental change in our social structure and reshaping both the political and economic landscape of our planet. Its immediate impact on the populations of Eastern Europe is now a historical reality. However, the effects of the information revolution reach far beyond social and political change. As Dr. Carver Mead of the California Institute of Technology points out: "The entire Industrial Revolution enhanced productivity by a factor of about a hundred, but the microelectronic revolution has already enhanced productivity in information-based technology by a factor of more than a million—and the end isn't in sight yet."

Clearly, the consequences of the telecommunications revolution will be felt in every facet and niche of civilized life, and will dramatically change the nature and structure of financial markets. Already, what were once dozens of scattered national economies are inexorably becoming linked into one interrelated, interdependent world economy. Sophisticated satellites, microchips, and fiber optics have changed the world from a confederation of autonomous financial markets into one continuous marketplace. There is no longer a distinct division of the three major time zones. Today's financial markets are worldwide in scope, ignoring geographic boundaries and time of day.

Today, as Mr. Wriston stated, by virtue of the information revolution "we are witnessing a galloping new system of international finance ". . . one that differs radically from its precursors" in that it "was not built by politicians, economists, central bankers or finance ministers . . . it was built by technology . . . by men and women who interconnected the planet with telecommunications and computers . . ." The consequences are global as well as regional and affect public as well as private financial policy objectives. That is good news for futures and options markets.

Indeed, the markets of futures and options were the first to read the handwriting on the wall and discern the meaning as well as potential of the new information standard. The financial futures revolution, launched in Chicago in 1972, blazed the trail for much of what has since followed in world capital markets. It established that there was a need for a new genre of risk management tools responsive to institutional money management and modern telecommunication technology, it led to the acceptance and integration of futures and options within the infrastructure of the financial establishment, it acted as the crucible of ideas for new off-exchange products, it became the catalyst for the development of futures markets worldwide, and it induced the introduction of risk management as a regime.

It is the latter consequence that will have the greatest impact on the use and expansion of futures and options markets during the coming years. Because more globalization, greater interdependence, instant informational flows, immediate access to markets of choice, more sophisticated techniques, and intensified competition are the trends of the future, the management of risk is bound to be at the core of every prudent long-range financial strategy. Two decades ago, financial risk was apt to be defined by most in fairly simple terms as the possibility of suffering financial loss. At that time, it was doubtful that many thought of risk management as a discipline. Nor is it likely that many outside of academia or the actuarial business spent much time tinkering with mathematical models in order to weigh different strains of strategic exposure; that is, a firm's sensitivity to changes in tax rates, interest rates, exchange rates, the price of oil, and so forth.

Two decades ago, the identifiable risks were the rough equivalent of what Claude Rains in the final scenes of *Casablanca* told his lackeys: "Round up the usual suspects." Farmers, for example, have always been at the mercy of the weather. Beyond that, there were all the usual insurable risks: fire, theft, natural disasters and so on. And recessions came and went. But at the end of the day, it was an era in which Treasury instruments yielded about 5 percent and foreign exchange rates were fixed.

Defined in the context of the world of commerce as we know it in the 1990s, risk is not merely a potential drought, earthquake, gas leak, or even oil spill. In today's interdependent world—where two contaminated grapes are found in Philadelphia and, a hemisphere away, Chilean farmers suffer $100 million in losses as a result; where Europeans worry about growth hormones fed to cattle and American beef growers suffer the consequences; where Bundesbank monetary policy must be weighed right along with that of the Fed; where a head tax imposed in London can affect the corporate bottom line every bit as readily as a value-added tax levied by Washington; where a drop in the Nikkei average can trigger a decline in every other stock market in the world; where the U.S. budget and trade deficits impact not just the American economy, but the economies of all nations and all those who are business participants; where the third world debt is everyone's burden; and where every action in any part of the world is immediately known by everyone else, its impact swift, and sometimes (as in the case of Iraq's invasion of Kuwait) of critical significance—risk is radically more complicated, intensely more concentrated, and devastatingly swift. Risk, today, is any one of a myriad of contingencies that could negatively impact an enterprise, thereby altering its value, its cash flow, or its future. And, since the implicit counterpart to risk is opportunity, the complexity of the world of tomorrow is good news for the markets of futures and options. Moreover, as Dr. Mead said, the end isn't in sight yet.

Futures and options markets are ideally suited for a world where innovation and competition will intensify, where demand for tailored risk management strategies will increase, and where opportunities will rapidly appear and disappear on a constantly changing financial horizon. Indeed, while in the coming years the lines between exchange-traded and off-exchange traded products may become somewhat blurred, no markets other than futures and options offer a blend of so many credible instruments to safeguard or enhance the trader's assets.

Consider for a moment the salient properties of futures and options markets: the widest array of agricultural and financial instruments, from beans to bonds, from cattle to crude, from stocks to silver, from euros to yen, from coffee to CPI; a measure of liquidity not available anywhere else; a cost-efficiency of incomparable narrow bid/ask spreads; an ability to swiftly institute a variety of strategies, programs, or fine-tuning techniques; the ability to cost-effectively adjust portfolio exposure by moving back and forth between securities and cash; a flexibility to choose between the most fairly priced alternative instrument at any time; a facility to preserve credit lines within a system offering the highest degree of creditworthiness; a fluency to access all markets on a global basis; a speed and certainty of execution difficult to duplicate; and, soon, market coverage on a 24-hour basis—these represent a uniquely impressive array of components in the arsenal of tools imperative for the financial manager to possess.

At least two more profound consequences brought about by the technological revolution have a material impact on the markets of futures and options as well as significant financial implications for the decade. First is the growth of institutional investment funds. Scientific and technological advancement have forced the world to become highly specialized, expertise oriented, and professional—a trend that will not abate, but rather will accelerate, and is nowhere more obvious than in finance. In the United States, investment managers now represent more than 23 million mutual fund shareholders and control a trillion dollars in assets for them. U.S. pension funds now total 60 million plan participants plus beneficiaries and hold $2 trillion for them, compared with only $400 billion a decade ago.

Investment and pension funds managed by professionals who apply complex strategies will increasingly dominate the markets. These managers will continue to invent investment techniques and demand instruments of trade—principally found in futures and options—that serve their needs. It is important to note that many trading activities will not be conducted relative to strict fundamental evaluations. With respect to equity investments in particular, portfolio management is likely to continue with the current trend of following index enhancement strategies—the 200 largest U.S. pension funds now have 30 percent of their assets committed to some form of indexation. These investment strategies may require adjustments to portfolios that sometimes cause price movements in individual stocks that bear little relationship to fundamental values. Thus the debate between fundamental and technical investment philosophies will continue for the foreseeable future.

Moreover, financial management will continue to become increasingly more disciplined, professional, and preprogrammed. To meet the demands of competition, financial engineering will become an exacting art form, and money managers will need to continuously refine and upgrade the process by which they make investment decisions. There will be no time simply to react during a moment of panic or pressure. To succeed in the coming decade, managers will have to employ precise blueprints and models for all eventualities. Investment strategies, protective hedging techniques, or decisions with respect to asset allocation will need to be in place long in advance of the time they are necessary. It goes without saying that professional management will need the most efficient tools, the know-how to use them, and the technology to apply them.

Second, the loss of dominance by American financial markets is striking and will continue to have a pivotal influence on money management. In the fixed income markets, the Japanese have become major participants. For instance, Tokyo's trading of Japanese government bond futures—which did not exist five years ago—is currently nearly twice as great in dollar value as Chicago's trading of U.S. Treasury bond futures. In 1988, Japanese investors accounted for 44 percent of the nearly $50 billion net foreign purchases of U.S. government notes and bonds. Similarly, the U.S. equity market is no longer the dominant force that it was years ago. In 1975, the United States accounted for 57 percent of the capitalization of world equity markets; today the figure is only 31 percent. Japanese investors alone represented nearly 30 percent of the $360 billion in U.S. stock transactions made by foreigners in 1988, while in 1983, Japanese investors accounted for less than 3 percent of the $135 billion in foreign transactions. And, bear in mind, the foregoing erosion of American market dominance occurred prior to the effects of "Europe 1992" and the revitalization of the emerging nations of the Pacific Rim, Eastern/Central Europe, and the Soviet Union.

Many significant national sovereignty consequences will flow from this altered financial panorama, but one of the most profound effects on the United States will be that American businesses and their markets—the same as foreign businesses and their markets—must adopt a global posture if they are to survive in the coming decade. "The multinational of the 1970s is obsolete," said *Business Week* in its May 14, 1990, issue. "Global companies must be more than just a bunch of overseas subsidiaries that execute decisions made at headquarters." Enter in its place: "the stateless corporation," a company that "does research wherever necessary, develops products in several countries, promotes key executives regardless of nationality, and even has shareholders on three continents."

And as *Business Week* might have added, enter also the risk management discipline. Because the international marketplace will no longer be dominated by a single nation as it was in the past century, no international entity will continue to exist for very long unless it has mastered the ability to manage risk on a global scale. Market coverage will have to be worldwide as well as on a round-the-clock basis. As *Business Week* concluded, "in this world of transparent borders, governments and nations that fail to create the right climate will find their living standards and well-being short-changed. But those that can extract the benefits that stateless corporations can offer will emerge clear winners." Once again, this is highly constructive for the markets of futures and options. President Gorbachev knew this when he recently called for the establishment in the USSR of both securities and commodity exchanges.

Finally, one sobering caveat and one fascinating prospect: Obviously, crystal-ball gazing is both difficult and dangerous. When we reflect that few predicted the cataclysmic European events of autumn 1989 even days before they occurred—although they represented a happening that will totally reshape the world of the coming decades; when we consider that we ignored all warnings about Iraq's invasion of Kuwait until hours before it occurred—although the event portends financial upheavals reminiscent of the early 1970s with threatening consequences for all financial markets; it becomes obvious that we must make predictions only with a carefully defined set of qualifications and caveats. Indeed, in the volatile and rapidly changing world in which we live, there are few easy prognostications. Every prediction is subject to unforeseen events or forces over which we have no control.

Clearly, the international economic repercussions stemming from the upheavals in the Soviet Union and Eastern Europe cannot be underestimated. As Professor Joseph A. Grundfest, Stanford Law School, and former SEC Commissioner, recently wrote, "It is difficult to overstate the severity of the problems faced by the Soviet Union and its temporarily constituent republics, on either the political or economic front. . . . As a practical matter, the economic condition of the USSR is indistinguishable from that which would exist had the USSR lost a conventional hot war—its economy has to be rebuilt from the bottom up and top down." The financial reverberations will undoubtedly be serious and global.

Even when focusing on only one segment of the revolution that swept over Europe—the reunification of Germany—we must conclude as did Professor Grundfest, that it "may well turn out to be the most significant single economic development over the short term economic horizon. Indeed, from a macroeconomic perspective, it can be compared to West Germany conducting a leveraged buy-out of East Germany, its physical plant, and its 16.6 million people." Can there be any doubt that such an LBO when coupled with the attempted emergence of neighboring economies will have profound ramifications to the financial future of all of Europe and beyond? Its economic consequences for the world at large cannot be estimated and must be viewed with extreme caution.

Aside from the foregoing, there are heavy clouds in the sky above us. "We enter the decade of the 1990s," writes Charles R. Hulten in the May issue of *The American Enterprise*, "riding one of the longest economic expansions in our history. But far from being the source of great optimism, other economic trends are the cause of much gloom: America is no longer competitive, we save too little and are burying the future under a mountain of debt, the standard of living of many workers has not risen in a decade."

Indeed, the decade of the 1980s is often described as one of excesses. The world accumulated debt as if it was on a unlimited credit card. But as Milton Friedman taught us, there is no such thing as a free lunch. Debt must ultimately be paid and that process can be long and painful. When you add to the fragile and problem-ridden state of the American economy the oil crisis that recently exploded in the Middle East with its grave financial implications on the economies of the entire world, a recession seems certain, perhaps of a severity we fear to spell out. Even if the Iraqi–Kuwaiti oil crisis turns out to cause but temporary dislocations, more "fundamental financial forces are now inexorably pushing their way to the surface," says financial columnist John Liscio (*Barron's*, August 13, 1990). Fundamentals that are of a much more permanent and serious nature and a consequence of our decade-long "unprecedented reliance on debt to fuel economic growth."

Alan Abelson, editor of *Barron's*, strikes an even more ominous tone (August 13, 1990) by suggesting that the coming recession will be "a credit-contraction recession," and quite different than the inventory recessions with which we are so familiar. "A credit recession," says Abelson, "is something there's no modern memory of, and hence one can only conjecture at its workings and its consequences. At worst, it would seem to encompass an unraveling of 30 years of debt abuse and entail, among other unpleasant things, an epidemic of bankruptcies. At least, it would be attended by more financial dislocation than we've experienced since the end of World War II."

Of course, not everyone subscribes to an America-in-Decline thesis or even to the gloomy picture portrayed by the global debt structure. States Herbert Stein, Senior Fellow, American Enterprise Institute, "The most important thing to know about the American economy is that it is very rich . . . in real terms, after allowing for inflation, the GNP now is six times as high as in 1929, and three times as high per capita . . . the GNP of the U.S. is probably two and one-half times that of Japan and five times that of Germany. . . . Some people think that the U.S. is becoming poorer because Americans and their government borrow a good deal abroad. But actually Americans are becoming richer. The productive assets owned by Americans—at home and abroad—are rising much faster than their liabilities to foreigners."

The discussion continues, one that is of great relevance to us. The fortunes of futures markets, no different than any other market sector, are highly dependent on the state of national as well as global economic conditions. Should the United States—and thus the world—fall into a state of severe depressed economic activity, futures and options markets could very well suffer with the rest of the financial community. Of course, in the past somehow the world always seemed to muddle through, and, even if there are some rough years ahead, beyond them is certainly a brighter tomorrow. Moreover, as in the case of Saddam Hussein's oil grab of Kuwait, world upheavals are often fuel for the fortunes of our markets and spell a continued and even greater demand for the features of futures and options.

As an unyielding consequence of the telecommunications revolution, the tomorrow we foresee will unquestionably include automated electronic systems for the execution of not only futures and options but every other financial medium including stocks, securities, options, or cash market instruments. In this respect, true to their tradition, futures markets again blazed the trail.

Indeed, back in 1984, recognizing that the financial world was at the threshold of increased international competition as a consequence of Wriston's information revolution, the Chicago Mercantile Exchange (CME) became the first futures exchange to respond by establishing a mutual-offset arrangement with another exchange in another time zone—the Singapore International Monetary Exchange (SIMEX). And, not much later, the Chicago Board of Trade (CBOT), with the same purpose in mind, instituted an evening session for its U.S. Treasury bond futures.

Ultimately, however, both Chicago exchanges, as well as most of the others in the world, concluded that futures and options markets must make the giant leap toward automated technology if they are to respond to the demands of globalization. The breakthrough occurred in 1986 when the CME initiated its development of GLOBEX with Reuters Holdings PLC as a joint-venture partner. This revolutionary direction for our industry was irrevocably confirmed when the CBOT subsequently also set about to develop an electronic after-hours system. With the recent agreement between the CME and CBOT to unify their separate after-hours electronic trading systems, and with the Paris-based *Marché à Térme International de France* (MATIF) already a member of the same system, GLOBEX will become the premier international futures and options trading mechanism. Indeed, when GLOBEX becomes operational, it will automatically include more than 50 percent of the world's financial futures and options business. Ultimately, GLOBEX envisions the linkage with a number of other world markets, affording these markets the capability to present their unique product lines on an international system.

GLOBEX represents the logical extension of the financial futures revolution that began in the early 1970s. It is the only realistic response to the demands for an efficient and cost-effective capability for managing risk on a global basis. It will integrate the open outcry sessions of the regular business day with state-of-the-art computer-generated screen technology. It will offer the world a 24-hour risk management regime that includes all the vital features of futures and options markets—their products, liquidity, trade clearing capability and credit-worthiness. It will facilitate competitive prices, a centralized marketplace, access, and a continuous flow of price information to the public. It represents the *avant-garde* of the financial services arena and the precursor of market systems that will serve every segment of the financial world. In a word, GLOBEX will offer the world a transaction capability that is as advanced as the imagination will allow and as far-reaching as the future itself.

As the old Chinese curse admonished, we live in interesting times. That is particularly true for those of us in markets, be they securities, options, or futures. Indeed, the markets developed in the United States over this century are at the epicenter of that which toppled the Communist order. They are at the heart of why the American standard of living—its social structure, its potential for the future—are the envy of other nations and the quintessential component of any successful global economic system for the coming era.

# The New World Order

*To appreciate the new world order that dawned with the last decade of the 20th century, it is necessary to understand the fundamental cause that induced all the revolutionary changes. More than any other single influence, the telecommunications revolution was the catalyst.*

*Modern communications penetrated every sphere of society in total disregard of geographical boundaries, economic principles, or political systems. It offered a stark uncompromising comparison of economic and political realities around the globe and became the common denominator of all the recent world upheavals.*

*It is also important to understand that the same common denominator is—and will continue to be—the single greatest influence on markets within the new world order. Telecommunications will continue to dictate globalization and a 24-hour market regime. Those who dare ignore this march of technology will cease to be competitive.*

---

**Presented at the 3rd Annual Tokyo International Finance Symposium, Tokyo, Japan, May 23, 1991**

---

On November 9, 1989, twenty-six years after President John F. Kennedy stood at the Berlin Wall and shouted, *"Ich bin ein Berliner,"* hundreds of thousands of East Germans began pouring with impunity through the Berlin Wall. The unbelievable had occurred without a shot being fired. The Berlin Wall had fallen. President Kennedy's historic pledge was no longer a symbolic gesture. The unification of Germany was soon to be a reality.

A continent away, on February 18, 1990, at the Victor Verster Prison Farm, an event transpired that South Africa's blacks had spent twenty-seven years praying for and many whites had spent just as long dreading. On that day Nelson Mandela emerged from the prison gates, raised both fists in the air, and climbed into a waiting car, a free man. The inevitable followed: a sea of changes that will inexorably lead to the abolishment of all forms of

246

apartheid. President F. W. de Klerk summed it all up correctly as "the historic turning point in the history of South Africa."

Only a few months later but again a continent away, another earth-shattering eventuality was unfolding. It was May 1, 1990, and it seemed like just another traditional May Day celebration in Moscow's Red Square. As usual, all the government top brass were present, there were banners and marches and songs, and there was all the expected pomp and circumstance. But something was drastically different. The banner's colors were right—yellow letters on a red background—but the message was all wrong. "Communists: have no illusions—you are bankrupt," it blatantly proclaimed! Right there, in the middle of Red Square on May Day.

On January 16, 1991, less than a year later, President George Bush announced from the White House: "In conjunction with our coalition partners, the United States has moved . . . to enforce the mandates of the United Nations Security Council. As of 7 o'clock PM, Operation Desert Storm forces were engaging targets in Iraq and Kuwait." Thirty-seven days later, by virtue of a coalition of multinational forces and the unqualified support of all free nations, the war was over. The Middle East, perhaps the world, will never be the same.

The foregoing four separate world occurrences are unequivocal evidence that the world changed quite profoundly during the past 24 months. Indeed, these events will have an incalculable impact on human history and, as President George Bush suggests, represent a new world order. But are these four incredible events of the past two years independent of each other? Are they isolated phenomenon, or does a common denominator tie them together?

The significance of the May Day parade and its disruptive banner—that this incredible event occurred and that it occurred without fear of retribution—is first and foremost vivid and commanding testimony of the failure of Communism. Conversely, it represents the magnificent triumph of capitalism, democracy, market-driven economic order, and of Adam Smith, Ayn Rand, Milton Friedman, and Merton Miller. The Cold War is at an end. Communism has failed. Eastern European nations are newly liberated. Germany is unified. South Africa has finally moved to enter the twentieth century. And the Gulf War—at a minimum—will force the next would-be dictator to reconsider any attempts to extend by force his tyranny unto a neighbor.

Are these events independent of each other? Are they isolated phenomena without connection? Of course not. The evidence is unequivocal: There is a strong common thread between all the cataclysmic happenings of the past 24 months that has formed the cloth of the new world order.

To Alan Greenspan, Chairman of the U.S. Federal Reserve, most of what happened in the Soviet Union was pure economics. And surely there is a ring of truth to what he suggests: "It is almost as if a great economic experiment had been undertaken some 70 years ago. The world was divided into two parts. In one part, there would be a market-driven economic order, and on the other, a centrally planned economic system. Today we can compare the results." They are, of course, stunning. On one side, a standard of living so high it was unimaginable when the experiment began, on the other side economic bankruptcy."

The Red Square banner is testimony to still another truth, one that has even greater implications to the new world order. While the failure of Communism is not news—it failed long before the autumn of 1989—what is news is that the populations hostage to this economic and political order suddenly had the temerity and courage publicly to denounce the system that had enslaved them; that the truth about the economic failure of that system, officially kept secret within a world isolated by the Iron Curtain, was out. Unquestionably, economic forces were fundamental to the revolution that transpired within the Soviet Union. Unquestionably, Andrei Sakharov, Mikhail Gorbachev, Lech Walesa, Boris Yeltsin, and many others deserve a substantial measure of the credit. These giants of human history forged a political environment that made the events of 1989 possible. However, their monumental achievement was not conceivable without the parallel consequence of yet another human endeavor: the inexorable march of technology. While this has been stated before many times and in many ways, it bears repeating: Those who ignore the march of technology will soon be history.

The telecommunications revolution—more than any other single factor—made it impossible to continue the charade and hide the unmitigated bankruptcy of the Communist order. Modern communications techniques, coupled with massive media penetration in disregard of national boundaries, offered a stark, uncompromising comparison of economic systems. As celebrated journalist David Halberstam states in his book, *The Next Century*, "It is increasingly difficult to censor thought in an age of sophisticated electronic media. Modern communications inevitably define modern conscience and speed across national borders. The oppressed can call attention not merely to the iniquities . . . but also to the price of such tyranny."

This leads us to the inevitable conclusion that the common denominator of the world upheavals of the past 24 months was the technological revolution of the past several decades. Modern telecommunications provided world citizens the ability to judge their governments, compare economic systems, examine moral codes, scrutinize cultural freedoms, and weigh them against that of their neighbors. No government could any longer hide the truth from its people. Clearly then, the technological revolution of the past decades made *perestroika* inevitable and brought the end of the Communist regime. By the same logic and as a consequence of the same force of information flows, the telecommunications revolution brought down the Berlin Wall and was the pivotal force that caused the immoral walls of apartheid to crumble.

And if technology was a fundamental factor in assisting half the world to break its chains of tyranny, was not technology the single fundamental factor that made the Gulf War different from every other war: high-tech weaponry, Tomahawk sea-launched cruise missiles, Patriot anti-missile missiles, F-117 Stealth fighter-bombers, laser guns to spot targets, missiles that can take a 90-degree angle to find their target, vision devices that turn night into day, and listening gadgets that read the enemy's every radio transmission. What nation could afford to duplicate, develop, or keep current with this high-tech weaponry? With the Soviet Union bankrupt, with capital scarce and in demand around the world, with high technology so costly, would it be so far-fetched to muse that, *perhaps*, no nation would be able to match this might, and this consequence would make major wars obsolete for the foreseeable future of humankind.

As it has throughout human history, technology again is dictating fundamental and revolutionary change in our social structure and reshaping the political and economic landscape of our planet. Its immediate impact on the populations of Eastern Europe and the Middle East is now an historical reality.

However, the effect of the information revolution reach far beyond social and political change. It has significantly altered the world financial markets and demanded instruments that can accommodate the new world order.

Enter GLOBEX. It is the only realistic response to the demands for an efficient and cost-effective capability for managing risk on a global basis. While it may take time to become accepted, GLOBEX will integrate the open outcry sessions of the regular business day with state-of-the-art computer-generated screen technology. It will offer the world a 24-hour risk management regime that will facilitate competitive prices, a centralized marketplace, access, and a continuous flow of price information to the public. It represents the *avant-garde* of the financial services arena and the precursor of market systems that will serve every segment of the new world order.

With the recent agreement between the CME and CBOT to unify their separate after-hours electronic trading systems, and with the MATIF already a member of the same system, GLOBEX should become the premier international futures and options trading mechanism. Ultimately, GLOBEX envisions linkage with all other world markets, affording all markets the capability to present their unique product lines to the international trading arena.

Financial futures are not a panacea, nor is the new world order free from the possibility of serious economic storms ahead. The Soviet Union is in chaos, the economic repercussions stemming from the German unification cannot be underestimated, the ramifications resulting from economic woes of emerging Eastern European nations will be serious, the monumental debt in the American economy is of critical significance, and the U.S. recession is not yet over. Whatever lies ahead, the markets of futures and options are prepared to play an important role in the new world order. Not only were they an essential ingredient in the economic revolution that recently swept over Eastern Europe and the Soviet Union, not only are they a quintessential component of any successful future global economic system, not only are they invaluable in times of upheaval and uncertainty such as may lie before us, they are in synch with the inexorable march of technology—a force that has been the common denominator and pivotal catalyst of change throughout the history of humankind.

# Markets of
# the Pacific Rim

*Financial futures markets have been fully embraced by the nations of the Pacific Rim. This was of no small significance in the evolution of futures markets. The Pacific Rim accounts for nearly half the world's population and represents an economic force equal to any region of the world. The action of the Chicago Mercantile Exchange in 1984 in forging a unique link with the Singapore International Monetary Exchange was unquestionably a most influential event in hastening the acceptance and growth of financial futures in Asia.*

*Of similar influence was our continuous assistance and encouragement of the Japanese government to open its doors to our markets. Clearly, the potential of financial futures in Asia could not be fulfilled without complete Japanese acceptance of this market regime. Recent actions of the Japanese government—including its liberalization of commodity fund rules—provide compelling evidence that Japan recognizes the importance of our markets in risk management and the need to allow its utilization by their citizens for investment purposes. Similarly, the Japanese Ministry of Finance apparent approval of GLOBEX for use by its nation's financial community can be viewed as a giant step toward the integration of world markets and of Japan's acceptance of this reality.*

---

**Foreword to *The Pacific Rim Futures and Options Markets*, October 1991**

---

"The Mediterranean is the ocean of the past, the Atlantic the ocean of the present, and the Pacific the ocean of the future," so said John Hay, the American Secretary of State at the turn of the twentieth century. And while it can certainly be argued that the future took its good time getting here, make no mistake, the future of the Pacific Rim has arrived. Today, the countries of the Pacific Rim represent a combination of developed and developing nations that jointly embody an economic force equal to any region of the world. "Today," states John Naisbitt, in his *Megatrends 2000,* "the Pacific Rim is undergoing the fastest period of economic expansion in history, growing at five times the growth rate during the Industrial Revolution."

The geographic area involved is as large as it is diverse. By its all-inclusive definition, it accounts for two fifths of the world's surface and nearly half the world's population. By any standard, the nations that encompass the Pacific Rim are dissimilar in many fundamental respects, with differences ranging from culture to political systems to economic orders. Their differences also run the gamut from those, in the words of the *Economist,* that are "as rich and stable as Japan and as poor and turbulent as China, as big and open as America and as small and closed as North Korea."

Japan is the financial colossus of the region, encompassing a vast and complex business infrastructure that includes some of the world's largest securities firms and banks. Australia and New Zealand provide the anchor on the South. Australia, almost as large as the continental United States, is more British than Asian, but its location makes it imperative for the continent to think Asian. The newly industrialized countries (NICs) include Singapore, Hong Kong, South Korea, and Taiwan. Hong Kong will revert to China in 1997 and become a uncommon segment of this vast and underdeveloped giant. Then there are the members of the Association of South East Asian Nations including Indonesia, Malaysia, the Philippines, and Thailand.

Although there are many ties other than geographical among these nations, there is a sufficient common denominator based on a similar economic evolution that brought some of these states to employ or consider employing the markets of futures and options. While their current experience with these markets is of recent vintage, futures markets are not new to the region. Indeed, it was in Japan during the Edo period (1600–1867) that centralized futures markets were born. The locale was Osaka, where feudal lords established warehouses to store and sell rice that was paid to them as landtax by their villagers. In 1730, to protect themselves from wide price fluctuations between harvests, these merchants established the Dojima Rice Market, the first organized futures exchange.

More than 200 years later, futures markets officially returned to the Pacific Rim with the birth of the Sydney Futures Exchange (SFE) in 1960. The SFE was also the first Asian futures exchange to launch a financial contract in 1979. However, the critical catalyst in the modern development of futures and options markets in the Pacific basin was the revolutionary link in 1984 between Singapore's SIMEX and the Chicago Mercantile Exchange (CME). It served to spur the race for financial futures dominance in the region. A year later, Japan reentered the futures markets arena when the Tokyo Stock Exchange (TSE) launched its successful Japanese Government Bond contract. This important event was quickly followed by the inception of futures trading at the Osaka Securities Exchange (OSE) and the birth of the Tokyo International Financial Futures Exchange (TIFFE). There was no stopping the process now. The community of nations of the Pacific Rim had fully embraced the financial futures revolution.

Nor could it be otherwise. The vibrancy and native talent of the Pacific-based populations, the wealth achieved as a consequence of decades of successful manufacturing and export, and the resulting potential of their financial centers all combined to make the region a vast store of financial strength and a force equal to any in the world. This expanding base of capital markets could not continue very long or compete on a global scale without the development of futures markets. The advent of globalization, greater interdependence, modern telecommunications capabilities, instant informational flows, immediate recognition of financial risks, and opportunities and intensified competition made the management of risk an essential prerequisite of success for every financial community. To address this new financial imperative, it was mandatory for the nations of the Pacific Rim to turn to the unique mechanisms provided by futures and options markets.

It was axiomatic. The financial futures revolution, launched in Chicago in 1972, blazed the trail for much of what has since followed in world capital centers. The CME was the first major exchange to recognize the significance of the demise of the

Bretton Woods Agreement, the post-World-War-II pact that instituted a fixed exchange-rate regime for the major world nations. To capture the potential of the free market epoch that was about to ensue, the CME created the International Monetary Market (IMM), the first futures exchange for the specific purpose of trading in financial instruments. The era of financial futures was thus born. While the new wave of futures began with currency contracts, it was quickly followed by futures contracts on U.S. government securities— Treasury bills at the Merc, and Ginnie Mae certificates and Treasury bonds at the Chicago Board of Trade (CBOT). Later, when in the early 1980s the concept of cash settlement in lieu of physical delivery was instituted, the stage was set for the CME's introduction of Eurodollar futures. This paved the way for stock index futures and initiated the era of index markets.

The financial futures revolution was destined to alter profoundly the history of markets. It established that there was a need for a new genre of risk management tools suitable for sophisticated strategies and responsive to professional and institutional money management. It proved the necessity of futures and options within the infrastructure of finance and alongside other traditional structures of capital markets. From their inception, the markets of futures and options understood and embraced the common denominator of recent world upheavals—the spectacular advances in technology. Clearly, no other single factor was more instrumental in influencing political and economic change than was the technological revolution of recent years.

On the political front, modern telecommunications fostered instant informational flows in total disregard of national boundaries, offering a stark, uncompromising comparison of political and economic life and making it nearly impossible for governments to hide the truth from their people. On the economic front, modern telecommunications made instantaneous price information available globally and fostered massive capital flows in an unencumbered fashion. It dramatically changed the nature of global capital markets forever. The markets of futures and options recognized this march of technology, understood its inexorable impact on commerce and trade, and willingly adapted to its demands. Thus it is no accident our markets represent one of the greatest growth arenas of the past two decades.

Events in Eastern Europe and the Soviet Union during recent years have dramatically confirmed the significance of the financial history of these past two decades. The bankruptcy of command economic order, the downfall of Communist rule, and the collapse of the Soviet empire serve as undeniable testimony to the value of capitalism and market-driven economics. The markets of futures and options are integral to that victory. Indeed, what markets better epitomize price determination by virtue of the free forces of supply and demand than do the markets of futures and options?

During the past decade, beginning with the 1982 establishment of the London International Financial Futures Exchange (LIFFE), new financial futures exchanges have opened in virtually every major world financial center, including the *Marché à Térme International de France* (MATIF) in Paris, the Swiss Options and Financial Futures Exchange (SOFFEX) in Zurich, the Deutsche TerminBörse (DTB) in Frankfurt, not to mention the exchanges in the Pacific Rim itself. The dramatic success of this history prompted Nobel laureate Merton Miller, University of Chicago professor of finance, to nominate financial futures as "the most significant financial innovation of the last twenty years."

Indeed, if financial futures and options were not yet invented, they would need to be. They are indispensable in a world that demands the ability to swiftly institute complex strategies or to cost-effectively adjust portfolio exposure between securities and cash. They are ideally suited for a world where tailored risk management strategies are on the increase and where opportunities rapidly appear and disappear on a constantly changing financial horizon. They are a vital option in a world in which it is often imperative to utilize a creditworthy mechanism that preserves credit lines. They are without equal in providing a vast array of products combined with an envious measure of liquidity and an incomparably narrow bid/ask spread. They are the *avant-garde* of market innovation and soon, as a consequence of GLOBEX—the after-hours electronic trading system being developed by the CME and the CBOT in conjunction with Reuters PLC—will achieve market coverage on a 24-hour basis. And most significantly, they are well-positioned for a world where professional money management is the wave of the future.

What was imperative for the financial structures of other global regions has become equally imperative for the Pacific basin. And this process is not yet complete. Some of the Pacific Rim communities are just beginning to emerge from their formative development stage. More to the point, the vast financial potential of mainland China has yet to be unleashed. Is there any doubt that the same forces that brought about the downfall of command order economics in the Soviet Union will achieve a similar result in China? Is there any doubt that its highly competent people will someday join the market rebirths occasioned by the other Asian populations? And when it happens, it will exponentially affect the strength and vitality of the Pacific Rim.

Although there are some heavy macroeconomic clouds overhead, the long-term direction in the evolution of global markets is unmistakable. In a world where the distinctions between the major time zones have vanished, where geographical borders that once could limit the flow of capital are but history, and where traditional internal protections that could insulate citizenry from external price and value influences are no longer valid—a market-driven economic order is quintessential and futures and options are a critical component. For expanding regions such as the Pacific Rim—with its vast and diverse cultures and infrastructure, and with its still untapped and developing potential—there can be no other course.

# Tomorrow's Technological Tidal Wave

*The impact of technology on the human race during the past two decades is near impossible to fathom or quantify. Its inexorable march materially affected every aspect and nuance of civilization and the lives of the inhabitants of this planet. It would have been impossible to stand in its way or ignore its demands.*

*The next 20 years may prove even more dramatic. It is now quite clear that the technological world is on the threshold of a quantum leap in the application of capabilities that will once again materially change the face of civilization. Nowhere will this change be more dramatic or more consequential than in world markets. Futures markets must not stand in opposition or they will be left in the historical scrap heap of industries that failed to embrace reality. Rather, they must anticipate and stand ready to apply the demands of this unceasing evolution.*

Presented at the First Annual London International Finance Symposium Conducted Jointly by the Chicago Board of Trade and the Chicago Mercantile Exchange, London, England, November 7, 1991

Futures markets, as their name implies, should provide a glimpse into the future. However, in truth, they often don't. The future is habitually too clouded and burdened with too many imponderables to be seen clearly.

At the end of the twentieth century, we are in the midst of a global rebirth that should offer an unequivocal picture of a bright tomorrow—Soviet Communism has been slain, the tyrannical order of the Soviet Union has been dismantled, Eastern European nations have been freed, market economic order has been embraced by all, apartheid is in retreat, nations are emerging in the Pacific Rim, and the European Economic

257

Union is in formation. But something prevents an unguarded optimistic prediction for the world, perhaps because we recognize humankind's contradictory and uncertain nature or because we know the steep price tag of all that lies before us, or because we are concerned that the global credit spree of the 1980s will demand payment in the 1990s.

Instead, allow us to stay clear of the unknown, to discuss the inevitable, and to predict that whatever ensues, the role of futures and options will be significant and that these markets are about to be engulfed by a technological tidal wave.

> Robin Maxwell settled back and buckled the safetybelt around her as the British Airways 787 taxied out to the runway at Kennedy. She pulls from her briefcase an IBM IAM-Port, her interactive multimedia portable system, and turns it on. After the screen in front of her comes to life, she executes a few directions using the system's electronic mouse and is instantly connected to the Equity Information Center at her Goldman Sachs office in New York. A few more clicks on the mouse gives her the information she requested as well as an on-line data-feed to various markets around the world. Robin studies the information, then calls up a trader friend in Chicago, who appears on her on-line video screen for a brief discussion of her market theory.
>
> As the airplane levels off at 55,000 feet, Robin checks the time in London, calls up for a GLOBEX connection on the screen, and initiates orders to buy December S&P 500 contracts on the CME; to sell March FTSE contracts at the LIFFE and CAC-40 contracts on MATIF; to institute a complex DAX/Nikkei options spread on the Deutsche Terminborse and Osaka exchanges; and to buy February U.S. Treasury bond puts at the CBOT.
>
> When she is finished with the transaction, Robin watches the market for a while, sends a fax to her London office, takes a sip of the coffee the stewardess provided, and asks her IAM-Port to review the current crop of theater plays showing in London so that she can make reservations for that evening.

Science fiction? Don't bet against it. Interactive multimedia—a multidimensional vehicle of communication representing the coalescence of key communications technologies: television, telephone, personal computers, and laser storage systems—is coming. And when these technologies merge, life as we know it will never be the same.

While Robin Maxwell's interactive multimedia system is not yet available, what *is* available is quite amazing: Robin can easily install a calling card that provides her with 24-hour real-time market information in stocks, futures, options, and mutual funds, or install a real-time spreadsheet system that will display, analyze, and monitor continuously current financial data with electronic on-line data-feeds, or install a portfolio information management system designed to document and control transactions and positions in actively managed portfolios or funds, or install a software product providing a host of analytical calculations, regression analysis, and exponential smoothing from single or multiple data-bases, or install software that provides daily investment performance calculations by account, currency, group, sector, and industry.

These are not the esoterica of a future tomorrow but just a small portion of present day *avant-garde* technology. A dozen years ago, these systems were the product of someone's overactive imagination; a few years ago, they were on programmers' drawing boards; and today they are reality.

The markets of futures and options understood the consequences of the new technology. And because our markets embraced and adapted to its demands, they have blazed the trail for much of what has since followed in world capital markets. We established that there was a need for a new genre of risk management tools responsive to institutional money management and modern telecommunications; we introduced the idea of risk management as a regime; we fostered the concept of financial engineering as a commercial necessity; we became the catalyst for the invention of a multitude of new products, both on and off the exchange; we promoted the acceptance and integration of futures and options into the infrastructure of the financial establishment; and we engendered the development of futures markets worldwide.

That was just the first phase. And while exciting and highly successful, it was only the beginning. For our markets are continuously evolving and the breathtaking speed of technological innovation is not likely to abate. What technology will bring in the very near future will again completely transform our marketplace and make trading unrecognizable from its form today. What is coming is a computerized trading competence undreamed of but a mere decade ago.

Some of it is structural. Computer-aided systems engineering—CASE—represents a new wave in programming. CASE moves systems development away from its traditional art form and into the realm of science by applying engineering discipline and computer support to systems building. CASE allows software development to focus on solving business problems. Its applicability is boundless. The Paris Bourse, for example, used CASE to overhaul and streamline its clearing system to establish a competitive edge in Europe. Similarly, Paine Webber—by enlisting CASE—will become one of the first wire houses to attempt to retool itself for the 1990s with a state-of-the-art distributed computer system that will provide round-the-clock on-line availability for trading, marketing, and customer data.

Some of it is being developed by the exchanges. For instance, the Chicago Mercantile Exchange and the Chicago Board of Trade are jointly developing systems to accept trading instructions from market participants worldwide that will be delivered electronically directly into the trading pits. Orders will be routed through the CME's TOPS or the CBOT's EOS system for electronic switching to the proper pit broker who will then utilize a computerized broker's workstation to organize and instantly report trade status back to the customer. Independent traders in the pits will utilize the latest innovations in hand-held technology to do their proprietary trading and instantly report their trades for clearing. AUDIT terminals will use advances in pen-based hand-held computers including handprint recognition.

But most of it is in software. Intelligent agents will reside in computers to create a world we can hardly envision. Craig Torres of the *Wall Street Journal* recently reported that during the past five years, major American market participants have spent millions of dollars to advance their computing potency. Indeed, one estimate says U.S. securities firms will spend some $7.5 billion on technology in 1991. Firms such as Morgan Stanley, First Boston, O'Conner & Associates, Salomon Brothers, Kidder Peabody, Goldman Sachs, and others are using automated development tools to build new software programs. They are venturing to achieve a new generation of analytics— sophisticated mathematical computer models that act as giant think-tanks to identify hundreds of never-before-imagined trading strategies in securities, futures, and options.

Though the trend is still in its infancy, its direction is unmistakable. Until now, computers were used mostly as spreadsheets, as fast calculators, to analyze risk, or to run accounting and other programs. In the coming age, computers will no longer act within the framework of their traditional competence, they will have gained artificial intelligence. The next generation of analytics—currently being developed at sophisticated research laboratories—seek to apply new financial theories that allow the trader to apply them to markets on an ongoing basis. The evolving mathematical formulas will imitate the way in which traders think and look at markets—but at a rate several thousand times faster than that of humans. A new supercomputer has just been unveiled that runs at a speed of one teraflop, a trillion floating point operations per second.

Computers are on the verge of generating a wave of pristine trading strategies that will offer heretofore unheard of opportunities. Computers are searching for price correlations and connections between markets that traders never thought possible—or never thought about at all. Computers will invent virgin tactics within a complex set of transactions inconceivable for the human mind to have perceived. Computers will create synthetic options and futures far beyond human imagination. Computers will find ways to blend these new analytical transactions with traditional strategies to produce even more complex possibilities. And while the bulk of the new wave of technological transactions will be utilized off-exchanges—within the cash markets—the markets of futures and options are bound to be substantial beneficiaries as well.

For example, computers recently created a synthetic option on the Nikkei Index by combining Nikkei stock index futures and exchange-traded stock index options. The synthetic Nikkei option cost less than the real option and allowed the traders who recently used it to make $500,000 on a single trade. In another example, a managing director of a major securities firm recently created a 2-year option that gives an investor the right to buy the S&P 500 stock index at its lowest point of 1991 in Swiss francs. Without analytics, such products could not even be imagined.

IBM's mathematical sciences department—very much involved in the development of analytic market math—is working on a mathematical model that will allow investors to assemble hundreds of portfolios in seconds and have various shadings of investment risk and reward. Anticipating a constant 24-hour market, IBM has also been working on a mathematical model for the past two years that will scan the trading pattern of stocks or bonds around the world and around the clock. Says the department's director, "time shouldn't be measured by how the clock ticks, but by the level of trading activity." By creating a model that uses trading activity as a measure of time, IBM hopes to create a new vantage point for spotting price trends.

As might be expected, competition in this emerging field will be fierce. Every new analytic is a most closely guarded secret. The only proprietary component for the inventor is the mathematical formula he devises that offers unique profit opportunities in extremely efficient and competitive markets. Consequently, while many of the major firms are working feverishly to develop analytic competence, most of it is behind secured doors. But the secret is out anyway. New computer-generated mathematical analytics are coming whether we like it or not. Says Myron Scholes of the coming new age in trading, "People who don't have analytics are going to be relatively obsolete."

Not only will analytics achieve a myriad of new trading opportunities, they will also result in a myriad of new regulatory concerns, issues, and problems. *How* will these new transactions be regulated? *Will* they be regulated? *Can* they be regulated? What dangers do they pose for the financial structure of the world? Can the financial risk of innovations applied to off-exchange instruments on a global scale be accurately measured or assessed? Does this not pose a great unknown financial risk to the international banking community? These are legitimate and important issues yet to be recognized by the federal regulatory bodies of the world and the traditional exchanges. Very few understand the full scope and nature of the coming technological tidal wave.

The new technological trading competence will be structured to capitalize on the coming global 24-hour market. The revolutionary GLOBEX concept fostered by futures markets has now become part of the status quo even for the securities markets—and before our own international system is functional. Consequently, the New York Stock Exchange is moving in the desired direction with after-hour trading sessions, the Nasdaq International (a trading system for U.S. stocks on an electronic screen) has been launched, the Japanese Over-the-Counter market is launching a similar system, the Italian securities market is leaving the traditional open-outcry stock trading for computerized screens, and similar systems are springing up all over the world, at LIFFE, MATIF, the Sydney Futures Exchange, TIFFE, SOFFEX, and the Deutsche Terminborse.

The forthcoming technological age—when combined with greater globalization, instant informational flows, 24-hour trading, immediate access to markets of choice, and intensified competition—offers immense opportunities for the markets of futures and options. In such a world—where financial risk is constant, financial volatility is commonplace, innovation is rewarded, financial engineering is prized, opportunities rapidly appear and disappear on a constantly changing financial horizon, demand for unique risk management strategies is increasing, and professional management continues to demand efficient instruments of trade—the role of futures and options is fundamental.

# Protectionism—The Scourge of Markets

*Protectionism—no less than intervention in exchange rates and other forms of government interference with free market processes—represents a dangerous and slippery slope. Such endeavors often come unannounced in small insidious increments, sometimes in the form of sophistry and fallacious reasoning. If we are not vigilant in our opposition to these man-made encroachments to market-driven economic order, they will take us down this slope and snatch defeat from the jaws of victory.*

Presented at the Chicago Mercantile Exchange and Chicago Board of Trade Annual International Finance Symposium, Tokyo, Japan, April 8, 1992. Entered into the *Congressional Record* by U.S. Senator Phil Gramm on May 5, 1992 (page S-5933)

It represents a paradox of unimaginable proportion. At the very moment in history when the triumph of free markets is nearly global; at the very moment in history when market-driven economic order is embraced in such unlikely places as Moscow, Sofia, and Prague; at the very moment in history when the Communist world has discarded the manifesto of Karl Marx in favor of the principles of Adam Smith—at this same moment in human history, some of the staunchest champions of a liberal world economy, free trade, and uninhibited competition have suddenly developed a severe case of second thoughts.

Even as the bust of Lenin unceremoniously disappears from every pedestal in the Communist world, even as endless teams of economists from Eastern Europe travel to America to study market-driven economic order, even as central planning becomes a ridiculed concept throughout the former Soviet

Union, some within the bastions of free market economics in the United States and Europe are talking of industrial policies, protectionism, and tariffs. The philosophical incongruity of this phenomenon is difficult to comprehend. It would be comical were it not so tragic.

What happened? Have we lost our faith? Our nerve? Or have we simply lost our memory and are condemned, as Santayana suggested, to repeat past mistakes?

Surely our memory cannot be so short that we have forgotten Senator Reed Smoot of Utah and Congressman Willis Hawley of Oregon who together devised the so-called Smoot-Hawley Tariff Act of 1930, which resulted in a trade war and according to most economists helped plunge the world into the great depression of that era.

Those who suddenly again question our liberal global economic philosophy suggest that the United States has been duped in a world that does not operate according to classic economic principles. That we are naive fools in a cut-throat competitive world that has few rules and that is ruthlessly unfair to nice guys. No question some of this has the ring of truth. There exist areas of unfair global competition. There exists a network of protected industries that take advantage of American goodwill. But there is nothing new about that, nor is the United States itself free from unfair trade practices. While we must be unrelenting in our efforts to erase such sins, they are meaningless in the sum total of our successful global course over the past half century. What has brought the protectionist voices to the fore has been the special economic circumstances of current vintage—principally the long and difficult American recession. It has created an emotional environment based on fear and distrust; it has created an atmosphere fertile for sophistry and demagogues.

Specifically, antiliberal economic theorists advance two major myths to support their views: that protectionism is justified by U.S. trade imbalances and that protectionism saves jobs. Both myths are false. They have again come into fashion, as Daniel Oliver the former Chairman of the U.S. Federal Trade Commission observed a few years ago, by virtue of special interests in America; that is, some industries adversely affected by foreign competition have invented a national problem to advance their own self-interests.

That protectionism will create jobs is a claim that Herbert Stein, the American Enterprise Institute scholar, has characterized as "best-selling fiction." While it is true that a protectionist policy will create jobs in the particular industry being protected, it is equally true that it will have a devastating effect and cost jobs in the economy as a whole. Saving jobs through trade protectionism in (say) the machine tool industry or the computer chip industry will be at the expense of jobs in manufacturing or jobs in electronics. Because when a foreign country cannot export its products to the protected country, it has less money to spend on imports from the protected country. The protected country will thus lose some other export market that will force some other corner of its industry to reduce its labor force. As Milton Friedman told us in *Free to Choose*, "The gains to some producers from tariffs and other restrictions are more than offset by the loss to other producers and especially to consumers in general."*

Similarly, the myth about the U.S. trade deficit negatively affecting the U.S. economy is simplistic and equally untrue. As should be obvious but is often misunderstood, a trade deficit (the so-called current account deficit) is not something that is good or bad per se. It is merely the counterpart to a capital account surplus. Exports are not by themselves good nor are imports bad. A favorable balance of trade basically means exporting more than we import; that is, shipping goods abroad of greater total value than the goods we get from abroad. In other words, sending more than we receive. If the reverse occurs—when we receive more than we send—strange as it may seem, it creates an unfavorable balance of trade.

During the 1970s, for instance, the United States had a trade surplus and a deficit in the capital account, partly because of large U.S. investment overseas. Was that good? In the 1980s, however, the United States began running a surplus in its capital account; the favorable climate for investment in the United States was causing an influx of foreign capital. This was used to partially finance a major retooling of American production capacity. Is this bad? If the rest of the world is to invest—on net—in the United States, the United States will necessarily run a trade deficit. As most economists and scholars will tell

---

*Milton and Rose Friedman, *Free to Choose* (1980).

you, this is neither good nor bad. Nor does the trade deficit take away jobs as protectionist rhetoric in the guise of national concern will attempt to tell us. For instance, during the 1980s, even as our trade deficit continued to mount to record levels, the United States continued to produce new jobs at a very high rate.

As everyone in Japan is aware, the brunt of the current protectionism attack has been directed at that country. Japan's economic miracle of the past several decades has made the rest of the world envious. Thus the tapestry of free trade is shamelessly being rewoven into something called fair trade, a buzz word for protectionism. An America-first syndrome, the equivalent to a fortress-Europe mentality, is disgracefully trampling on the sacred precepts of global competition; and the time-honored principles of a market-driven economy are outrageously attacked in favor of short-term solutions, political expediency, and emotional rhetoric. Japan has become the whipping boy for the world's economic problems.

Does anyone care to listen to the truth? For instance, although the U.S. 43-billion trade deficit with Japan is blamed for the American recession, in truth its impact on the American economy is relatively small—equal to 2 day's worth of U.S. output. Excluding autos, the U.S. deficit with Japan is not much more than it is with China. In fact, the U.S. total trade deficit—66.2 billion in 1991—fell below the 100 billion mark for the first time in 8 years. At the same time, U.S. exports surged to a record 422 billion and the United States captured a greater share of worldwide manufactured exports than Japan. Indeed, the United States exports more to Japan than it does to Germany, France, and Italy combined. Conversely, Japan imports more per capita from America and at a higher percentage of its gross national product than the United States imports from Japan.* In truth, the U.S. export picture has been the one bright spot in the American economy; if a recession or an economic slowdown is occasioned by U.S. trading partners or if protectionism has its way, the American economy will be hit even harder.

However, the rationale for protectionism and tariffs is unencumbered by the truth; it is built on false assumptions, inaccurate impressions, and demagogic sentiments. For

---

*U.S. News & World Report, March 12, 1992.

instance, Japan is said to be an unfair trader. This is an erroneous accusation. While Japan is not without guilt, it is on the whole no different than other industrial countries. In fact, on average, Japan trade barriers are lower than other industrial nations. Its average tariff for industrial products is 2.6 percent—compared with 3 percent for the United States—and its nontariff barriers, such as quotas and licenses, are similar to those in America.*

These facts are not well understood or publicized in the United States, nor are they sufficient to offset the frustrations resulting from our long and deep recession, unemployment in excess of 7 percent, and an ongoing U.S. election process. This combination of circumstances has created a climate ideal for those motivated by self-interests. Indeed, sophistry and demagogic polemics are highly effective tools in times of economic stress, especially in a political year. Take the American auto industry as an example. Some of its executives would have us believe that the problems occasioned by their industry are not caused by competitive value comparisons on the part of U.S. consumers, but are the result of a Japanese government plot that has caused the current U.S. trade deficit. Consequently, the problem, they argue, is of national concern.

Of course there is nothing new about the use of such sophistry by merchants and manufacturers to advance their own special purposes in the guise of a national necessity. Sophistry in commerce has been applied throughout the ages. It was best described by Adam Smith in 1776, in *The Wealth of Nations:*

> In every country, it always is and must be the interest of the great body of the people to buy whatever they want of those who sell it cheapest. The proposition is so very manifest, that it seems ridiculous to take any pains to prove it; nor could it ever have been called in question had not the interested sophistry of merchants and manufacturers confounded the common sense of mankind. Their interest is, in this respect, directly opposite to that of the great body of the people.†

---

*The Economist, January 11, 1992; World Bank.
†Adam Smith, *The Wealth of Nations* (1776).

As Milton Friedman will tell you, "These words are as true today as they were then."* It is always in the best interests of the vast majority of the people to buy from the cheapest source and sell to the dearest. Yet, sophistry, motivated by special interests, will attempt to tell you that this is not the case and that there are national priorities at stake. The national priorities just happen to coincide with the special interests of the merchants and manufacturers Adam Smith wrote about.

Nor is protectionism, sophistry, and demagogic polemics exclusive to the United States or Europe. Such endeavors know no geographic boundaries. Here in Japan, the same or similar political expediencies, sentiments, and actions are exercised for a wide range of commercial enterprises including the protection of domestic industries at the expense of international trade, exclusive arrangements among Japanese companies, *keiretsu* transactions, and even the blaming of the futures index market in Osaka for falling stock prices in Tokyo. Such actions are the cause of the unwarranted image Japan has earned. For instance, the proposed Japanese restrictions on derivative trading activities can be assessed by financial markets as an attempt to punish the profitability of foreign brokers—primarily U.S. institutions. Is this other than protectionism? Is it not sophistry to suggest that such measures will correct the perceived problems in Japanese markets? Similarly, when a Japanese official recently stated that American workers are "lazy and illiterate," his words were not only a disservice to the cause of free trade, they were blatantly false.

While Japanese do have more working hours than Americans—225 hours per year more than U.S. workers—American workers rank second in the number of work hours of any nation in the industrialized world. Americans work about 320 hours more per year than workers in Germany or France. Indeed, working hours in the United States have increased substantially over the past 20 years. From the end of the 1960s to the present, Americans' work hours have increased by about 160 hours (or nearly one month per year). This is true for women as well as men.†

*Free to Choose.*
†*Newsweek,* February 17, 1992.

Similarly, it is a fallacy that the productivity of American workers has fallen. The level of productivity of the U.S. worker has more than doubled since 1948. And as for leisure time, American and Japanese workers on average receive the same 10 days' vacation time—well behind the 30 days of vacation for Swedish or Austrian workers, or the 25 days in France, or the 22 days in the United Kingdom, Switzerland, and Spain, or the 18 days in Germany.*

And while the negative comments about American workers were probably made for domestic rather than foreign consumption—possibly to forestall the growing pressure from Japanese laborers to reduce working hours (just as many of our negative comments about Japan are made for domestic U.S. consumption)—they nevertheless can cause serious difficulties for the relations of our two nations. It therefore behooves public officials on both sides of the Pacific to bear this in mind. Particularly during times of recessions—as the United States has endured, as most of Europe is experiencing, and as may yet be felt here in Japan—it is imperative that the voices of our public officials be less shrill and that they not unwittingly lend ammunition to those who have a special protectionist agenda.

We know that protectionism has popular appeal. We know that in times of economic strain protectionism can gain a following. But we also know that protectionism is the scourge of markets everywhere. We know its consequences are devastating and ubiquitous. Dare we allow the near global triumph achieved by free markets in recent years be diminished? Dare we endanger the new world order we have fought so long and valiantly to achieve? Dare we allow the protectionists of the 1990s to lead us down the Smoot-Hawley path of the 1930s? Sophistry and demagogic polemics can snatch for us defeat from the jaws of victory. We, of free markets, must not allow this to transpire.

---

*Ibid.

# Index

271